Japan's early parliaments, 1890–1905

The Nissan Institute/Routledge Japanese Studies Series

Japan's early parliaments, 1890–1905

Structure, Issues and Trends

Andrew Fraser, R.H.P. Mason
and Philip Mitchell

Routledge
Taylor & Francis Group

LONDON AND NEW YORK

First published 1995
by Routledge

2 Park Square, Milton Park, Abingdon, Oxon OX14 4RN
711 Third Avenue, New York, NY 10017, USA

Routledge is an imprint of the Taylor & Francis Group, an informa business

First issued in paperback 2016

Transferred to Digital Printing 2005

Typeset in Times by
Ponting–Green Publishing Services, Chesham, Bucks

British Library Cataloguing in Publication Data
A catalogue record for this book is available from the British Library.

Library of Congress Cataloging in Publication Data
Fraser, Andrew.
  Japan's early parliaments, 1890–1905: structure, issues, and trends/Andrew Fraser, R.H.P. Mason, Philip Mitchell.
  p.   cm. – (Nissan Institute/Routledge Japanese studies series)
  Includes bibliographical references and index.
  1. Japan. Teikoku Gikai–History.   2. Legislative bodies–Japan–History.   3. Japan–Politics and government–1868–1912.   I. Mason, R. H. P.   II. Mitchell, Philip, 1961– .   III. Title.   IV. Series.
  JQ1654.F73   1995
  328.52'07–dc20   94–12044

ISBN 978-0-415-03075-5 (hbk)
ISBN 978-1-138-97370-1 (pbk)

Contents

Preface and acknowledgements

The separate chapters of this book have a varied provenance. Andrew Fraser's have been freshly written; Philip Mitchell's was originally an Honours research dissertation; and Richard Mason's are revisions of already published papers. Details of original titles and places of publication, where relevant, can be found in the Bibliography. In a significant way, too, the present volume is an outgrowth of an earlier study of the 1890 election (Mason 1969). Despite this heterogeneity, it is hoped that there is sufficient commonality of approach, style, theme and purpose to give the book more than a semblance of unity; and the Introduction and Conclusions have, of course, been composed to that end. The question of datedness hardly arises; because all the chapters have been written from primary sources, and the precise topics covered have either not been treated elsewhere or not in anything like the same detail.

And so to acknowledgements: first, on the institutional side, all three authors are or have been connected with the Australian National University, and we owe it an additional measure of thanks for a generous publication subsidy; the Japan Foundation has helped finance two research visits to Japan in the case of Mason, and Mitchell received similar aid from the Australia–Japan Foundation; and the Oriental Society of Australia kindly gave permission for reproduction of the material on poor relief. On the directly personal side, warm thanks must go first of all to Peter Sowden of Routledge for his unflagging support through years of delay and frustration for all concerned; also to Gordon Smith and James Whiting of Routledge for all their invaluable help with getting the book actually printed and published; to Junji Banno for his learned advice so willingly given; to Arthur (J. A. A.) Stockwin for his initial and continued interest and encouragement; to the efficient and ever kind and helpful staff of the Meiji Newspaper and Magazine Archive at Tokyo University; and, finally, to a group of keyboard staff whose support was often sadly discontinuous through no fault of their own but none the less vital. Among these last special mention must be made of Ms Katrina Anne Blight, Mrs Oanh Collins, Mrs Jean Harlen and Miss Panida Thamsongsana.

Introduction

The year 1990 marked the centenary of the Japanese Diet, originally known as the Great Japan Imperial Diet (*Dai Nihon Teikoku Gikai*), which was opened by Emperor Meiji on 29 November 1890. At the time, this event aroused great official and popular attention, along with much goodwill. Newspapers of all kinds, from about the middle of the month, were increasingly filled with lively comment and speculation. On the day itself, congratulatory telegrams poured in from the provinces, and the capital was the scene of general rejoicings as well as the Imperial procession. These included widespread street decorations and a special Diet Inauguration Concert held at the Tokyo School of Music (newspaper files; Wigmore July 1891). On occasion, the hyperbole could be taken to extremes, as the following extract from *Chōya shimbun* (25 November) shows:

> The opening of the Diet is truly a major event, which has no precedent down the ages. As an auspicious occasion, it surpasses even the great day of the inauguration of the Constitution; because this is the day when the Constitution will truly begin to come into effect. Anybody with any claim to be Japanese must welcome this development with the utmost fervour and rejoicing. If people are going to disapprove of our cheerfully celebrating the Diet, then there is no point in opening it. What objections can there be to hearing His Majesty's subjects, overcome with delight, raising their voices in jubilation throughout the land? How can the people who last year jumped for joy at the time of the promulgation of the Constitution not [now similarly] leap in ecstasy at the time of the opening of the Diet?

In striking contrast, little or no notice was given to the hundredth anniversary even in Japan – not even a postage stamp being issued to mark the occasion[1] – still less elsewhere.

This lack of interest no doubt reflects the fact that in the 1930s the parliamentary political parties ceased to govern the country, with awesome results; but it is none the less remarkable on at least two interconnected counts: the Diet as national archive; and the Diet as national stage. One can note first that the Diet, its membership, proceedings and role in public affairs have all been the subject of ample record and comment, official and otherwise. Apart from any other significance it might have, this great body of materials represents a wonderful and largely unlooked-through window on to Japan's national life during the past century or so. Wars have been won or lost; armies have come and gone; politicians of all stripes and colours have had their seasons, some extraordinarily long, and their flowerings, usually comparatively short. Groups committed to purely local interests have on occasion exercised much authority; while the great national parties, with their constituent factions, have, like the nation itself, persisted and thrived, often against the odds. All this has been acted out within the confines of the Diet or, more broadly speaking, in conjunction with the Diet as the supreme legislative body. Even so, that recent anniversary went virtually unremarked, and primary materials relating to the Diet remain largely unused by historians in Japan and overseas.

The Diet as central to national politics from the outset is a common theme that runs implicitly through the chapters of this book, even when not treated explicitly. Therefore, of its many aspects, only that of the Diet as a training-ground – 'sustaining-ground' would be an equally apt expression – for national leadership need be touched on here. After it opened, all incumbent or aspiring Japanese political leaders had to make at any rate part of their way through the Diet; and for dedicated parliamentarians such as Ōkuma Shigenobu, Hara Kei, Inukai Tsuyoshi, Saionji Kimmochi, and Katō Kōmei, Diet life and Diet politics proved to be a major route to high government posts, culminating in the office of Prime Minister (Oka 1986). On such figures parliament conferred a wide, if variable, degree of popularity. It also gave them the vital support of elected Representatives who had strong local ties, often forged by years of experience as local assemblymen before moving on to the Diet.

Linked with centrality there is another characteristic of continuity, which cannot be given the attention it deserves in a work concerned with only the first decade and a half of Diet history. Continuity has manifested itself in various ways. In every year since it opened, the Diet has met, usually for several months, as one of its more important tasks is to approve the annual budget. Many Representatives have had extremely long periods of service, seeking and winning re-election time and again. Ozaki Yukio and Inukai Tsuyoshi were particularly noticeable in this regard, the former holding the world record (sixty-four years) for continuous membership of an elected assembly. This is a feature of Diet politics that is still present. Furthermore, the close connection between membership of the prefectural assemblies and the national Diet, which was such a distinctive feature of the opening stages of the latter's operation, has been maintained, but not to the same extent as previously and in a way that makes it characteristic of the mass of Representatives rather than their leaders. The structure and 'style' of the Diet also display strong elements of continuity. It has always been a bicameral legislature, with a Lower House plebeian and representative in function as well as name, and an Upper House (whether the earlier House of Peers or the later House of Councillors) distinctively senatorial. At the level of internal procedure and House rules, too, Diet business is transacted today very much as it has always been. Other obvious, and more important, ongoing characteristics have been the dominant part played by con- servative forces, especially rural landlord and farmer interests but also business big and small; the high level of education and personal ability of many individual Members; and the already mentioned powerful role of factions and parties. The major components among these last, despite at times bewildering successions of name changes, have indeed proved surprisingly durable. Thus, the present-day governing party in con- temporary Japan, the Liberal-Democratic Party (*Jiyū-Minshū-tō*) which held power from the mid-1950s until 1993, can be quite easily traced back to the original *Jiyūto* (Liberal Party) and *Kaishintō* (Progressive Party) of the 1880s. Similarly, the Social Democratic Party of Japan (former Japan Socialist Party) derives from the *Musan Seitō* (Socialist) factions founded in the early 1920s, several of which first gained Diet representation in 1928.

In some respects, the early Diets differed from the general pattern sketched here. To put first things first, women were debarred from a direct role in Japanese politics until after 1945, a situation which they have gone a long way to making good since. Another notable area of difference concerns the House of Peers, which played a far more active role in its own right in its first thirty or so years of existence than it did later. In the House of Representatives, rural landlords, many of whom were also country businessmen, disappeared as a class as a result of the post-1945 land reform, and had in fact already lost much of their power in the Great Depression of the late 1920s and early 1930s. Moreover, the overall level of ability of the early Representatives is often considered to have been higher than in subsequent parliaments, owing, some would say, to the relatively large numbers of former samurai among the Members of that time. Certainly, as will be made clear from what follows, Members of both Houses in the period under review were strongly individualistic in their approach to politics and far less bound than their successors by party and factional discipline, even though organizational allegiance was an important factor in the conduct of the Diet from the beginning. In the first House of Representatives, for example, no fewer than forty-five of the total of three hundred seats were occupied by Independents (Mason 1969: 195). The range of occupations of Members, and the wealth of experience they brought to their new role as Diet men, goes a long way to explaining their sturdy divergences of outlook.

Over a longer perspective, the Diet, like all major institutions, and indeed all successful parliaments, has shown a readiness both to initiate and to accept sometimes quite radical change, along with the continuities. In times gone by there has been much experimenting with such matters as the size of constituencies and the number of Members to be elected from each. A separate but related development has seen the electorate for the Lower House grow from a minuscule 1.14 per cent of the adult male populace in 1890, to manhood suffrage in 1924, and to universal suffrage (for both Houses) in 1946. Within the shorter timeframe of 1890–1905, the total population of Japan rose from 40 million to 46 million; the number of electors to the House of Representatives grew from just over 400,000 to 762,445[2] as a result of a lowering of the property qualification in a new House of Representatives Election Law which was enacted in 1900; and the same legislation saw many of the original small and single-Member constituencies replaced by larger, multi-Member districts.

Elsewhere in the Diet structure, the mainly hereditary, and by the 1930s – it must be admitted – generally reactionary, House of Peers (*Kizokuin*) was replaced by a totally elected House of Councillors (*Sangiin*) as part of the post-1945 Occupation reforms. Indeed, the whole basis and framework of Diet politics, though not so much the politics themselves, were altered when, in 1946, it itself substituted (albeit at the behest of the Occupation authorities) the present Constitution for that promulgated in 1889 by the Meiji Emperor.

The same adaptability allowed the Japanese Diet throughout its history, and again like other parliaments, to accommodate new groups and interests, in keeping with the general development of society. Apart from the Socialists, who rose from their fragmented and meagre beginnings to become the major post-Second-World-War opposition party, even forming the government for a while in 1947–8, there has been a Communist movement in Japan since just after the First World War. Suppressed under the Peace Preservation Law of 1924, and its adherents later imprisoned, the only Diet representation it managed to achieve at the time of its first formation was in collaboration with the Socialists. After 1946, however, the Communists were quite strongly represented in the Diet in their own right; and over time, the 'new religion' of Sōka Gakkai (*Kōmeitō*) has become an even more powerful influence in the Diet through winning relatively large numbers of seats.

But first and last, truly as the alpha and omega of the situation, it is the old, established parties of a conservative-liberal or liberal-conservative stamp that have made the Diet their own; and its story is largely theirs. This is so largely because of the general circumstances just outlined. Diet history and politics have not been simply a point counterpoint of old and new, a brittle co-existence of tradition and modernity: melding, cumulative change, institutional growth and expansion have all been essential components. By far the most significant of these changes has been the way political parties, which date back to the heady days of the Liberty and Popular Rights Movement (*Jiyū Minken Undō*) of the 1870s and 1880s, have evolved from being (in)subordinate elements in the Emperor-centred political structure to junior partners in bureaucrat-led administrations and finally to mastery of government in their own right. This road to power has been long and stony, though ultimately successfully travelled. Its starting point was the parties' consistent majority in the Lower House of the Diet from 1890. Such majorities have not only represented a starting point but have also served as a position of enduring advantage because it was from the Lower House that the conservative parties continued to rule; and the same majorities provided a place of return and refuge in times of trouble as in the 1930s and early 1940s (Berger 1977). This long-term trend in favour of government by parties ensconced in a parliament – together with the central, continuous, and increasingly representative nature of the Diet – can clearly be regarded as a major factor in the political development of modern Japan. The years from 1890 to 1905 mark no more than a beginning, as the parties, emboldened by their dominant position in the House of Representatives, attempted to come to preliminary terms with bureaucratic, non-party cabinets led by seasoned Meiji statesmen. This initial stage was to last until the great Taishō political crisis of 1912–13 opened a new era under a new Emperor.

Turning from prospect to retrospect, the historical formation of the Diet represents a generally benign confluence of foreign and native traditions, as well as native aspirations. 'Foreign' means, of course 'European', in particular, the constitutional monarchies that flourished there in the second half of the nineteenth century. The Meiji constitutional system, as inaugurated in 1889, was not so very different in form and operation, or even in its actual wording and many of its underlying assumptions, from that of contemporary Belgium say, or the united Kingdom of Italy; and it both reflected and was put to work in a comparable social and economic environment. By 1890, Japan was also on the verge of taking a full and independent part in the Western-inspired international order of the time.

Even in foreign affairs, the way had been prepared to some extent by the Tokugawa regime's adoption – along with so-called 'closed country' policies – of a theory of mutual recognition of sovereign independent national states, strikingly like that which had come into vogue in the sixteenth and seventeenth century West (Toby 1977). In domestic affairs, modern representative and consultative (in a word, parliamentary) institutions had at any rate loose antecedents in such well established Tokugawa practices as elections of village and urban ward headmen; ceremonial monarchy at all three levels of Emperor, *shōgun* and *daimyō*; administration by council;[3] and an increasingly *de facto* rule by law. Digging deeper, we see in ancient and Tokugawa times a fully functional Japanese tradition of institutional diversity that has been of prime importance in helping to bring about and nurture modern parliamentarianism. While this is too big a subject to go into here (Mason 1969), it can be argued that Japanese society, in addition to the authoritarian, hierarchical and even theocratic values that have characterized it, has also shown a strong tendency, in its institutional structures, to favour pluralist forms, and that these forms have carried with them their own distinctive but often undefined norms. In other words, pluralist structures bred a pluralist approach. Thus, to take but one example from Diet history, both Houses could quite easily find room for different social groups and divergent economic interests, in a manner which, in itself, had nothing to do with personal ambition or individual merit. In them, literally formerly warring political foes came together. Going further, it could be said that the House of Peers rendered a significant national service simply by bringing together at long last in a new institutional framework the old nobilities of civilian *kuge* and feudal *daimyō*, and merging them not only with one another but also with the topmost echelons of the 'upstart' post-1868 national leadership. In this connection, it is worth remembering that Prince Tokugawa Iesato, the grandson of the last *shōgun*, was for many years an esteemed President of the House of Peers. More generally speaking, in the rooms and chambers of the Diet building, prince mixed with commoner, bureaucrat with businessman, Westernized intellectuals and urban professional men with traditionally minded but shrewd landlord-farmers.

The Imperial Diet of the 1890s and early 1900s, then, may from this standpoint be thought of as a genuine culmination of Japanese as well as Western experience, and as crowning the events of the 1870s and 1880s when resolute domestic efforts had been made, as well as foreign pressure exerted, to catch up with and join the 'civilized' West. The Constitution, within which the Diet operated as one of its integral parts, reflected all this. Imbued with principles of dynastic sovereignty, as were the great majority of its European counterparts, it nevertheless was strictly binding and with its companion document, the Imperial House Law, seemed to have ushered in the full rule of law. In addition, the 1889 Constitution held in practice to the separation of powers, and firmly established the Legislative branch in the Diet. Members of both Houses had equal authority to approve or initiate legislation; to ask questions (including supplementaries) of cabinet ministers or their delegates; to censure the government of the day and to pass bills of no confidence; to frame and enforce internal House rules while generally managing their own affairs; to enjoy the accepted run of parliamentary privileges during sessions; and, in the case of the House of Representatives, virtually to choose its own Speaker and his deputy. The Executive and Judicial branches were allotted their own specific spheres of authority under the Constitution; but the precise relationship between the Legislative and the Executive was left – almost certainly by design – ambiguous. The Constitution equally allowed government by party and by non-party cabinets. This was to be the great bone of contention during the first two or three decades of Diet history. But the forces concerned had not only to contend with each other; they had to work together, if the system were to be sustained and the nation's cause advanced.

NOTES

1 Stamps were issued to mark such occasions as a Century of Japan–Turkey Friendship and the 38th International Youth Hostel Federation Congress.
2 This figure was 982,868 in 1902.
3 Again, these councils were key elements in internal Imperial Court administration, in the *Bakufu*'s rule of both the nation at large and the Tokugawa house-lands (*tenryō*), and the regulation of the 260 or so *han* by their respective *daimyō*. They were not elected, but appointment to them was highly selective and by due process. They operated in a systematic and bureaucratic fashion with proper attention to procedure; and they grew to a point where they could accommodate recognized cliques which alternated in power (Totman 1967).

1 The House of Peers (1890–1905)

Structure, groups and role

Andrew Fraser

When the first Diet convened in 1890 the stage was set for an epic contest between bureaucratic cabinets and political party opponents in the House of Representatives. Most Prime Ministers in the next decade were veteran Satsuma and Chōshū leaders with powerful weapons at their disposal: accumulated kudos as the founders of the Meiji regime and drafters of the Constitution; strong ties of patronage extending widely across palace, official, business, and political circles; all the resources of an efficient, highly specialized bureaucracy; powers to suspend Diet sessions and to dissolve the House of Representatives; strict regulations for the control of political associations, meetings and publications; prefectural governors and local police chiefs able to monitor and manipulate elections on their behalf. On their side, political parties with majorities in the House of Representatives could withhold approval for increases in government expenditure or for new legislation, while putting cabinets on the spot and even forcing their resignation by direct memorials to the Emperor or motions of no confidence and censure. In the end, both sides were forced to make important compromises and concessions; as if tired of the battle, bureaucratic and party leaders by 1905 had agreed to conduct government on a pragmatic give-and-take basis. Politics then settled into a fairly humdrum routine for almost a decade, though this gain in stability was accompanied by a perceptible loss of verve and idealism.

Over these fifteen years the Peers followed their own road, sometimes acting in concert with the Representatives, as when both Houses agreed to deliberate on specific bills in a Joint Conference of the Diet (*kyōgikai*),[1] but more often striving to uphold their independence both against cabinets that took their support for granted and political parties in the Lower House demanding more power under the Constitution. At most times playing a muted role as an umpire rather than a contestant, the House of Peers rarely held the spotlight of the political stage, then gradually declined in importance until swept away as part of the Occupation reforms of 1947. However, historians are now beginning to accord it detailed analysis as a significant force in the constitutional regime;[2] except for the right of the Lower House to consider the budget first, the Peers had the same powers as the Representatives; especially in earlier years it exercised all of them at one time or another, occasionally with telling effect.

But if equal in powers, the two Houses were very different in structure, in the kind of groups that formed within them, and hence in the role they played.

STRUCTURE

Table 1.1 provides a brief guide to House of Peers membership and how this changed over the years.

Table 1.1

Conditions	Grade	Age qualification	Nos 1890	Nos 1905
By right for life				
	Imperial Princes	Adult	10	13
	Princes	25 years	10	10
	Marquises	25 years	21	29
By election every 7 years				
	Counts	25 years	14	17
	Viscounts	25 years	70	70
	Barons	25 years	20	63
(one-fifth of total number by multiple-name ballot)				
For life				
	Imperial Nominees	30 years	61	125
By election every 7 years				
	High Taxpayers	30 years	45	46
(mutual election from top 15 in each metropolitan city and prefecture)				
Total			251	373

Source: Sakeda Masatoshi, *Kizokuin kaiha ichiran 1890–1919* (Tokyo, 1974)

Members by right and for life, the top three grades differed from others in both character and role. Imperial Princes were the sons, brothers or nephews of the Emperor, sharing his exalted status. Unlike all others, they took their seats when 'adult', as if a specific age limit was undignified, though later it was ruled that the Crown Prince could sit at age eighteen, and Imperial Princes at age twenty. Over the centuries, both at the Imperial court in Kyōto and within the military regime of the Tokugawa *shōguns*, a few aristocratic families had established a social and political supremacy that set them far above all others. In an almost equal mix the Princes and Marquises were their direct heirs. No mere privileged ciphers, many of them had been educated overseas after the Restoration of 1868,[3] and on average their level of ability was quite equal to that of lesser grades. But high social status and palace connections in most cases kept them aloof from the routine business of the House of Peers; even on important issues they rarely attended or voted. In particular, the Imperial Princes were so lax in attendance that they hardly counted as Members at all; with several notable exceptions, the Princes and Marquises were much the same. The slight increase in Marquises by 1905 had its reason: the veteran Satsuma and Chōshū statesmen, now known as the *genrō*, had risen into the upper aristocracy despite their lowly origins as ordinary samurai. These new arrivals, too, were noted for a lofty indifference to House business.[4]

Next come the Counts, Viscounts and Barons, all hereditary peers and most of them guaranteed generous incomes for themselves and their heirs paid from the ample resources of the Imperial Household Treasury. Sitting not by right but by mutual elections from one-fifth of their total number held every seven years, they also divide almost equally between the heirs of lesser court nobles and *daimyō* on the one hand; elder statesmen, top civil and military bureaucrats, famous loyalists and talented young officials on the other. Many of those elected to the House of Peers had experienced overseas study; by no means outshone in ability by career bureaucrats, the former *daimyō* among them often had practical experience in running smaller domains, in some ways a more testing background than the civil service. Competitive and ambitious, these grades contended fiercely at elections and played a vigorous role in the running and politics of the House. Within them, Barons more than trebled between 1890 and 1905, while the Counts and Viscounts remained steady in number. For as the Meiji regime prospered, more and more rising bureaucrats and prominent businessmen gained elevation to this bottom grade of the hereditary peerage. In these years over twenty Barons also found places in the House of Peers as Imperial Nominees.

Required to be men of 'meritorious service to the state or scholars of distinction', Imperial Nominees were appointed for life. They were expected to form an independent meritocracy commanding respect from the nation as a whole. At first this was indeed the case: many of them were famous scholar-patriots active in the loyalist movement of the 1860s or former members of the *Genrōin*, or Senate, an institute set up to review government legislation before its functions were taken over by the Privy Council and the Diet after 1890. While not so inflated in numbers as the Barons, by 1905 they had nearly doubled. The Emperor nominated them after recommendation by the current Prime Minister, and successive cabinets found this a useful way to reward adherents and to build up a bureaucratic following in the House of Peers.[5] As older ones died, or younger ones got promotion, vacancies were frequent; their numbers were limited, though, by the regulation that they and the High Taxpayers should not exceed in total the titled Peers. As a grade they contributed much to the House, by regular attendance and official expertise. Here we see a balance of a different kind. The framers of the Constitution kept in mind the possibility of obstinate resistance by hereditary peers to government measures occasionally experienced by other states such as Britain and Prussia where the right of the sovereign to make new appointments to the Upper House of the Legislature was a useful resource.[6] But in Japan's case, the rule that Imperial Nominees and High Taxpayers could equal, but never exceed, the titled Peers shows rather more optimism on this point.

Although each High Taxpayer was elected from the top fifteen of their number in every metropolitan city or prefecture, in their case membership of the House of Peers was by the Emperor's favour and not by right, a reminder that they were appointed to provide a specific quality, not some kind of representation. Their wealth was required to be 'in land, industry and commerce'; shareholders in companies and banks and owners of large sums in public bonds were specifically excluded.[7] Limitation to existing administrative boundaries kept their numbers constant at around forty-five, and they provided both contact with the wealthy and a geographical spread over the whole nation.

Total membership of the House of Peers increased from 251 in 1890 to 373 in 1905, largely owing to the influx of new Barons and Imperial Nominees, whose numbers were then fixed in the reforms of that year (see below).

Prime Ministers could recommend Imperial Nominees and award promotions in the Order of Merit, but appointment to hereditary peerages remained the jealous preserve of palace circles, monitored by elder statesmen beyond Diet interference or control, preventing any danger of political intrusion on an exclusive aristocracy.

The framers of the Constitution took one more precaution against untoward changes in the House of Peers; unlike the House of Representatives, which was constituted by a law of election that was able, like all other laws, to be changed by Diet resolutions, the House of Peers was regulated by imperial ordinances, giving the cabinet power to recommend changes, though these had to be approved by the House itself.[8]

Seats in the House of Representatives were allocated by lot, provoking many a bout of impromptu fisticuffs when heated opponents rubbed shoulders, until division by party was allowed in 1904.[9] But the Peers sat in order of rank at court, Princes at the front ranging back in a widening semicircle of benches to High Taxpayers at the rear, this regular progression broken by a few individuals with court ranks above normal for their grade. Since the Imperial Princes and other great nobles so rarely attended, the empty front benches must often have given the assembly chamber a rather deserted look. At the same time, renowned for the friendly relations between its Members at the personal level, even between competing groups, the Peers with a few rare exceptions were spared the angry debates, noisy interjections and florid displays of violence that often agitated the Representatives, coupled on occasions with hectic mobbing by bodyguards and party activists in the Diet corridors and adjacent grounds. While the Representatives normally held their sittings in the afternoon, extending till early evening, the Peers met in the morning and sat till mid-day, perhaps a further inducement to placid behaviour.

Especially in early years, Members of the House of Peers often declared themselves with pride to be 'Protectors of the Dynasty' (*kōshitsu no hampei*), claiming a close relationship with the Emperor and his family, though by the 1920s hostile critics were asking just what the sovereign needed to be protected from. Surely not from the people, they exclaimed, whose loyalty was besmirched by such an expression.[10] A richly furnished enclosure reserved for the Emperor when he opened Diet sessions towered above the Peers' assembly chamber; its heavy drapes were kept open while the House was sitting, the Emperor's throne in full view, as if to remind Members that his august presence was always with them. By custom, the President and visiting officials turned towards it and bowed as they entered or left the chamber.[11]

The electoral system of the lower-grade peers and provisions for Imperial Nominees and High Taxpayers were carefully framed on Western examples,[12] but the House also had traditional roots. It reminds one of the ceremonial assemblies of former military rulers; the lord and family members presiding over hereditary retainers who held their posts for many generations, joined by able bureaucrats employed for life, together with a number of medical doctors, scholars and leading merchants with specialized skills. Like many other endeavours of Meiji Japan, the constitutional regime was an ambitious attempt to combine the best models of the past with new forms needed to create a modern state, and the House of Peers is a good example of this.

GROUPS

Government leaders – and many Members of the House of Peers itself – hoped that factional strife and the formation of groups could be avoided. They were swiftly disappointed. The creation, if not entirely the creature, of Satsuma and Chōshū statesmen with antipathies and rivalries of their own, the House of Peers could hardly remain unaffected by movements in official and political circles or indifferent to seeking a share in the rewards of government.

For example, the President of the House of Peers was not elected by its Members like the Speaker of the House of Representatives; he was appointed by the Emperor on the recommendation of the current Prime Minister for a five-year term. Itō Hirobumi agreed with some reluctance to be President for the first session only. His successor Marquis Hachisuka Mochiaki, former *daimyō* of the Tokushima domain and generally regarded as a Chōshū protégé, was put up by Prime Minister Yamagata Aritomo in 1891. Prince Konoe Atsumaro, equally obliged to Satsuma patrons,[13] watched over Hachisuka's elevation with jealous eyes. In 1896, when the Satsuma leader and current Prime Minister Matsukata Masayoshi offered him the post of Education Minister, Konoe suggested a neat exchange. Hachisuka stood down to take this post, then Konoe replaced him as President on Matsukata's recommendation.[14] If Satsuma and Chōshū influence and manipulation was so evident at the very top, little wonder that it extended a lot further down.

Competition within the electoral grades of the peerage also made grouping almost inevitable. Counts, Viscounts and Barons were far too numerous for them all to have seats, so to restrict total House membership to around three hundred, roughly the same as the Representatives, each of these grades elected one-fifth of their number. Term elections were held every seven years, but a few vacancies occurred before each Diet session and these were hotly contended, making electoral competition endemic. While drawing up a ballot system for the Peers, government experts found themselves in a common dilemma when relatively small groups compete to elect a sizeable proportion of their number. If the ballot was restricted to one candidate per voter, the result would probably be a few Members elected by massive majorities but many by a handful of votes, a ludicrous discrepancy unless several subsidiary elections were held. So they settled for a multiple-name ballot, each voter filling in a set form with as many names as places to be filled, thus making elections a contest between lists of candidates rather than between individuals, providing the additional advantage of the speed and dignity of a single poll. This also ensured that all Members were elected by a respectable number of votes.[15] Such a system had the drawback that between competing lists of candidates the one with most aggregate votes would elect all its nominees, perhaps by a very small margin, depriving many able men of seats. The framers of the electoral regulations were well aware of such a possibility and did not rule out changes to a more equitable system in the future.[16] But as they hoped, common sense prevailed; electoral organizations within each grade negotiated with their competitors before major elections, aiming for a higher proportion of seats rather than outright monopoly,[17] saving the system from falling into contempt. Even so, the losing side after elections often raised strident cries of unfairness and manipulation. But despite demands by critics and legal scholars for reforms, this multiple-name ballot system was to endure for the whole history of the House of Peers.[18] Within it, electoral organizations were quick to appear among the Counts, Viscounts and Barons, run by powerful bosses adept at drawing up effective lists and canvassing out-of-town Peers who voted by proxy. These electoral organizations also played political roles, until by 1905 all grades in the House of Peers were characterized by groupism, with the exception of forty or so Princes

Table 1.2

Pro-cabinet		Moderates		Opposition		Independents
1893						
Kenkyūkai	59			*Sanyōkai*	28	127
Sawakai	18			*Konwakai*	50	
Total	77				78	127
1898						
Kenkyūkai	55	*Mokuyōkai*	16	*Sanyōkai*	15	165
Sawakai	11			*Konwakai*	52	
Hinotorikai	13			*Asahi Club*	14	
Total	79		16		81	165
1905						
Kenkyūkai	80	*Mokuyōkai*	49	*Doyōkai*	46	85
Sawakai	46	*Mushozokuha*	45			
Total	126		94		46	85

Source: Sakeda Masatoshi, *Kizokuin kaiha ichiran*; for the internal composition of groups, see Sakeda (1978): 176

and Marquises who sat by right, a handful of lesser Peers and twenty-nine Imperial Nominees holding seats for life. From around this time the Chief Secretary of the House of Peers regularly drew up lists of Members divided into groups.[19]

As a rough outline – complicated by shortlived formations, shifting allegiances and plural membership – groups within the House of Peers can be classified as in Table 1.2:

PRO-CABINET

With the exception of the bitter confrontation of 1900 to 1901, when all major groups in the House of Peers united to reject the fourth Itō cabinet's budget bill, these Members supported successive cabinets as conservative defenders of the Constitution against attempts by the House of Representatives to expand its powers. Sneered at by opponents in both Houses as time-serving opportunists, they also gained official posts in reward for their support. The most solid and enduring group was the *Kenkyūkai* (Study Club). About one-third of them were Marquises, Counts, Imperial Nominees or High Taxpayers; but the majority were Viscounts: twenty-four in 1893, forty-nine in 1898 and sixty-one in 1905. Not just in numbers, but as a combination of the best traditional and new talent of the Meiji regime, Viscounts were a formidable class. When collected together as Members of the House of Peers they organized with speed and efficiency. No other group could match the *Kenkyūkai*'s hierarchy of directors, standing committees and specialized subsections, lodged in a club headquarters near the Diet compound and maintained by regular levies accumulating in a central fund. Their electoral organization, the *Shōyūkai* (Esteemed Friends Club), effortlessly returned all its candidates in polls for vacancies and at seven-year terms.[20] Its first leaders were Viscounts Okabe Nagatoshi and Hotta Masayoshi, both former *daimyō* of middle-sized domains. Okabe, educated in England and previously a councillor at the Japanese Legation in London, had useful official connections. Of all the Members of the House of Peers he was the nearest to being a political boss on the lines of Hoshi Tōru in the House of Representatives, though his forceful leadership was marred by public displays of drunken, insulting behaviour. Hotta, much more modest and accommodating, started out as ward head in Tokyo, later forming business links.[21] Among the Imperial Nominees who joined the *Kenkyūkai*, the most important was Kiyoura Keigo, a henchman of Yamagata and several times a minister in Chōshū cabinets in the 1890s and early 1900s, who kept it in touch with top bureaucratic circles. As a vital support for any administration, *Kenkyūkai* leaders gained important official posts: Okabe as Governor of Tokyo from 1897 to 1898, Hotta as Communications Minister in 1906.

Supporting the *Kenkyūkai* as a Pro-cabinet force, and sharing its links with the Chōshū leaders, the *Sawakai* (Tea Talk Club) in 1893 had eighteen members, all of them Imperial Nominees.[22] Four years later a group of High Taxpayers with similar views and connections formed the *Hinotorikai* (1897 Club). By 1905 they had merged with the *Sawakai*, increasing its numbers to forty-six. Devoted followers of Yamagata like Hirata Tōsuke, Ōura Kanetake and Komatsubara Eitarō were now leaders of this group. As appointees for life these Imperial Nominees had no need to form an electoral organization, and they were a powerful force in House of Peers politics, differing from their *Kenkyūkai* allies only in being a non-Viscount group.

MODERATES

This broad classification begins with the formation of the *Mokuyōkai* (Thursday Club) in 1897. Several Barons broke away from the *Kenkyūkai* during the term election of this year, setting up an electoral organization of their own. Motivated by ambition rather than any settled principle, moderation for them implied flexibility and compromise. Their acknowledged leader was Baron Senke Takatomi. Hereditary high priest of the Izumo Shrine in West Japan, widely respected as a Shintō religious leader, Senke was none the less an adept politician on friendly terms with the Chōshū leaders, supplying them with detailed information on the inner workings of the House of Peers.[23] He was rewarded with a series of official posts: after 1894 he was successively governor of Saitama and Shizuoka Prefectures, then of Tokyo, finally becoming Justice Minister in 1908. This last appointment reinforces his classification as a moderate, for it was made in the first Saionji cabinet supported by the *Seiyūkai*, a political party anathema to the more rigid *Kenkyūkai* from which he had broken away. The steady increase in the number of Barons after 1890 provided Senke with a fruitful base for recruitment. A handful of Counts, Imperial Nominees and High Taxpayers could be found in the *Mokuyōkai* at any given time, but Barons formed its core: forty-four out of forty-nine members by 1905.

Harder to classify, drawn from a wide range of grades and deliberately loose and informal in organization, the *Mushozokuha* (Independent Club) can also be termed a Moderate group. When Ōkuma Shigenobu formed Japan's first party cabinet in 1898 it became obvious that political forces were on the move in ways that threatened to swing the balance of power towards the House of Representatives. In response, many Members previously listed as pure Independents began to draw together.[24] By 1905 they numbered forty-five and were a force to be reckoned with. Top-ranking member was Marquis Matsudaira Yasutaka, former *daimyō* of the powerful Fukui domain. Educated in England, he then indulged in landscape gardening at his family castle, while also head of the Japan Farmers Association. Some Counts, Viscounts and Barons joined this group, but most were Imperial Nominees, thirty-two of them in 1905. Over the years Imperial Nominees increased steadily, from sixty-one in 1890 to 125 in 1905, and now outnumbered all other grades. A solid core of Pro-cabinet Imperial Nominees were to be found in the *Sawakai*; the twenty-nine who joined the *Mushozokuha* in 1898, mostly ex-bureaucrats, were less rigidly aligned, though members of both these groups joined together to set up a social club (*Saiwai Kurabu*) in 1899.[25]

OPPOSITION

This is a blanket term for all those Members determined to resist Chōshū domination, cabinet arrogance and downgrading the role of the Diet. The *Sanyōkai* (Three Days Club) was led by Prince Konoe Atsumaro, in close association with Prince Nijō Hiromoto, Marquis Tokugawa Yoshiakira and Count Shimazu Tadaakira, all of them court nobles or former *daimyō* of the highest pedigree. Its twenty-eight members in 1893 included fifteen Viscounts, four Barons and five High Taxpayers. Konoe's family stood at the very pinnacle of the court aristocracy, with a lineage almost as ancient and distinguished as that of the Emperor himself, his prestige reinforced by family ties with the Shimazu, former *daimyō* of the Satsuma domain. After long years of study in Germany, Konoe returned to Japan in 1890 determined to make his name as an independent statesman and a champion of 'virtue' and 'justice'.[26] Animated and combative, he gave successive Chōshū cabinets no quarter, hammering away at them on every contentious issue. His special *forte* was diplomacy, presiding over popular anger against what he regarded as spineless concessions to the Western Powers, such as unrestricted residence allowed to foreigners in the new treaties signed by the second Itō cabinet in 1894. On the other hand, he advocated friendly relations with China as a fellow Asian nation and championed Korean independence. Feelings of contempt for China and the mood of chauvinistic euphoria after Japan's victory in the war of 1894–95 aroused his ire, as did the huge increase in military budgets that followed. Yet for all Konoe's verve, the political tides were running against him. The *Sanyōkai* steadily lost numbers and finally dissolved in 1899. One reason for this was the lofty disdain of Konoe and his allies for the electoral machinations of the *Kenkyūkai*; their lack of organization brought about a humiliating defeat in the seven-year term election of 1897. Paradoxically, as the *Sanyōkai* collapsed, Konoe's popularity outside the House of Peers reached its peak. In 1900 he launched a People's Alliance pledged to demand Russia's withdrawal from Manchuria and to uphold the independence of Korea. With a headquarters in Tokyo and branches in many localities, this movement swept across the nation until the authorities ruled it to be a political association, whereupon Konoe's allies in the House of Peers deserted it, as did Konoe himself, leading to an ignominious collapse in 1902.[27] Already a very sick man in 1903, choked by throat cancer and barely audible during public speeches, Konoe led a final campaign for an Anti-Russia League, now ironically finding himself on the same side as Yamagata and other Chōshū military leaders who had successfully concluded an Anglo-Japanese Alliance against Russia in preparation for an all-out war.[28] His death in 1904, aged forty-two years, deprived the Peers of a courageous, if erratic, leader.

The other pillar of Opposition was the *Konwakai* (Friendly Talk Club). It, too, had a charismatic leader in Viscount Tani Kanjō, heroic defender of Kumamoto garrison against the Satsuma rebels in 1877, who had resigned from active service as a major-general in 1881 in protest against the control over top army posts progressively applied by Chōshū generals Yamagata Aritomo and Katsura Tarō. After a spell as Agriculture and Commerce Minister from 1885 to 1887, Tani took up the cause of Japan's heavily-taxed farmers, proud to call himself a 'peasant' in his letters and speeches. Like Konoe, he advocated a strident, self-confident nationalism to combat predatory Western Powers bent on destroying Japan's economy and draining away its wealth by their unequal treaties. Also a friend of China, though not so rabid an opponent of Russia, he joined Konoe in bitter protests against runaway military expenditure beyond the power of the nation to sustain. Equally with Konoe, Tani commanded a strong following among the common people. In February 1889, coinciding with the promulgation of the Constitution, he joined with others to launch the *Nihon* newspaper, which in the 1890s was often ordered to suspend publication after vitriolic attacks on cabinets and government leaders. The *Konwakai* had fifty members in 1892; highest in rank was Prince Shimazu Tadanari, former branch *daimyō* of the Satsuma domain, followed by one Marquis, three Counts, nine Viscounts, four Barons, fifteen Imperial Nominees and sixteen High Taxpayers. Nothing like so well organized as the *Kenkyūkai*, this group with a wide spread of grades drew its strength from unity of principle. For a brief moment in 1899 its numbers rose to sixty-eight, four more than the *Kenkyūkai*. Yet there was little chance that Tani, any more than the fastidiously aristocratic Konoe, could muster political-party forces behind him in a nationwide movement against the Chōshū leaders. His fervid nationalism inclined him to disparage foreign concepts of democracy advocated by most political parties. Formerly a rural samurai of the Tosa domain, he also bore a personal grudge against fellow countryman Itagaki Taisuke and other castle-town leaders, who in pre-Restoration days had on occasion ordered the execution or imprisonment of unruly loyalists like Tani and his friends. After 1890 he remained critical of Itagaki's brand of Western-style liberalism and his party followers in the House of Representatives. On the other hand, he did not share the fierce chauvinism of Konoe's Anti-Russia League; swamped by dilemmas both political and diplomatic, the *Konwakai* suddenly dissolved in December 1900 when its bewildered members joined a new, but much weaker, Opposition group.

This was the *Doyōkai* (Saturday Club). Its fifty-four members included Princes Konoe and Nijō, two Counts, seven Viscounts (including Tani) and five Barons. But most of its members were Imperial Nominees (seventeen) and High Taxpayers (nineteen). Tani's concern for the farmers had always attracted strong support from the last of these. When thirteen High Taxpayers formed the *Hinotorikai* in 1897 and later joined the *Sawakai*, fourteen others in opposition set up the *Asahi* Club, and then formed the *Doyōkai*'s core in 1900. By 1905 *Doyōkai* numbers had fallen to forty-six, reducing a once strong Opposition to a shadow of its former self. Chōshū Prime Minister Katsura Tarō could now boast, 'The House of Peers is mine'.[29]

INDEPENDENTS

In numbers, these were a sizeable component of the House of Peers. At the outset most Members did not join groups; indeed, for a few years after 1890 Independents actually increased, peaking at 170 out of 331 Members in 1897. But as groups grew more powerful and political alignments hardened, many Independents took sides or joined others in loose associations like the *Mushozokuha* of 1898. As a result, Members in this category fell to eighty-five in 1905; once reduced to this hard core, numbers remained at around this level for the next two decades, a touching reminder of what government leaders had once expected all Members of the House of Peers to be.

Independents came in two main kinds, at opposite ends of the social scale but both sitting for life: top-level aristocrats and Imperial Nominees. In 1905 some thirteen Imperial Princes, nine Princes and twenty-seven Marquises are listed as Independents, along with twenty-nine Imperial Nominees. At this time, in the electoral grades of the peerage, only two Counts, one Viscount, two Barons and two High Taxpayers had held out against the pressure to join groups. But Independents were now unimportant in the politics of the House; many of them, beginning with the Imperial Princes, well known as consistent absentees.

It is easy to imagine why lofty aristocrats did not join groups, often led and managed by their social inferiors, or why some Members in lower grades were content to keep out of things. When specific Independents are studied more closely, however, some interesting facts emerge. For example, Marquis Hachisuka Mochiaki, President of the House of Peers from 1891 to 1896, is always listed as an Independent. Membership of the Privy Council after 1897 might also have inhibited him from playing an active role.[30] Former *daimyō* of the Tokushima domain, five of his ex-retainers became Members of the House of Peers between 1890 and 1905. They joined a variety of groups: Viscount Yoshikawa Akimasa (*Kenkyūkai*); Imperial Nominee Komuro Shinobu (*Sawakai*); Baron Nakajima Masutane (*Konwakai*); Imperial Nominee Matsuoka Kōki (*Mokuyōkai*); High Taxpayer Miki Yokichirō (*Doyōkai*). While all these men remained Hachisuka's loyal followers at the personal level, attending regular garden parties at his spacious Tokyo mansion along with other leading men of their province, they held diverse political views and were obliged to different Satsuma and Chōshū patrons in their official and business careers. Yet between them, they spanned the entire political spectrum in the House of Peers, a very strategic network if held together by Hachisuka, co-ordinating them as an Independent. In 1900 he launched a monthly magazine called *Meigi* (Loyalty) pledged to defend the constitutional regime against further political-party inroads and to ward off threatened reforms to the House of Peers. The list of subscribers printed in the first few issues bears the names of many prominent *Kenkyūkai*, *Sawakai* and *Mushozokuha* members.[31] If, as seems likely, other lordly Independents played roles as positive as this, then as a class they were perhaps more active and less aloof than might be supposed.

ROLE

The crucial battles between Sat–chō cabinets and the House of Representatives were fought over the budget. Yearly government expenditure rose steadily from ¥82 million in 1890 to ¥464 million in 1905; successive cabinets each demanding heavier taxes than the last had to resort to all measures, fair or foul, to get their budgets passed. Political parties with majorities in the House of Representatives gave their consent to budget increases only in return for concessions: relaxation of the laws controlling political associations, meetings and publications; higher salaries for Diet members; wider electoral qualifications; cabinet posts and special places in the bureaucracy for party members. In 1898 the Satsuma and Chōshū elder statesmen had to hand over the prime ministership to Ōkuma Shigenobu, leader of the *Kenseitō* party, though his cabinet collapsed within a few months as a result of bureaucratic obstruction and internal feuding. A few years later, in 1900, Itō Hirobumi launched his own political party, the *Seiyūkai*, and formed a cabinet in which most ministers were members of it. Thereafter for over a decade cabinets were formed in alternation between Katsura Tarō with non-party ministers and Saionji Kimmochi, Itō's successor as President of the *Seiyūkai*, who continued to appoint party members to ministerial portfolios.

The House of Peers played a subsidiary but important role in these developments, all the while trying to maintain its independence and to avoid being treated like a pawn in the grander contest between bureaucratic cabinets and political-party forces. When its powers were first mooted, most framers of the Constitution envisaged that the House of Peers should receive budget estimates for debate after the Representatives, approving them as a whole without going into specific details. But one of them successfully objected to such a disparaging restriction,[32] and finally both Houses of the Diet were given equal rights of budget review. Even so, when the Peers restored cuts made to the navy estimates in June 1892, the Representatives refused to accept its right to do so. As the budget bill shuttled between the two Houses, the Peers appealed to the Emperor on the issue. He referred the matter to his own advisory body, the Privy Council, which ruled that the House receiving the budget estimates second was not bound in any way by the first, and that cuts made by one House were quite able to be restored by the other.[33] The fact that the Peers had to confirm this right against objections from the Representatives reminded its Members that equal partnership between the two Houses could not be taken for granted, though most Peers at this time shared the Representatives' outrage at the Matsukata cabinet's interference in the last general election, and promptly agreed to hold a Joint Conference of the Diet which approved the cuts that had caused the rift between them.

Especially in budgetary matters, most Representatives viewed the

Peers with hostility as a pro-cabinet bastion of bureaucratic privilege, as indeed was mostly the case. With the exception of this Joint Conference of both Houses in June 1892, which slashed nearly ¥1 million from the cabinet's proposed expenditure on warship construction, it was a fact that until 1900 all budget bills passed the House of Peers with only minor amendments and cuts. Unable to command a majority in the House, Viscount Tani and his followers had to frame objections to budget increases in the form of Diet memorials (*kengian*) that when reported in the newspapers brought their views to public attention. In December 1891 Tani and seventy-five followers drew up a memorial demanding savage cuts in government expenditure and a policy of strict retrenchment, but after two days of debate the House of Peers rejected it by 97 votes to 78, an ominous defeat for the Opposition forces.[34] A few years later, in February 1896, Prime Minister Itō went before the House of Peers budget committee to explain his proposal for an army increase of six divisions. Prince Konoe was head of this committee and Viscount Tani one of its members; they determined to refuse approval, but after heated debate Itō's budget was finally passed without amendments.[35] The Opposition tried again in March 1897, when Viscount Tani and forty-six followers drew up a memorial to the Emperor pleading for a reduction in military expenditure, now running at nearly 50 per cent of the budget. Even in the most competitive Western nations, they pointed out, this figure rarely exceeded 30 per cent. But when put to the ballot, only a minority seventy members voted for it.[36] Cuts made in the budget estimates by the House of Peers later that month were very modest,[37] and Viscount Tani's memorial strangely muted; both he and Konoe had to face the fact that the current Matsukata cabinet, for all its promises of retrenchment and anti-Chōshū complexion, had no real desire to cut military expenditure; indeed as Finance Minister in the previous Itō cabinet, Matsukata had been largely responsible for drawing up the armaments-expansion programme.[38] Any hope that Opposition forces in the House of Peers could join with their allies in the House of Representatives to halt runaway military expenditure was now dashed. The fact that both Itō and Matsukata had formed coalitions with the leading parties in the House of Representatives to get these budgets passed left Konoe and Tani even more isolated and depressed.

By now Pro-cabinet and Moderate groups, led by the *Kenkyūkai*, were strong enough to ensure that budgets put up by bureaucratic cabinets would always be passed by the House of Peers. In return, leaders of such groups, beginning with Baron Senke Takatomi in 1894, were appointed to local governorships and official posts. The only hostile memorial on budgetary matters passed by a majority of the House was delivered to the Emperor by President Hachisuka in March 1895, a protest against improper tendering by the Communications Ministry as had appeared in the final budget accounts for 1891.[39] This was long after the event, however, and hardly an issue of current importance.

But if getting budgets passed was the final test of who was the master in politics, more combative Members of the House of Peers found other controversial issues on which to challenge successive cabinets. The first of these erupted when Baron Ozawa Takeo resigned from his commission as lieutenant-general in December 1891. An Imperial Nominee, he had given a speech in the House of Peers pointing out with graphic detail defects in Japan's military organization and national defence. Army circles took umbrage at what they decried as leaking strategic secrets, then contrived to obtain Imperial approval for Ozawa's 'voluntary discharge', a form of retirement not stipulated in Army Regulations. Members of both Houses were guaranteed unrestricted freedom of speech by the Constitution during Diet sessions, so the issue remained contentious for the next few years. Tani and his followers drew up a memorial to the Emperor in January 1893 protesting against Ozawa's dismissal, declaring that Prime Minister Matsukata was to blame even though the Emperor had approved it, the earliest attempt to question Imperial orders and to define ministerial responsibility, key points in Japan's future political development.[40] Tani's memorial was rejected by 83 votes to 45, ending further debate on the matter in the House of Peers, but it remained a pivotal event none the less.

Then there was the issue of electoral interference. The first Yamagata cabinet of 1890–91 just managed to pass its budget against a hostile House of Representatives; the Matsukata cabinet that took over determined to put down political-party opposition. When his budget was rejected, Matsukata ordered a Diet dissolution; in the ensuing general election, under orders from Home Minister Shinagawa Yajirō, prefectural governors and their police chiefs harassed party candidates, provoking disturbances that left in their wake twenty-five dead and over three hundred wounded across the nation. Despite this, almost all the previous Representatives were re-elected and the cabinet in its next Diet session faced a House thirsting for revenge. Many Members of the House of Peers shared their outrage; in April 1892 even the normally Pro-cabinet *Kenkyūkai* set up a committee to investigate, and in May a majority of eighty-four Members passed a memorial urging the cabinet to enforce official discipline in the matter. The House of Representatives went further: it passed a bill for cabinet censure, whereupon Matsukata ordered a Diet suspension, rejecting its right to question the status of cabinet ministers. Members of all groups in the House of Peers then sent a letter of admonition to the Prime Minister remonstrating against this evasive action.[41] True, Matsukata was able to get his supplementary budget bill passed by a Joint Conference of both Houses, though with a savage cut to the naval estimates, together with a number of other bills on less controversial issues. Even so, Shinagawa had been forced to resign in March 1892, taking responsibility for the election debacle, soon followed by Matsukata and all his cabinet in August.

In the field of diplomacy feelings grew heated after November 1892 when the warship *Chishima* collided with a British merchant vessel in the Inland Sea and sank. For legal reasons, the suit for compensation had to be made in the Emperor's name; when the Privy Council in London rejected Japan's claim for ¥850,000, awarding it a miserable £10,000 sterling (less than one-tenth), a popular outcry erupted. Party opponents of the current Itō cabinet were quick to take this up, as an action damaging to Japan's sovereignty and an insult to the Emperor, who had been forced to sue a merchant company in a foreign court with such humiliating results.[42] Konoe and Tani, as leaders of the *Sanyōkai* and *Konwakai*, joined in the chorus of protest.[43]

This rumpus coincided with negotiations for treaty revision; in return for a number of tariff advantages, among other concessions aliens were to be allowed unrestricted residence in Japan after 1899. By October 1893 hostile groups in the House of Representatives, supported by Konoe and Tani, demanded that the right of aliens to reside outside the open ports should be strictly controlled; they should also be liable to tax and required to obey Japanese administrative regulations. When Itō as Prime Minister went before the House of Representatives in December 1893 to explain his policies, he was hissed and booed from the assembly chamber. His angry response was to order a dissolution of the Lower House without further ado, forcing the Representatives to the costly and enervating necessity of a general election.

Not only Konoe, Tani and their followers but many other fair-minded Members of the House of Peers resolved to protest against Itō's action, maintaining that to dissolve the Diet without giving any reasons was arrogant and unconstitutional. Thirty-eight prominent Members drew up a memorial in January 1894 warning Itō that the opposition his cabinet was receiving from the House of Representatives over its treaty revision proposals was not simply the result of ignorant anti-foreign feeling; it sprang from a sincere concern for the national interest. While conceding that many Representatives in earlier Diet sessions had concentrated all their strength on cutting the budget estimates, there had recently been an improvement in quality, they maintained. As the leading men of their localities, Representatives could not just be written off as all holding mistaken views. In questioning foreign policy they were quite sincere, and if their resolutions were troublesome, that was their proper office. When the Emperor granted the Constitution, he had intended to promote unity and co-operation. Although to suspend the Diet and dissolve the House of Representatives was part of the Imperial prerogative entrusted for a time to Itō as Prime Minister, this power was not to be used wantonly, so they urged him to reconsider his decision.[44]

Itō replied that various party factions had determined to resist the cabinet even before the Diet met, and had then simply attacked the government without considering facts or reasons, irresponsibly demanding the strict enforcement of existing treaties regardless of details. Having given up all hope for this Diet session, he had therefore dissolved the Lower House. In a further letter of February 1894 Konoe and Tani again remonstrated with Itō for taking a low view of the Diet as merely an advisory body to the cabinet and seeking to subordinate it to the Executive. Itō's final reply, both flippant and condescending, was that they would simply have to disagree.[45]

Konoe and Tani had not finished yet, joining with anti-cabinet political forces to launch a Strong Foreign Policy Convention in April 1894. Itō went in person to give his reasons for the previous dissolution to the House of Peers on 29 May, one day before the Representatives passed a bill for cabinet censure. So Itō dissolved the Lower House for a second time; in June 1894 he published his reasons for this. Konoe sent him a prompt rejoinder, while Members from all groups in the House of Peers resolved to support the current Representatives in the forthcoming general election.[46] Just when it seemed that both Houses of the Diet were firmly united against the cabinet, relief came to Itō from an unexpected quarter: after military skirmishes with Chinese troops in Korea, Japan declared war on 1 August 1894. When the new Diet session opened in October both Houses suspended all opposition to the cabinet as a patriotic gesture, and a budget bill for huge increases in military expenditure passed without question.

Thereafter, as we have seen, Konoe and Tani kept up their objections to military increases after peace was restored in March 1895. But they were never again able to achieve an alliance between both Houses of the Diet to resist subsequent cabinets. Within the House of Peers itself, Konoe's following was reduced to a mere fifteen Members after the seven-year-term election of 1897, at a time when cabinets and political parties were reaching accords that threatened to bypass the House of Peers as an independent force in politics.

Meanwhile some notable initiatives of the Peers were supported by all its groups; for example, improvements in education. In February 1895 the House of Peers resolved that a National Education Convention should be set up, and secured the approval of the House of Representatives for this.[47] Thereafter it memorialized the cabinet in March 1896, requesting that ¥10 million of the China Indemnity should be used to fund local primary schools.[48] Konoe took a special interest in education; he became principal of the Peers Academy in 1895 and for a few years was President of the Japan Education Association. Members of the House of Peers with their high levels of academic achievement were well qualified to take the initiative in pressing for educational improvement, not just for special schools but for those at the city, town and village level. A little later, *Kenkyūkai* leaders in January 1899 drew up a memorial advocating more middle schools and universities, then secured large increases for education in the budget of January 1900.[49] These endeavours show the House of Peers at its best, promoting the national interest on a non-partisan basis.

Many leading Members also sought to defend the independence of the Judiciary against cabinet manipulation. Japan had acquired Taiwan in 1895 as part of the spoils of its victory over China; for the next few years the new colony weltered in violence, maladministration and corruption. Takano Takenori, the first Chief Justice of the Taiwan Supreme Court, opted to hear a prosecution involving a high official of the colonial administration in 1897. He was recalled to Tokyo for discussions with cabinet ministers; they attempted to dissuade him by blandishments and threats, then ordered his retirement. Under Article 58 of the Constitution, judges were immune from involuntary transfer or dismissal except on the grounds of criminal conviction or incapacity, so Takano stuck by his rights and returned to Taiwan. The day before the corruption case was due to come before him, twelve policemen cordoned off the courthouse. Four constables then arrived at the bench with Takano's designated successor and ordered him to stand down. Other judges present urged him to resist; after a violent scuffle the dejected Takano stalked out of the High Court and returned to Japan to vindicate himself as best he could.

The current Matsukata cabinet had meanwhile ruled that henceforth judges in the colony were to be appointed, retired or transferred by the Justice Ministry in Tokyo, and in July 1897 summarily abolished the Taiwan Supreme Court. Such savage browbeating of the Judiciary unleashed storms of protest; impassioned speeches were made against the cabinet in both Houses of the Diet, while Takano found many supporters in newspaper and academic circles. In December cabinet ministers faced harsh questioning in the House of Peers.[50] Both the

Opposition and normally Pro-cabinet Members joined the general outcry; for example, Imperial Nominee Matsuoka Kōki, a prominent Justice official, whose carefully reasoned indictment rose to its disdainful climax with:

> Pleading ignorance of the law as an excuse to escape from blame is stupid and idiotic. Nobody should have to apply names like these to cabinet ministers. If simple rustics cannot make such a defence, how much less can ministers of a proud empire with a duty to implement the Constitution. They must correct improper actions and make a speedy amend for their faults. How dare they attempt to justify themselves with arrogant rebuttals and insolent faces![51]

Matsukata dissolved the House of Representatives and resigned a few days later after it passed a no-confidence bill in his cabinet, so the matter lapsed. For the next few years Takano appealed to court after court in vain, while Diet interpellations on his behalf bogged down in the mire of political turmoil. His direct pleas to subsequent Prime Ministers Ōkuma and Itō also fell on deaf ears. Even so, many Members of the House of Peers, much to their public credit, had championed his cause.

The House of Peers also made a modest contribution to relaxing the strict official regulations over political associations, meetings and publications. Especially when faced by a hostile House of Representatives in the early 1890s, cabinets applied such controls to the full. The fact that the Peers blocked bills passed by the Representatives for greater freedom in these areas was, together with their compliance in passing budget estimates, a source of much bad feeling between the two Houses. In December 1892, for example, a special committee of the Peers rejected out of hand a bill passed by the Representatives for the abolition of the Peace Preservation Law.[52] Two years later, by a unanimous vote, the House of Representatives passed a bill abolishing temporary bans on publication, often imposed by cabinets to suppress hostile newspapers. When this bill came before the House of Peers many Members argued that such bans violated the spirit of the Constitution, but it was rejected by 94 votes to 91.[53] Even so, the result was close. By 1896 Pro-cabinet and Opposition forces in the House of Peers were evenly balanced; Tani with his allies was able to defeat a bill proposed by the Itō cabinet of this year strengthening the Peace Preservation Law; then in March 1897 they overcame *Kenkyūkai* and *Sawakai* objections by 96 votes to 66 in passing a bill for liberal revisions in the newspaper regulations,[54] put up by the second Matsukata cabinet in order to conciliate its party supporters in the House of Representatives.

When Yamagata formed his second cabinet in 1898, Opposition groups in the House of Peers had lost many Members in the term-election of the previous year, and the new Prime Minister had a strong following in the *Kenkyūkai* and *Sawakai*. By now the right of foreigners to reside in the interior under the new treaties of 1894 was due to become operative. As a preparation for this, the cabinet drafted a law to regulate religious affairs; an influx of Christians was in the offing and their legal rights needed to be defined. Prime Minister Yamagata took a special interest in the bill for this law, which he submitted to the House of Peers first; rather than sending his Home Minister to introduce it, he did so himself. The bill granted equal rights to Buddhists and Christians; when first projected, newspaper and academic opinion was friendly rather than hostile, so Yamagata expected it to pass without much opposition. But Buddhist groups across the nation were outraged that their religion, propagated in Japan for over a thousand years and so much part of its history and culture, should be put on a par with an alien creed only grudgingly tolerated for the last two decades. Supporters in the House of Peers were quick to echo these objections; even Pro-cabinet Members and personal followers of Yamagata combined with others to defeat the bill in February 1900 by 121 votes to 100 in a contest that cut across all group lines.[55] A confounded Yamagata simply had to abandon it, leaving the House of Peers to revel in glory as the defender of national traditions.

In order to pass his budget Yamagata formed an alliance with party leaders in the House of Representatives who demanded a high price for their support. Many Members of the House of Peers who had rejoiced at the collapse of the shortlived Ōkuma cabinet in November 1898 now found that the political parties were to gain most of their current demands from Yamagata, of all people. They did their best to resist. When a bill for revisions in the electoral law of the House of Representatives was put to the Peers in February 1900 they amended several of its key proposals: small electoral constituencies and signed voting papers (very advantageous to the larger political parties) were revised to large multi-member constituencies with secret balloting; the proposed increase in Representatives was cut from 478 to 337, and the tax-paying qualification to vote raised from ¥5 to ¥10 per annum. Angry exchanges ensued as committees from both Houses met to argue these points,[56] but the Peers stuck fast, and when the cabinet promulgated the new electoral law in February 1900 their amendments carried the day. A separate bill to increase the yearly salaries of all Diet Members from ¥800 to ¥2,000 passed the Peers in March 1899, but only after heated debate and a close vote of 96 to 90.[57]

Yamagata had considerable trouble in getting his budget bills through the House of Representatives, but the Peers approved them promptly with only minor amendments despite their large tax increases. Having successfully checked some of the political parties' electoral aspirations, Yamagata's powerful following in the Peers could also take heart from new measures to restrict outside appointments to the regular bureaucracy, and to the rule, confirmed by an Imperial ordinance of 1900, that Army and Navy Ministers must be serving officers of flag rank (lieutenant-general, rear admiral or above), thus ensuring strong powers for the military in cabinet formation, another check on future attempts by leaders in the House of Representatives to form party cabinets.

When Itō succeeded Yamagata as Prime Minister in September 1900 an icy wave of hostility swept through the House of Peers. Whereas Yamagata had formed an alliance of necessity with former Liberals gathered for a time in the *Kenseitō* party, Itō came to power as President of his own party, the *Seiyūkai*, with a strong majority in the House of Representatives. This new formation threatened to reduce the House of Peers to a political cipher. Most ministers in Itō's cabinet were party members, headed by the notorious Hoshi Tōru whose vituperative insults had angered the Peers on many occasions.[58]

Itō could look forward to his budget bill skating smoothly through the House of Representatives despite its hefty tax increases. His problem was to get the Peers to pass it. Unlike Yamagata, he had never sought to build up a following in the House of Peers,[59] though quite a few Members had risen under his patronage. Even so, only seven of them joined the *Seiyūkai*, and in the next few years when Itō's supporters got together to form a group they never numbered more than twenty.[60] On 17 December 1900, a week before the new cabinet faced its first Diet session, Itō's opponents in the House of Peers fired the first shot: 187 of them, drawn from all six major groups, sent him a letter of admonition demanding the dismissal and prosecution of Communications Minister Hoshi Tōru, alleging that his corrupt manipulations of Tokyo government while a city councillor made him utterly unfitted to hold a cabinet post.[61] Hoshi was compelled to resign a few days later.

When Itō's budget bill came before the House of Peers in February 1901, it faced a towering rampart of opposition: sixty *Kenkyūkai*, seventeen *Sawakai*, nineteen *Mokuyōkai*, fifty-four *Doyōkai*, and assorted Independents; in total 170 Members. Of the 251 people who attended the budget debate, only fifty approved, thirty-one abstained;[62] the rest handed Itō one of the harshest budget rejections in Diet history, almost as humiliating as the one he suffered in 1894 at the hands of the House of Representatives.

Prime Minister Itō went before the Peers to make a speech of complaint, then ordered a Diet suspension for twenty days. His next move was to seek help from fellow elder statesmen Yamagata and Matsukata, but to no avail. Although Yamagata remonstrated with his numerous followers in the House they refused to submit,[63] and by early March 1901 things had reached complete deadlock.

But the beleaguered Itō still had two trump cards to play. His genius as a legislator and renown as the 'father' of the Meiji Constitution made his views on structural change almost paramount. Egged on by party followers eager to cut down the House of Peers to manageable proportions, he had already drawn up proposals for sweeping reforms. Membership by hereditary right was to be abolished for all grades of the peerage, with merit as the sole criterion. Most Members were to be military or civil officials, or heads of universities, sitting by virtue of their posts; Imperial Nominees were to sit for a seven-year term, not for life, with a weeding out of old and worthless ones. High Taxpayers were to be removed altogether, as better placed in the House of Representatives. Itō planned to complete these reforms by 1911; only a rough draft of his plan remains, and was never made public,[64] but knowledge that the cabinet was considering such radical reforms helped to unnerve Itō's opponents.

Then there was his other card, in the event an ace: the Imperial throne itself. Over the years Emperor Meiji had developed a deep trust in Itō, who for all his bombast and tendency to sudden veering impressed his sovereign as a most loyal, patriotic and farsighted statesman.[65] In the past, Itō as Prime Minister had several times managed to persuade the Emperor to issue orders commanding political opposition to cease, though this was regarded even in official and palace circles as improper and against the spirit of the Constitution. Now he resorted once more to this unchallengeable expedient. On 12 March 1901 President Konoe was summoned to the palace, where the Emperor handed him an Imperial rescript expressing the hope that the House of Peers would submit promptly to the cabinet's budget proposals. When the Diet reopened two days later, Konoe read out this rescript to a packed House of Peers. All Members listened in frozen silence, then unanimously authorized Konoe to present a letter of compliance to the Emperor; Itō's budget bill was re-submitted to the House special committee and approved on 17 March without revisions.

Yet Itō's victory was a last throw; now he had to back down. To the disappointment of some party ministers in his cabinet, all plans to reform the House of Peers were scrapped. Then he resigned in May 1901, handing over to Katsura, who like his patron Yamagata was a professed opponent of party cabinets. That same month, as if to vindicate the House of Peers, their arch-enemy Hoshi Tōru was stabbed to death by an outraged critic of his corrupt dealings in Tokyo City government. Itō's own political career was now near its end. Two years later, in a neat manoeuvre, Yamagata and Katsura persuaded the Emperor to appoint him President of the Privy Council, forcing his resignation from the *Seiyūkai* leadership.

As Prime Minister, Katsura cultivated friendly ties with the House of Peers,[66] where in any case the balance had swung towards Pro-cabinet groups. Konoe by this time was engrossed in his People's Alliance pressing for strong measures against Russia, leaving Tani isolated, his demands for cuts in military expenditure now swept aside as Japan nerved itself in preparation for an all-out continental war. Already very ill in 1903 when his term as President ended, Konoe died next year. His successor was Prince Tokugawa Iesato, direct descendant of the last *shōgun*. Educated in England, and a respected, cordial President, he was to hold his post continuously until 1932, bringing a sedate calm to the House. Tani remained active as chairman of the House general committee until his death in 1911, aged seventy-three years, removed this twin pillar of a formerly vibrant Opposition.

After the confrontation of 1901 the need for some reforms of the House of Peers was generally admitted, so Prime Minister Katsura drafted an imperial ordinance and put it before the House for approval in 1905. Barons had more than trebled in numbers over the last decade, threatening to alter the balance of House membership. Imperial Nominees had doubled, though restricted by the provision that they and the High Taxpayers should not in total exceed the titled Peers. It was now proposed to set definite limits: Counts seventeen, Viscounts seventy, Barons sixty-three, Imperial Nominees 125. The multiple-name ballot for electoral grades continued, but voting was to be secret. These changes in fact did little to alter the *status quo*; Barons and Imperial Nominees were granted a slight increase over current numbers, and the Viscounts in the *Kenkyūkai* could continue to use their electoral organization to good effect. In March 1905 the Peers approved this draft by a very close vote of 129 to 128, and it was promulgated as Imperial Ordinance No. 58 later in the month.[67]

POSTSCRIPT

This new-found stability in the House of Peers came at a price. Over the next two decades a few new groups formed and old ones vanished but the basic structure remained the same: the *Kenkyūkai* and *Sawakai* continued to dominate House politics as a solid bloc, bargaining with successive cabinets for a share of power. Prime Ministers Yamamoto Gonnohyōe in 1914 and Ōkuma Shigenobu in 1916 resigned after the House of Peers took a hostile attitude to government bills, but both of them were in deep political trouble anyway and found this a convenient pretext to leave office. By the 1920s, as demands for mass democracy grew strong, the House of Peers was often denigrated as a useless anachronism and its hereditary Members as lacking the ability of their forebears, a fact ruefully admitted by some of its own leading men.[68] In 1924 Prime Minister Kiyoura Keigo made a farcical attempt to form a cabinet centred on his followers and allies in the House of Peers. He was a longtime member of the *Kenkyūkai* and its link with high government circles but this was no use to him now. Backed by a hostile outcry from the public, the major political parties united to bring him down. In the general election of early 1925 they won a sweeping majority, forcing Kiyoura to resign with all his cabinet before he had achieved anything of note. This humiliating debacle triggered off renewed demands for radical reforms, which the House of Peers was perhaps lucky to evade.[69] The only structural change of these years, most unfortunate in its results, was to widen the suffrage for High Taxpayers, increasing political strife among them and leading to a marked decline in the quality of elected Members.[70]

Thereafter the House made two pathetic attempts to improve its reputation. By an Imperial ordinance of 1925, professors of the Japan Academy elected four of their number to be Members for a seven-year term. Then, early in 1945, as Japan lay in ruins awaiting its inevitable surrender, its empire in tatters, Korea and Taiwan were allotted three nationals each as Imperial Nominees. The Occupation reforms of 1947 put an end to the Peers as a separate social order and replaced them politically by an elected House of Councillors.

The Peers Club, a handsome building set in spacious parkland, was taken over by the Occupation authorities for a few years as a club for women officers, who helped themselves to many valuable artefacts and fittings.[71] Then it was sold when made subject to municipal taxes as a private institution in 1951. Today its scholarly heir, the *Kasumi Kaikan*, publishes historical studies on the House of Peers from an office in central Tokyo. The *Kenkyūkai*'s electoral organization, the *Shōyūkai*, is still lodged in its former headquarters near the Diet building. Now a social club with a small library, its archives section has recently published a list of members, a year book, and a useful history.

If the passage of time has dealt so harshly with it, did the House of Peers ever have a real chance to grow and flourish as a vital institution of modern Japan? Perhaps not, when one considers that so few aristocratic Upper Houses have survived in our century; even Britain's House of Lords awoke to discover in 1911 that it could survive only as a review body for legislation within strict constraints. Konoe and other leading Members foresaw from the start that unless the House of Peers commanded genuine respect for usefulness and ability it could not expect to endure, well aware of the downward drag of mere privilege.[72] From the outset, the Peers had to struggle hard to uphold their dignity against the wry condescension often shown for them by the Meiji meritocracy. Several of the leading Sat–Chō statesmen were Counts when the House first convened; their lofty refusal to seek election, and consistent non-attendance when they rose to Marquis or Prince and sat by right, was a bad omen for an institution they themselves had created. Kaneko Kentarō, one of the framers of the Constitution, and the first Chief Secretary of the House of Peers, outraged prominent Members when he gave them a condescending lecture on their duties and responsibilities just before its first session, warning them that in contribution to constitutional progress, ability and experience they were clearly inferior to the former samurai and commoners of the House of Representatives.[73] Next, in 1891, a government spokesman lost his temper when explaining a bill and dubbed the Members 'parasites' (*yakkaimono*) to their very faces.[74] If that was not enough, Tani's newspaper *Nihon*, when reporting heated debate in the Upper House over the bill to increase Diet Members' salaries in March 1899, quoted a speech that castigated the beggarly behaviour of out-of-town Peers with a sneering disdain quite as vitriolic as anything a commoner could say about them.[75] Meanwhile party leaders in the House of Representatives, especially Hoshi Tōru, lost no opportunity to bombard the Upper House with abuse whenever it got in their way.

In fact, whether Members of the House of Peers or not, over the years most nobles managed to maintain respectable levels of education and employment,[76] but no really forceful leaders emerged after Konoe and Tani. Son of Atsumaro and expected to match his illustrious father, Konoe Fumimaro was President of the House of Peers from 1936 to 1937, and Prime Minister from 1940 to 1941. But for all his popularity with the crowds he was simply a puppet of the Military, much to his private shame and regret.[77] He died by suicide in 1945 just before he was due for arrest as a war criminal.

Another grave weakness of the House of Peers was its ineptitude in drafting legislation. Unlike the House of Representatives, which drew up many successful bills, between 1890 and 1905 the Peers initiated and passed a mere handful, all of them on minor issues. Over the next two decades it scarcely drew up any bills at all. Its role in legislation was a very negative one,[78] often blocking bills passed by the Representatives, or at the most requesting a bill on a given matter to be drawn up, leaving it to the cabinet with its team of specialized officials in the Bureau of Legislation to frame and present it. Social restraints on noblemen playing active roles in politics, the confusion of grades and electoral systems, compliant attitudes to bureaucratic patrons, reluctance to change a system that supported them so well – perhaps these among other factors combined to restrict the House of Peers to such a passive role, then doomed it by political inertia to a decline in authority and respect.

Yet the first fifteen years were fresh and invigorating. Despite cabinet influence and internal grouping, the balance of votes on many important bills was very close, following debates that set out the pros and cons with careful thoroughness. Even experienced observers often found it difficult to foresee what action the House of Peers would take on any political question or to discover divisions within it along consistent lines, except for a general inclination to support bureaucratic cabinets.[79] And if the House of Peers failed to fulfil its earlier promise, so perhaps did Japan's political world as a whole.

NOTES

1　For a list of all such occasions after 1890 see Taguchi Sukekichi (1931: 337ff.).
2　Notably Banno Junji (1971) and Sakeda Masatoshi (1978). For an earlier study, still very useful, see Hayashi Shigeru (1951).
3　Short biographies of all members of the House of Peers are given in Shūgiin Sangiin (comp.), *Gikai seido nanajūnenshi: Kizokuin sangiin giin meikan* (1961).
4　*Tokushima nichi nichi shimbun*, 4 August 1898, puts the number of these consistent absentees at seventy out of a total of 320 Members.
5　Takahashi Hidenao (1985: 34–70). See also Maeda Renzan (1971: 441–3).
6　Hayashi, p. 52.
7　Ibid., pp. 50–1.
8　Ibid., p. 52.
9　Masumi Junnosuke (1966), vol. 2: 176–7.
10　Iwasaki Uichi (1921: 44).
11　Taguchi, p. 11.
12　Satō Tatsuo (1943: 236, 249–51). *Kyūkizokuin 50 nenshi hensan shūshū monjo*, MS (Kenseishiryōshitsu, National Diet Library, Tokyo), item 21.
13　Konoe Kazankai (1924: 84).
14　Konoe Atsumaro Nikki Kankōkai (1968), vol. 1: 66–7, 70.
15　For an inside critique of Viscount elections see *Toki Akira monjo mokuroku*, MS (Kenseishiryōshitsu, National Diet Library, Tokyo), item 30. Speech

of Ogyū Yuzuru, 17 September 1891. See ibid., item 48 for June 1890 procedure and ballot paper. For a list of votes cast for all Viscounts elected in July 1890, see Meiji Nyūsu Hensan Iinkai (1984), vol. 4: 144.

16 Satō, p. 244.

17 For example, see *Tōkyō nichi nichi shimbun*, 9 July 1897.

18 Sawada Minoru (1924: 223–5). Duus, Peter (1968: 210).

19 See *Kondō Eimei monjo mokuroku*, MS (Kenseishiryōshitsu, National Diet Library, Tokyo), item 96.

20 See Shōyū Kurabu (1971), (1983).

21 For Okabe and Hotta, see Yamaguchi Aikawa (1932: 105–6); Sakamoto Tatsunosuke (1930b: 80).

22 For the formation and development of this group and others, see Sakamoto Tatsunosuke (1930a: especially 62–3).

23 See for example, Kokuritsu kokkai toshokan, *Kenseishi hensankai shūshū monjo mokuroku* (Tokyo, 1960), item 673, 'Inoue kōshaku ke shozō shomeika shokanshū', 6, 90. Senke to Inoue, 16 January 1894. Later this month Senke was appointed governor of Saitama Prefecture; Home Minister Inoue must have recommended him for this post. For Senke's character, see Yamaguchi, p. 106.

24 Hanabusa Sakitarō (1942: 16–17).

25 Kobayashi Kazuyoshi (1987: 69).

26 Konoe Kazankai, pp. 44–6.

27 Sakeda, pp.165–8. Meiji Hennenshi Hensankai (1936: 168–9, 294, 408).

28 Sakeda, pp. 264–5.

29 Oka Yoshitake (1958: 110).

30 Privy Councillors were not officially allowed to hold seats in the House of Peers, but top aristocrats like Hachisuka and the leading Meiji statesmen, sitting by right and for life, still remained Members.

31 Ōyama Ujirō (1934: 207). *Kondō Eimei monjo*, item 97. *Nomura Yasushi monjo*, Shokan 11.6 (Kenseishiryōshitsu, National Diet Library, Tokyo).

32 Shumpo Kō Tsuishōkai (1943), vol. 2: 626–8.

33 Sakamoto, *Nihon teikoku*, p. 16.

34 Hisho Ruisan Kankōkai (1935), vol. 1: 434–5.

35 Sakamoto, *Nihon teikoku*, p. 35. Ōtsu Junichirō (1927), vol. 4: 665–8.

36 *Meiji nyūsu jiten*, vol. 5 (1985: 110–11).

37 Sakamoto, *Nihon teikoku*, pp. 39–40.

38 Banno, pp. 135–7.

39 Nihon Kokusei Jiten Kankōkai (1953), vol. 2: 97.

40 Yasuda Hiroshi (1990: 43–4). *Meiji nyūsu jiten*, vol. 4 (1984: 107).

41 Sakamoto, *Nihon teikoku*, pp. 15–16. *Nihon kokusei jiten*, vol. 1 (1953: 659).

42 Uzaki Rojō (1915: 156–7). Washio Yoshinao (1959: 72–3).

43 Inoue Kiyoshi (1955: 209).

44 *Hisho ruisan*, vol. 1, pp. 560–5.

45 Ibid., pp. 571–88.

46 Sakamoto, *Nihon teikoku*, p. 28.

47 Ibid., p. 31.

48 Ibid., p. 36.

49 Ibid., pp. 55, 84. Sakamoto Tatsunosuke (1930: 13).

50 Sakamoto, *Nihon teikoku*, p. 43.

51 Ōyama, p. 225.

52 *Shimbun shūsei*, vol. 8, p. 335.
53 Ibid., vol. 9, p. 76. On this particular bill, the Peers opted to vote by name rather than to stand and be counted; the list for and against published here is a rare example of known personal divisions in the House.
54 Hirao Michio (1935: 729–32). Takahashi, p. 39 and note 3.
55 Kobayashi, pp. 65–81. Matsumoto Shigetoshi (1926: 148–51). Katō Fusazō (1927: 86–9).
56 Sakamoto, *Nihon teikoku*, pp. 51–2.
57 *Meiji nyūsu jiten*, vol. 6, pp. 129–30. Quoting *Nihon*, 9 March 1899.
58 Sakamoto, *Nihon teikoku*, p. 51.
59 Maeda Renzan, pp. 441–2.
60 Itō Hirobumi Kankei Monjo Kenkyūkai (1973–4: 434–6).
61 Sakamoto, *Nihon teikoku*, p. 57.
62 Maejima Shōzō (1964: 212–13).
63 Tokutomi Iichirō (1933), vol. 3: 444.
64 Satō, pp. 34–6.
65 Oka Yoshitake (1986: 20, 22–3, 25).
66 Shōyū Kurabu (1983: 61).
67 Sakamoto Tatsunosuke (1940: 16–17); (1930b: 51).
68 Kanazawa Makoto (1968: 143).
69 Shinobu Seisaburō (1954: 1276ff.).
70 Sawada, pp. 79–83.
71 Kasumi Kaikan (1967: 721–2). Mrs MacArthur, wife of the Supreme Commander, is said to have made off with some choice items.
72 *Hisho ruisan*, vol. 2, pp. 566–70, 422–8.
73 *Tōkyō nichi nichi shimbun*, 29 August, 2, 3 September 1890. *The Japan Weekly Mail*, 6 September 1890.
74 *Shimbun shūsei*, vol. 8, p. 169.
75 *Meiji nyūsu jiten*, vol. 6, p. 130. For a later and even more harsh criticism of this kind, see Noma Gozō (1926–7), pp. 139–42.
76 Senda Minoru (1986: 31).
77 Oka, *Five Political Leaders*, pp. 215–18, 221.
78 Banno Junji (1973: 44). Also, Taguchi, pp. 188–91. For specific bills, see *Gikai seido Nanajūnenshi. Teikoku gikai gian kemmei roku* (1961).
79 Iwasaki, p. 48.

2 Land tax increase

The debates of December 1898

Andrew Fraser

Land tax provided 60 per cent of government revenue when the first House of Representatives met in 1890. Suffrage restricted to male adults paying ¥15 per annum or more in direct national taxes ensured that at least half of those elected would be rural landlords. As such, they were a formidable occupational lobby, certain to challenge the first cabinets headed by Satsuma and Chōshū leaders to a head-on fight over budgetary issues.

For many years Japan's farmers had smouldered with resentment at their tax burdens. In July 1873, at a time when the new Meiji government was still rather insecure, the Emperor issued an edict announcing that their tax would be levied at a rate of 3 per cent on land price assessments but progressively reduced to 1 per cent as commercial and other taxes rose to significant levels.[1] While having to sell 20–30 per cent of crop to pay land tax, farmers also faced rising local taxes; to quell massive farmer uprisings sweeping the nation another Imperial edict reduced the former rate to 2.5 per cent in January 1877. At that time land tax provided 90 per cent of government revenue; by 1890 new consumer and income taxes had reduced this percentage by one-third, yet no reduction had been made in land tax despite the Emperor's promise. When surveys were carried out – at great expense for local farmers – to fix land prices over the whole nation in the later 1870s, the Finance Department had also promised re-surveys every five years, then cut out all mention of this in the revised Land Tax Regulations of 1884 when the time had become due[2] (though in all fairness many farmers had prospered in the inflationary years of 1878 to 1881).

Well aware that land tax in the advanced nations of Europe and North America rarely provided more than 20 per cent of government revenue, and in Britain only 1 per cent, most rural landlords in the House of Representatives were determined from the outset to press for immediate and future reductions, while demanding heavier taxes on commerce and industry to share the revenue burden more equally. But government leaders, though regretful that land tax remained so heavy, insisted that it must remain at the current rate. They pointed out that customs dues were still restricted to low levels as a result of unequal treaties forced on Japan by the Western Powers in the 1850s, while commerce and industry remained too backward to pay heavier taxes, needing all the support they could get.

Several bills for land tax reduction passed by the House of Representatives after 1890 were rejected by the House of Peers, where a majority of Members shared the government's view. Meanwhile in these years rural landlords grew more prosperous for a variety of economic reasons, though how far small farmers and tenants shared in this was a contentious issue at the time and remains open to conjecture.[3] In particular, the price of rice rose steadily from ¥8 per *koku* (180 litres) in 1890 to ¥13 in 1898, when rural landlords certainly had to sell much less crop than before to pay their tax, still fixed at 2.5 per cent of land values assessed on the basis of much lower prices in the mid-1870s. The huge indemnity of ¥360 million received from China after its defeat in 1895 fuelled an economic boom; while prices of agricultural products rose, rural landlords found new opportunities to invest in spinning, railways and other enterprises, making them less dependent on farming for their income.[4]

But if the wealthier rural landlords after 1890 grew less determined to reduce land tax, any attempt by a cabinet to increase it was political suicide, as Prime Minister Itō Hirobumi discovered when his budget bill came before the House of Representatives in June 1898. Needing to make up a deficit of ¥36 million per annum in government revenue, Itō proposed to raise the rate of land tax from 2.5 to 3.7 per cent of assessed value, which would bring in nearly half of it. He went before the House of Representatives several times to plead for this in person, then resigned in despair when handed the most humiliating budget defeat in Diet history: sweeping rejection by 247 votes to 27. In office for barely three months before forced to resign by internal feuding, the Ōkuma Shigenobu cabinet that followed Itō's did not have time to conduct a Diet session, but its budget plans proposed to raise the extra revenue by higher taxes on sugar, tobacco and *sake*.[5] When Yamagata Aritomo took over in November 1898 to form his second cabinet he returned to land tax as his chief resource, proposing to increase its rate to 4 per cent levied for the next ten years. In such circumstances Prime Ministers usually engineered a general election to get a more subservient House of Representatives, but Yamagata disdained to do so; he intended to get his bill for this increase passed by the very same people who had so overawed Itō earlier in the year.

Opposition was quick to flare. Viscount Tani Kanjō, a forceful leader in the House of Peers and a champion of Japan's small farmers, launched a formidable League Against Land Tax Increase. Massive delegations of local farmers arrived in Tokyo as Tani and his allies sponsored a national convention to protest against the cabinet's proposals; amidst mounting excitement and disorder, the police broke up demonstrations and forced meetings to dissolve.[6]

On the other hand, business groups led by Shibusawa Eichi mounted a Campaign For Land Tax Increase; they maintained that rural landlords as the most prosperous class in the nation must contribute more to the national treasury if economic development was to continue. The business world had slumped at the time, and the outlook for commerce and industry seemed bleak. Many of the new enterprises that had mushroomed during the postwar boom of 1896 collapsed into bankruptcy as interest rates rose steeply, stocks and bonds plummeted in value, and imports burgeoned. Meanwhile the currency switch from silver to a gold standard in 1897 posed a potential threat to Japan's export trade.[7] Small farmers and tenants had also suffered much hardship in the widespread crop failure of that year. To city businessmen, rural landlords in the House of Representatives were a selfish, greedy lobby indifferent to a grave crisis in government finance at a time when Japan desperately needed to build up its military strength as Western Powers encroached on east Asia and conflict loomed. Their views were echoed by famous economists such as Taguchi Ukichi, one of the Representatives from Tokyo.[8]

Yamagata could also expect support from the Land Price Revision League, headed by rural landlords willing to support some increase in land tax provided that the burden was fairly shared. In the land tax reforms of the mid-1870s each prefecture had been allotted a separate rice price, varying in accordance with proximity to the big city markets. This is turn put a higher or lower price on the land itself, on which all owners paid a 2.5 per cent tax. In some prefectures, notably Tokushima, despite all their protests, the rice price had been fixed at a level that farmers regarded as much too high.[9] In others such as Yamaguchi, home of Chōshū leaders Yamagata and Itō, earlier assessments were much more generous. Thereafter railway development, particularly in north Japan, caused real land values in some favoured localities to rise well above the mid-1870s assessments.[10] From the first Diet in 1890, Representatives from central Japan had put up bills for land price revision; by 1898, with strong support from local farmers, they formed a powerful lobby in the House of Representatives.[11] So while proposing an increase in land tax from 2.5 to 4 per cent, Yamagata drew up a separate bill for land prices to be revised over the whole nation; some prefectures would pay as little as 3 per cent and others as much as 6 per cent on the new assessments, correcting the anomalies of the last two decades. This assured him the support of at least one third of the farmer Representatives.

As a further tempting bait for local leaders, Yamagata announced that if the Diet approved his increase in land tax, the central government would take over a major proportion of prison expenses. In most prefectures these amounted to a large sum and were rising year by year as Japan progressively adopted Western legal standards and institutions. New treaties signed in 1894 allowed aliens to reside in the interior after 1899; hitherto special prisons in the metropolitan cities and treaty ports had coped with the problem of confining foreigners but the government was now anxious to have national control. This provided Yamagata with a very opportune *quid pro quo*. In places like Tokushima Prefecture, where the land price revision movement was very strong anyway, local leaders estimated that although land tax would rise by ¥66,000 per annum as a result of Yamagata's bills, they would save up to ¥80,000 a year in prison expenses.[12]

Even so, against all his political principles, Yamagata could only succeed by forming an open coalition with the *Kenseitō*, former Liberals now holding a majority of seats in the Lower House. This party was led by Hoshi Tōru, one of the Representatives for Tokyo, with a powerful following centred on the Kantō region.[13] In the contest with political enemies and rivals, both within his party and outside it, his closest allies were Representatives from Kōchi Prefecture such as Kataoka Kenkichi, elected Speaker of the House in December 1898. Unlike the beleaguered Itō earlier in the year, Yamagata could count on *Kenseitō* support provided he made concessions to keep Hoshi's followers loyal. The cabinet therefore drew up bills for electoral changes advantageous to the stronger political parties, while also proposing to increase the yearly salary of Diet members from ¥800 to ¥2,000.

Then there was outright bribery. Yamagata is known to have received ¥980,000 from palace funds when he became Prime Minister. In return for political support, Hoshi got at least ¥80,000 of this for his personal use.[14] Where the rest went is a mystery, but one Representative openly admitted having taken a bribe of ¥4,000, flaunting his written acknowledgement for this while pleased to announce that he had voted against the bills anyway.[15] Dark stories circulated that Home Minister Saigō Tsugumichi won over several Representatives from Yokohama with a lucrative contract for dock development,[16] and that Army Minister Katsura Tarō put money in the pockets of needier Members of the House of Peers.[17]

The stage was now set for one of the most startling upsets in Diet history, as Yamagata set out to achieve what all political observers would have regarded as impossible just weeks before.

THE HOUSE OF REPRESENTATIVES

On the afternoon of 10 December 1898 government-delegate (*seifu iin*) Mekada Tanetarō presented two bills to the general assembly for a first reading. Cabinet ministers were not required to hold Diet seats under the Constitution, so spokesmen like Mekada, a senior Ministry of Finance official, introduced legislative proposals on their behalf. In themselves these bills were quite simple: tables for revised land prices on wet and dry fields in every city and rural district of the nation, and an amendment to the Land Tax Regulations of 1884 raising the standard rate of tax from 2.5 per cent to 4 per cent. The bills were based on a rice price of ¥7.46 per *koku* as averaged over the last ten years, Mekada told the House, reminding Representatives that at the time of land tax reform in the mid-1870s the standard price of rice had been ¥3.86. He recounted the familiar story of how railway development and other factors had led to anomalies in land tax burdens over the nation as a whole and recommended the bills as the way to correct them.

To give the government-delegate a verbal roasting was all part of the political game, and Mekada's first questioner sought to tangle him in knots on the seeming contradiction of how tax could be increased while reducing the assessed value of land in some localities, an obvious quibble but pressed with venom. His next critic wondered why the government wanted to increase tax on agricultural land because its value had increased threefold in the last two decades, but allowed tax on urban dwelling land to remain the same although values had increased by as much as twenty times in the same period. Mekada replied that urban dwelling land differed fundamentally from agricultural land in leases, sales and situational values, while the Meiji government had in fact imposed taxes on it that had never been levied in the past.

At this point, anxious to move things on, another Representative proposed that the bills should be considered by a special committee of twenty-seven members of the House to be selected by the Speaker. When the votes on this motion were counted, it passed by 146 to 127, and the Speaker deferred continuation of the first reading to a later date.[18]

For the next ten days, members of the House special committee engaged in complicated bargaining and discussions of their own, both with the Finance Minister and among themselves. It was in such committees that the real legislative work of the House of Representatives was done, for although cabinet ministers and government-delegates attended plenary sessions to make explanations and answer questions, this process was often quite perfunctory.[19]

As the day for the first reading of the two bills approached, and Yamagata's many-pronged offensive reached its climax, diehard opponents of land tax increase mounted a last, desperate resistance. On 16 December, when Speaker Kataoka Kenkichi set a date for the forthcoming debate, they demanded its postponement, no doubt to allow more time for protest motions against the cabinet's flagrant use of bribery and police powers to overcome opposition. This quickly became a shouting match between Hoshi Tōru and Tanaka Shōzō, a political opponent equally notorious for rough-house tactics and abusive speech.[20] Clamouring for Hoshi to be ejected for insulting language, Tanaka lumbered up the steps to the Speaker's table and tugged Kataoka by the sleeve to reinforce his demands, only to be ordered out himself. When he refused to budge, four guards pinioned him, then dragged him out of the chamber, Tanaka all the time struggling and roaring in protest like a wild animal.[21] Meanwhile the entire assembly erupted in a pandemonium of mingled shouts of abuse or encouragement. This was all good fun, a spot of melodrama for the House, and was reported with gusto in the less staid newspapers.

Nevertheless, all was calm on the afternoon of 20 December when the first reading of the bills was about to commence. Speaker Kataoka called on the chairman of the House special committee to make his report. This recounted at some length negotiations with the Finance Minister and among the committee members themselves; as a result, a majority of them recommended that the bills should be amended to cut the proposed increase in land tax from 4 per cent to 3.3 per cent, and to reduce its term from ten years to five. They also agreed that the rate of tax on urban dwelling land should be raised from 2.5 to 5 per cent.[22] These revisions were a workable compromise: the cabinet could hardly expect to get all it demanded without any cuts at all, while a tax increase on cities pleased rural landlords.

Finance Minister Matsukata Masayoshi was present to answer questions. Despite his renown as a past Prime Minister and leader of the Satsuma clique, he got a drubbing from a grizzled old Representative from north Japan, where rural landlords were most determined to resist any increase in the land tax. Matsukata disputed his inquisitor's figures with wry contempt, but was challenged in turn 'to use his abacus'.[23] After further exchanges between Representatives, the Finance Minister and the government-delegate, the House was becoming impatient to move on to the main debate.

Kataoka now called on Taketomi Tokitoshi, an opponent of the bills, to speak first. For all his passionate concern for the farmers, Taketomi was in fact a former samurai, now a professional politician, a weak point his chief opponent in the debate later seized on. A native of Saga Prefecture, which he represented in the House, he was a fellow countryman and friend of Ōkuma Shigenobu, who had appointed him Chief Secretary of the cabinet a few months ago. As one of Ōkuma's closest advisors on matters of government finance and a member of the *Kenseihontō* party, Taketomi could be expected to oppose any proposals put up by a Yamagata cabinet, if only for reasons of political strategy; to him and his colleagues the Chōshū leaders were long term enemies. Taketomi's speech was as follows:

When the special committee of the House met to draw up a report on the government bills, I was one of the twelve opposed to them, as against the fourteen who approved. Some people mistakenly believe that we are blocking finances essential for the nation; to oppose an increase in the land tax is a rather different matter from that. Is the government's proposed expenditure of ¥220 million really needed? Cannot one cut a single mite from it? This should be debated at a later sitting to review the budget, and has no connection with these bills. Some say that anyone opposed to an increase in land tax at this time of looming crisis in east Asia can have no concern for the national interest, while only those in favour of it really care for Japan and its people, a confusion of two quite separate issues.

I oppose the bills because they are badly conceived, and because today the rate of land tax must on no account be raised. Even if the bills were perfectly drafted, I would still oppose them. To argue that an increase in the land tax will foster commerce and industry is quite wrong; farmers contribute very much to production and only they can increase prosperity. How can the national wealth be enhanced by oppressing and impoverishing them? Of course, certain merchants with government connections soak up a lot of tax money to enrich themselves, whether this comes from taxes on land, *sake* or tobacco. How can impoverishing twenty million farmers possibly promote the prosperity of a mere two million merchants and artisans in the big cities of Ōsaka and Tokyo! Japan today is a nation of farmers; they form over half the population and produce more than anyone else. If they decline, Japan's commerce and productivity do so too. Government revenue also falls, as a result of many things such as fewer passengers on the railways and reduced postal receipts. Quite apart from taxes, you all know how much good or bad harvests affect the economy.

Some people also argue that after Japan switched from silver to a gold standard two years ago, the value of currency has halved, and farmers now pay only half the tax they did before. This is quite wrong. The price of gold has risen in response to a fall in silver; it is not the cause of a decline in currency value but its result. Silver has lost value steadily over the last twenty years, and a further drop last year was not due to Japan's adoption of a gold standard; it fell from long-term tendencies. What was the value of currency around 1890 when strident demands were made for a reduction of land tax? The value of silver was higher then than it is now, yet in both Houses of the Diet voices were raised for land tax to be decreased. Silver now exchanges at ¥1 to 3 shillings sterling, and if you argued in 1890 that land tax was too heavy, you should do so now. How can you possibly advocate raising it? Silver has fallen by 33 per cent against sterling, but the increase in land tax proposed by the government is 60 per cent. In any case, it is quite wrong to maintain that because of this fall in currency value the tax burden on people has been reduced and so land tax should be raised. Having demanded a reduction in land tax for so many years, all of you who support increasing it now are guilty of gross inconsistency.

Another reason advanced by supporters of the bills is that in 1890 tax was 2.5 per cent of land value, so the rise in the price of rice from ¥8 per *koku* then to ¥13 this year has reduced its real incidence by between 30 and 50 per cent. This, of course, is a big mistake. Some government officials also maintain that an increase in the land tax will be paid only by rural landlords and does not affect tenant cultivators, a fatuous argument put forward by academic economists; it is useless as a foundation for government finance and quite at variance with actual conditions. Such a view may be valid for a nation like Britain where a small number of landlords virtually own the whole country and control agriculture while living the life of rich aristocrats in the big cities, and where farmers are just labourers. But Japan has 5,200,000 farmer households, a total of more than 20 million people. A little over half of these do not own land and are just tenants, but many of them are landlords as well. This cannot be compared to nations where most rural landlords are aristocrats.

To argue that a rise in the land tax affects only landlords but not tenants is therefore quite wrong. Any increase in land tax robs agriculture of resources and leads to a drop in production. Even if land tax was paid only by landlords, their tenants and servants must be adversely affected. The lot of farmers today is truly pitiful and they are condemned to it all their lives.

Academic economists like our fellow Representative Taguchi Ukichi also maintain that land tax is now very light compared with the Tokugawa regime. The government then had an income of 8 million *koku*, they say, while today it raises only ¥40 million from land tax. But the Tokugawa government behaved like a parent to its children, providing farmers with various forms of relief, such as loans for fertilizer and exemption from tax in times of disaster, as did the other territorial lords. Taxes on land were to some extent an insurance levy. Today farmers have to pay land tax regardless of good or bad crops; a heavy, cruel burden. Such economists also argue that in feudal times 40 per cent of the yield went to the government, 60 per cent to the farmers; but that after land tax reform in the 1870s these figures changed to 29.5 per cent and 70.5 per cent respectively. In this, too, they make a fundamental mistake, ignoring the fact that in 1878 a prefectural tax of up to one-third of land tax was imposed, while towns and villages had to raise an equivalent amount to pay for their own administration. Subsequently these local taxes have risen year after year. When city and prefectural assemblies were first opened in 1878, the budget for many prefectures was barely ¥300,000 per annum; today they pay ¥1 million or more. Prefectural tax alone has risen threefold in the last ten years, and now amounts to 60 per cent of the sum paid in national tax. Town and village taxes are harder to estimate, but government statistics make it clear that they have risen too; household, land and community levies are certainly a grievous burden on local people.

Another argument I must refute is that land tax is the only sure foundation for government income because consumer taxes are uncertain and variable. Both the Prime Minister and the Finance Minister said so at the opening of the current Diet session, and I believe that this is the kernel of their proposal to increase land tax. How reliable can a tax be on agriculture that can suffer losses of two or three million *yen* in a single flooding disaster? They argue that taxes on commerce and industry have risen steeply in recent years, and that to increase land tax from 2.5 to 4 per cent by the use of existing land registers would involve little administrative expense, ignoring the hardship this is bound to cause. In feudal days, land was the only resource for tax so perhaps they are dreaming of distant times. As the economy develops and population increases, the extra income they hope to gain from land tax is little security; they will have to raise revenue from other sources. The people have a duty to provide a proportion of their income to meet government expenditure, but this increase in land tax is no such thing; it amounts to a partial theft of the property itself.

The Finance Minister also calculates the income of rural landlords from tenancy rents at much too high a rate. Landlords must receive 12.5 per cent interest on the value of their land; if they cannot do so, they will shift their capital to another business. If land tax rises, they must therefore increase tenancy rents. And if as a result the price of land also falls, rural debt will rise. Tenant farmers already have huge debts. In 1893 these amounted to over ¥270 million, rising to ¥340 million in the two years 1893 and 1894. When the price of shares falls, their holders can mortgage them to get loans, otherwise they would go bankrupt. Farmers in the same position have to sell their land, depressing its price even further. Many of them who have tilled a piece of land for generations will be forced to part with their holdings. Dealers in shares have no such qualms, but the proposed increase in land tax will cause panic in farmer households. As a result the number of independent cultivators must decline and Japan's agriculture will stagnate, with tenants oppressed by a small minority of big landlords. At the moment, all over Japan, relations between rural landlords and tenants are very amicable. If a tenant complains that he has not enough fertilizer, his landlord will lend it to him; or if a member of a tenant's household is sick, provide him with money. Such admirable customs still prevail in the countryside. An increase in land tax will turn tenant farmers into wage labourers, and their landlords will treat them ever more harshly. To raise the rate from 2.5 per cent to 4 per cent amounts to a real tax increase of 60 per cent. Please consider the effect this will have on society, the economy and government.

Whether the increase is to 4 per cent or 3.3 per cent, it will have the same results. In particular, the virtual destruction of local government. Cities, prefectures, towns and villages with slender powers to levy indirect taxes can raise public funds only by extra taxes on land. As I said before, in many places prefectural tax has risen from ¥300,000 a year to over ¥1 million today. In 1894 prefectural tax totalled ¥32 million, rising to ¥38 million in 1895, then to ¥45 million in 1896, with town and village taxes running at the same level. As enlightenment advances, education, public works, police and hygiene cost more and more, no doubt with further rises to come. If land tax is increased now, the burden will almost all fall on the farmers. Where will they get money to pay for public undertakings in the future? At present local governments have debts of nearly ¥50 million. If the proposed increase in land tax is designed to bail out the national treasury for a few years, its result will be the destruction of local undertakings. I appeal to your fair judgement for these bills to be thrown out.

In 1873, when land tax reform was first announced, the Emperor issued an edict promising its progressive reduction to 1 per cent. I cannot understand how Finance Minister Matsukata and the government-delegate could maintain in committee that land tax is not heavy because of the 1877 reduction from 3 per cent to 2.5 per cent, saying that after land price revision, tax would return to the 1873 standard. Matsukata himself was in charge of land tax reform, and I can declare with all force that his present proposals are a violation of the Emperor's edict and breach a national compact.

The present cabinet maintains that land tax is secure and certain, while consumer taxes are not. If so, why should this be true of Japan only, and not of any other nation in the world? Government revenue is particularly large in Britain; there land tax brings in only 1 per cent of it. In France, Germany and Italy, with much more income than Japan from customs, land tax provides less than 20 per cent. This percentage is higher only in backward places like the interior of Africa where land tax is the only resource. What way is this to promote a nation? The advanced nations of Europe would collapse if land tax was the only basis of government revenue.

In committee, the proposed increase to 4 per cent was cut to 3.3 per cent and limited to five years, bringing in an extra gain of barely ¥7 million per annum to the national treasury. The government's original proposal was for ten years; well aware that funding from the China indemnity and government bonds would be exhausted by 1903, the government finally settled for five years, a dirty trick unlikely to deceive you clever Representatives. What use is a five-year limit? Even if approved by this Diet session, the next one can throw it out. For cabinet ministers to juggle with government finance in this opportunistic way is scandalous. We need to put the national budget on a firm footing; blundering about with 3.3 per cent for five years does not convince a single man at the top and violates the trust of the people below. If, as they always proclaim, cabinet ministers are sincere in their care for the nation and love of its people, conscious that they run the government in trust for the Emperor, they should immediately resolve to abandon this unreasonable and harsh increase in land tax. You three hundred Representatives from the same motives, I sincerely hope, will also resist these bills to the utmost . . .[24]

At this point, Bandō Kangorō, a Representative for Tokushima Prefecture and leader of the Land Price Revision League, interrupted to ask a question. Speaker Kataoka Kenkichi invited him to speak, as if judging that Taketomi had said enough and that it was time to move on with the debate. Bandō:

> I don't have time to ask all my questions about Taketomi's speech so I limit myself to just this one. He said that in 1873 an Imperial edict promised to reduce land tax to 1 per cent of land value, so the increase proposed now goes against the Emperor's orders. People objecting against an increase in the land tax often use this argument. But with all due respect to the Emperor, I cannot believe he has any such wish. The first legal codes were issued twenty-five years ago when men still wore long hair and carried two swords; quoting clauses in the laws of those times out of context is a very unsure guide as to what the Emperor, if I may humbly say so, thinks to day. I am not going to reprimand Taketomi for this; I simply ask him to withdraw his remarks.

After calls for this matter to be discussed further, Kataoka invited Taguchi Ukichi to speak. One of the Representatives for Tokyo, and proprietor of the influential magazine *Tōkyō keizai zasshi*, Taguchi was the very epitome of the academic economists Taketomi had so derided. Taguchi:

> We have just heard a speech of feverish opposition from Taketomi, the *Kenseihontō* party's leading expert on government finance. He went on for more than an hour, so I lack time to refute him point by point. First of all, I am inclined to doubt his sincerity. Taketomi served as a counsellor of the Finance Ministry during the Matsukata cabinet of 1896–97; as Chief Secretary, he is rumoured to have drawn up proposals for an increase in land tax during the Ōkuma cabinet earlier this year. After he left office, Ōkuma switched to become a strong opponent of this policy and I think that Taketomi objects to it now just out of spite against the present cabinet. I cannot help feeling deep down that if Taketomi was now a member of the cabinet he would approve an increase in land tax, or even draw up a bill for it himself. Men of his party are well known for trimming their arguments to suit calculations of political advantage.
>
> Among many points, I should like first to rebut Taketomi's assertion that land tax is an insecure base for government finance,

and that European nations all rely on consumption taxes, drawing as little as 1 per cent or at most 30 per cent from land tax. Conditions in that part of the world are very different from those here. Japan's rural landlords, thanks to government policy and the gracious favour of His Majesty Emperor Meiji, are extremely fortunate compared with those of Europe. Land tax is so small in Britain because the aristocrats never surrendered their land titles to the government, as those of Japan did in 1869. Farmers there are all tenants of noblemen, sitting in the House of Lords, who pocket the taxes paid to the central government here. I am well aware that land tax and tenancy rents in Japan today are a heavy burden. But our present rural landlords, who were all tenants of feudal lords before 1869, now rejoice in a proud title that deserves their gratitude. Moreover, subsequent rises in the price of rice and currency changes have resulted in very large tax reductions compared to what they paid to their former lords. However much people like Taketomi complain, you know this is a fact. Although British farmers pay little to the government, they pay a lot to aristocratic landlords. In Japan, for all that farmers pay to the government, the rest is income. They are now free from the oppression of former lords and live in a free realm. In addition, they received a generous reduction in tax; for all these things they should be very grateful.

We all know that in Britain the government raises huge sums in revenue from indirect, i.e. consumer, taxes. That nation has engaged in commerce for centuries and its foreign trade is very vigorous. Even a light tax brings in a big income there. In terms of our currency, the British government gains ¥200 million a year from barely eighteen items, a sum equal to Japan's total trade in both imports and exports. It is a big mistake to think that we can raise a tax revenue of such magnitude. Britain taxes imported goods such as wine at 20 per cent of their value; *sake* and tobacco taxes are heavy in Japan, but revenue is small because society is still backward and the level of consumer spending remains low.

As for land tax, in France, Germany and Holland this is heavy. Even when the aristocracy was dispossessed and the tax paid to the government it remained at high levels. In Britain too, it is heavy in some instances. There, so-called crown land was equivalent to the Tokugawa domains; mortgaged by kings to pay for wars, it is now owned by parliament and leased to tenants at stiff rents.

Taketomi says that advocates of a land tax increase today are merchants with government connections currying favour with the cabinet for their own profit, in defiance of public opinion. I must say something here in defence of truly independent merchants. Because prices have doubled after the recent switch to the gold standard, holders of government bonds or bank shares and those who lend money or work on business capital have all lost half their assets. As a result, the value of shares has fallen, business is stagnant and the commercial world reduced to a sorry state. But the value of agricultural land has gone up five or six times [a shout of 'Tokyo City one hundred times!']. In November 1887, over Japan as a whole, land sold for about one-third of its assessed value; it is now worth three times that figure, making rural landlords much better off than merchants in banking or commerce, whose wealth was reduced by half when the price of silver fell. So in today's difficult economic situation, where is the government to get its income? It can do so only from people with a surplus, and the Diet has a duty to bring this about.

Then there is the question whether an increase in land tax will cause hardship to tenant farmers. Taketomi emphatically maintains that it will do so, but I find this disputable. From the point of view of the economy as a whole, tenants are not adversely affected. I have argued this point with Viscount Tani of the House of Peers, but he simply cannot see it. I am surprised to hear Taketomi, a realistic and intelligent member of his party, put forward this argument again. I cannot explain the matter in detail because it is a principle of economics; though I wish you had all learned this at college, the House of Representatives is hardly the place to explain it. So let me ask one question to those who cannot understand. If land tax was completely abolished would tenant farmers get any benefit, or would all the profit go to the landlords? Today tenants of big landlords are certainly oppressed. To give you a current example, over Japan as a whole land tax is lightest in Yamaguchi and Miyagi Prefectures, and in the northern provinces of Ōshū, Dewa and Echigo. When I visited north Japan recently, tenants came to me with bitter complaints that they had never been so heavily burdened as at present. Had not the Tokugawa government of olden times upheld protests by farmers against their domain lord in the famous Sakura Sōgorō Incident? But now throughout Japan rural landlords can all get away with things that even the Sakura domain could not do. While their tax decreases year by year they levy the same rents on their tenants and even raise them. They never till the soil with their own hands or cultivate it themselves; they just skim off the profit from the land itself. Recently rich merchants and noblemen have also bought large agricultural estates, with tax exemptions to meet development costs even though profits are large, but they have invested capital so perhaps this has to be allowed. In matters of taxation they are more akin to shareholders in the Bank of Japan. My deepest sympathies are for the independent cultivator with just over half a hectare of arable land, worth ¥200 as a national average. Taketomi says that to increase tax on their land by 0.8 per cent is a great burden on them, advocating consumption taxes instead.

But these indirect taxes fall unequally on the rich and poor. The rich do not consume more *sake* than the poor, who like to have a drink now and again. Japan today has eight million households; they consume *sake* produced from four million *koku* of rice, an average of twenty gallons per household on which ¥7 of tax is levied. Making up half the population, tenant farmers on average pay ¥3.50 a year in *sake* tax. If, as Taketomi and his friends advocate, this was raised to ¥12 per twenty gallons, they would pay ¥6 a year. Yet he says that a tax increase of 0.8 per cent on a ¥200 land price is a hardship on poor farmers! *Sake* tax in particular is paid by a multitude of people who have no land. Fellow Representatives! All of you! Please remember that this is not just an assembly of rural landlords. Surely it is best to make taxes on the poor lighter and those on the rich heavier. To make things easier for the little people we should not levy higher taxes on *sake*, sugar and tobacco that fall so inequitably on rich and poor. That is no way to improve society or to open up a brighter future for the nation.

Taketomi's arguments are based on European models, where they are already outworn, and to adopt them in Japan will create a widening gulf between rich and poor [mingled cries of 'Hear, hear!', 'No, no!']. If this happens, business combines such as Mitsubishi and Mitsui, along with the rich in general, will no doubt rejoice while tenant farmers weep incessantly.

Rural landlords reaped great profits from the currency switch from silver to the gold standard two years ago, and I want to say one more thing about this. Without going into Taketomi's comparison of taxes under the Tokugawa with those of the Meiji regime in detail, I think we can all agree that before the reform programme of 1874 government income from land tax was 12 million *koku*. At today's rice price of ¥10 per *koku*, a comparable rate of tax would yield ten times that figure. But at present total tax on irrigated and dry fields over the whole nation, including Hokkaido and Okinawa, is a mere ¥35 million. Anyone can surely see that government finance cannot be sustained by this, especially those of you who approve military expansion, and even members of Taketomi's party. If they say that the burden must fall entirely on merchants and the general population, what kind of Representatives are these? As for the constant expansion of local budgets, the money for this comes not from land but from business and consumption taxes. Taketomi was a member of the special committee to report on the bills for land tax increase, so no doubt he knows the figures better than I do; while I cannot be certain of this, subsidiary taxes on land levied by cities, prefectures, towns and villages have legal limits and cannot be increased, so the extra revenue must come from local business and consumption taxes. Fellow Representatives! If tax on *geisha* rises, are farmers likely to be troubled? When household and commercial taxes are increased, do rural landlords suffer? Certainly not, though I lack time to refute those who put foward this argument.

Finally, what Taketomi says about the Imperial edict of 1873 is wrong. It certainly says nothing about a 1 per cent level of land tax. I do not have a copy to hand and I cannot give details, but from memory it was just a statement that the people would be spared harsh and unreasonable levies; there was no promise that when government income from taxes on commodities rose above ¥20 million a year, land tax would be reduced to 1 per cent. Stupid though this story is, from time to time it crops up in this House. It is up to us Representatives to decide on taxes; to quote now expedient statements made many years ago when the government was anxious to achieve reforms is a very shameful thing for members of the Imperial Diet to do. [Shout of 'Finish your speech!'] Just one more word. In a strident tone of voice, Taketomi demanded to know 'What is the financial policy of this cabinet?' I think it is the same as that of the previous Ōkuma cabinet drawn up by Taketomi and his fellows a few months ago, dished up to us now without full investigations. I agree that this cabinet should have done more research and come up with a rather improved plan. Taketomi dwells on the decrease from 4 per cent to 3.3 per cent as an example of fickle changes, but such revisions are the proper role of the Diet. I have gone on too long, so I cannot refute Taketomi further, and will end now. [Mingled cries of 'Finish your speech!', 'Go on, Go on!']25

Speaker Kataoka in response to the general mood of the House accepted Taguchi's offer to conclude. Hoshi Tōru, waiting impatiently for the bills to be put to the vote, reminded the House that it had previously resolved that the ballot should be secret (a wise precaution to shield turncoats). The opposition countered with demands for an open ballot; amid noisy interjections from both sides, a division was held on the matter. When Hoshi's proposal was declared passed by 157 votes to 138, the winning side burst into wild cheers, now certain that the bills would go through. The Land Price Revision bill then passed by 166 votes to 129 after a secret ballot, Kataoka and Hoshi bulldozing down all demands for a fuller second reading. To a jeering shout of 'No running away, cowards! Fight fair!' the opposition forces attempted to troop out of the chamber en bloc, but the Speaker ordered the guards to bar all doors. As the infernal uproar continued, the bill for Land Tax Increase then limped through by 155 votes to 15, most opponents abstaining from the ballot in disgust. A weary Kataoka announced business for the next sitting and closed the chamber at 7.35 p.m.[26]

THE HOUSE OF PEERS

Seven days later, on 27 December 1898, the two bills came before the House of Peers. Marquis Kuroda Nagamasa, chairman of the House special committee to report on the bills and a member of the powerful *Kenkyūkai* group, made the first speech. After conferring with the Finance Minister and the government-delegate, the committee had spent most of its time discussing the revisions made by the House of Representatives to the original bills, he reported. The Peers committee wanted them to come into effect from 1 January 1899 and not from April–May as in the amendments put forward by the House of Representatives. So they authorized three of their number to negotiate with the House of Representatives on this issue; they were also perturbed that the land tax increase was for five years only, despite the government's proposal for at least ten years. They regarded this as an obstacle to future military expansion and industrial development, and did not see why the cabinet should timidly accept these revisions and put such chopped and changed bills before the House of Peers. The committee regretted that for reasons of urgency it must recommend their passage as they stood despite the need for future planning.

Although military expansion was necessary, unjustified expenditure must be pruned. For example, the cost of uniforms and rations in Japan was much higher than in foreign armies, and savings here could be used to promote industry. And while committee members felt they must approve the bills in these times of national crisis, not one of them was fully satisfied. All, both for and against, urged that the national wealth must be increased by improving local education and administration, and hoped that the government would pay full attention to this. Marquis Kuroda finally declared that these bills were very important; views for and against ought to be fully debated. He regretted that before the Diet session when opponents of an increase in the land tax held public meetings to propagate their opinions, the government had ordered them to disperse. Yet the government itself should weigh the matter carefully and allow objections to be fully expressed; opponents of the bills, for their part, should adopt a conciliatory attitude. He urged Members of the House on both sides to state their opinions without reserve before deciding whether to approve the bills or not.

Imperial Nominee Tsuji Shinji, formerly a professor of foreign languages and a Ministry of Education official, agreed wholeheartedly with Kuroda's insistence upon the need to foster local education. How, he asked, were the funds for this to be found? Kuroda replied that the Finance Minister had assured him education would not suffer as a result of an increase in land tax. The committee had also discussed various plans for its expansion.

Other Members of the House then raised points of procedure, or questioned minor details, while regretting that the cabinet had been much too compliant in amending the bills to suit the House of Representatives.

As President, Prince Konoe Atsumaro then called on Viscount Tani Kanjō to speak. A longtime champion of small farmers, Tani had been leader of the recent League Against Land Tax Increase until it was forced to dissolve under police pressure. Tani:

> I was one of a minority on the House committee reviewing the bills who refused approval so I did not sign its report. But as Marquis Kuroda said, whether for or against, nobody was satisfied. I cannot fathom what the cabinet hopes to achieve; I feel compelled to make my own report on the matter, explaining why I oppose both bills. The bill for land price revision is supposed to correct unfairness and put government finance on a firm footing, while the cabinet also proposed an increase of land tax from 2.5 per cent to 4 per cent. What a contradiction to say, on the one hand, that national urgency requires a tax increase however harsh, while also maintaining that there is surplus enough for it to be decreased in some cases! For a number of reasons I do not agree that land prices should be revised in today's circumstances.
>
> As for the tax increase to 4 per cent, I flatly opposed this as bound to reduce the number of small, independent farmers with voting rights. Because of opposition in the House of Representatives, the rate was reduced to 3.3 per cent and limited to five years. What kind of basis for national finance is this? I found the explanations of the Finance Minister and the government-delegate most unsatisfactory, so I drew up a minority report opposing both bills. We agreed that

local education was of the utmost importance; many parents are prepared to cut down from three bowls of rice a day to only one in order to provide an education for their children; for them, to pay 5 or 6 *sen* for a textbook is a heavy drain. So any increase in the land tax is bound to weaken local education. Public works will also suffer: dykes will collapse, rivers flood, building and repairs fall into neglect. In opposing these bills and submitting a minority report, I am concerned above all else for local education and public works. Please listen with patience while I explain my views at length.

Military expenditure has risen to huge sums. In the ninth Diet session of 1895, both the *Jiyutō* party and the pro-government Representatives of the *Kokumin Kyōkai* party gladly co-operated with the cabinet in its programme for armaments expansion. In my opinion they were grossly deceived in this. When Taiwan became a Japanese colony at this time an increase of two army divisions was justified, but an increase of five divisions was most inordinate. The government's policy is like ordering rifles without the bullets to make them effective. Guns without ammunition are useless. The ninth Diet also approved an expansion of the military police. We Japanese, with the Emperor at our pinnacle, are people of the same race; there is no risk of rebellion, quite unlike recently unified states such as Italy rent by divided loyalties. Considering the many prefectures without a single army barracks, we can see how useless the military police are. The government should therefore abolish them and not seek to establish army barracks in new places. Military police cost around ¥700,000 a year; this would be better spent on universities, which are too few in number. Every year, as you know, more and more middle-school graduates cannot obtain university entry. While approving military expansion with such enthusiasm, the ninth Diet of 1895 neglected education, reducing it to the needy state it is in today. Much money will be needed for education in the future; we cannot be content with the present situation.

On the matter of military expenditure, the Finance Minister explained to me in committee that as a very rich nation France had no trouble in raising money for armaments; Germany, too, was always prepared for war and kept finances in reserve at all times. But Japan is an island cut off from the rest of the world; it could not raise foreign loans, nor even domestic ones in today's circumstances. Current talk of importing foreign capital, nationalizing the railways, and so on, is just hot air; foreigners regard lending Japan money as far too risky. In Japan's present situation a sailship is perhaps better than a steamship without coal, but anyway I hope great attention will be paid to military organization. If not, government finance will become ever more confused, and like some other nations we may not be able to provide our soldiers with pay. However much an army is expanded, it is useless without money. Yet people like me who oppose an increase in the land tax are denounced as 'disloyal', 'unprincipled' or 'rebels'! Even if, as I had hoped, army expansion had been restricted to two divisions and not increased to five, a great deal of money was still needed.

Around 1887 people began to brag about Japan's national wealth and progress in enlightenment, but in 1891 railway shares fell in value and proposals were made in the Diet for nationalization. I felt that it was very dangerous for the government to contemplate such airy-fairy measures and urged it to act with common sense. I drew up a memorial warning the cabinet on the matter, but most of you in the House of Peers voted against it, so it lapsed. The fever for railway construction erupted again after the 1894–95 war with China, with people believing that if only new lines were built here, there and everywhere, money would bubble up spontaneously. I criticized this at the time, on the grounds that Japan is an island nation and railways would turn out to be unprofitable. Proof of my view can be seen in the falling profits of the Turkish Eastern Railway when the Suez canal opened.

Despite the heavy blow to our national pride when forced to return the Liaotung peninsula to China in 1895 under concerted pressure from France, Germany and Russia which might have caused people to reflect, they boasted that Japan was rich. Public and private undertakings mushroomed until lack of capital brought them to a grinding halt. Unless Japan's economic development is orderly, it will be blown along on such futile gusts and just as quickly peter out. Now we hear florid talk of importing foreign capital, nationalizing the railways, and a rise in land tax. As the Finance Minister said in committee, we must reflect on this with care. When Japan raises money by domestic bonds the time of redemption is not fixed and interest is paid in paper money. Interest on overseas loans must be paid in British pounds or French francs every year. This optimistic talk of foreign loans at 5 per cent or 6 per cent damages Japan's international credit and is no way to promote useful undertakings. And at a time when the government is unable to raise domestic loans, nothing can be more stupid than proposals to nationalize the railways. Such a policy requires purchase in consecutive instalments of ¥10 million spread over fifty or sixty years.

Those who call opponents of an increase in the land tax 'rebels' or 'disloyal' are out for their own profit at great expense to the nation. As for people who argue that land tax is the easiest to levy and the most secure source of revenue, what they are really saying is that farmers are honest and tell the truth, so collection is no problem; income and business taxes are hard to raise because merchants are too cunning to pay them. In other words, money is easily extorted from simple children but hard to get from liars, so the honest should pay first. A lot of people calling themselves businessmen are nothing of the sort; they are dealers in shares whose noisy outcries for an increase in land tax can be reduced to 'Grab the farmer's money!' All they care about is to keep the price of their shares from falling. If successful on the three issues of importing foreign capital, nationalizing the railways and increasing land tax, the result will be a major disaster.

First of all, the rate of interest is bound to rise as a result of the boom in credit. For a time the price of bonds and shares may also rise, but then collapse when the initial blast of hot air deflates, leaving the nation stuck with a chronic malady. Today the lack of international confidence in Japan's commerce and the bad reputation of its products for quality in overseas markets are cause for alarm. Merchant speculators, parasitic grubs eating away at genuine commerce, are responsible for this evil; they destroy confidence in Japan's society, making real commercial and industrial development impossible, while turning genuine businessmen into figures of fun.

Then there is the argument that agriculture is very profitable so what harm is there in milking it? I have studied all the figures but to go over them in minute detail would take up too much time. So I will just state categorically that farmers are in no such prosperous condition. Small farmers can only make enough to feed and clothe themselves if they supplement their income by making straw sandals or by woodcutting. They hang on desperately to the irrigated fields created with great effort by their forebears. Who are these people who say that because agriculture is so profitable we need have no qualms about squeezing them? First of all, the academic economist Taguchi Ukichi. He attacked me in the House of Representatives but I have no respect for his views, which are simply those of a political enemy. He draws his argument from the Physiocrats of seventeenth-century France, a special breed of economists who advocated a single tax to be levied on land, just as in feudal Japan, putting the entire burden of government revenue on agriculture. At that time the French nobility and clergy held much of the land as private property and were exempt from tax, a very harsh imposition on the common people.

When the Physiocrats argued that land tax on its own was sufficient for government revenue as long as it was levied in full upon the privileged classes, they were quite right: it was the exemptions of the nobility they aimed to abolish. But to maintain that since all products originate from agriculture, rural landlords would pass this single tax on to goods and make no loss is far too simplistic. That might work on a remote island, but when communications are opened up and products like rice and barley come flooding in from other countries, special taxes must be imposed to control this. So the Physiocrats were soon forced to modify their principles.

Yet Taguchi bases his argument on this simple idea. Underlying it is a sort of worship for trade and merchants, with money as the cardinal deity. Overseas trade and domestic commerce are put on a pedestal, farmers despised as those at the bottom. By his own logic, if rural landlords are so hateful for imposing heavy rents and worthy of punishment, dealers in shares should be much more so. I find it quite abhorrent to castigate farming families that have built up their holdings over many generations from one, to two and then to three hectares. At official expense I have made detailed studies of the land for many years; whatever these academic economists say, I am convinced that if not decisively refuted their arguments will cause great harm in the future.

Some people in the government, and of course share dealers, also put forward the view that land should not be private property but owned by the state. If the government wants to buy all arable land for several billion *yen*, well and good. But if it is not prepared to do so, then clearly individuals are entitled to own land by the Emperor's gracious favour. People like myself believe that the small independent farmer should be protected as the backbone of a splendid agricultural system with admirable customs rooted in Japan's distant past. If we take Britain as an example, agriculture is given a very low ranking there. Even so, its scholars are now worried about this. As Germany, France, America and other nations build up their industrial strength, Britain faces strong competition in the future. India, and Canada too, may become independent. If agriculture declines in Britain, although it has money to buy cereals now it may not be able to do so when circumstances change. I hear that British scholars are therefore advocating encouragement for agriculture. In Japan, as the very basis of our nation, to foster it and protect farmers is the prime duty of all statesmen.

People like Taguchi also talk of Japan's farmers as if they were all tenants and assume that all rural landlords have big holdings. This is by no means true. I regret not having recent statistics, but around 1883 independent farmers declined in numbers. Part landlord/part tenant farmers numbered 2,315,000; pure tenants 1,340,000. Wealthy landlords paying large sums in tax amounted to barely 1 per cent of the farming population. Taguchi wrongly maintains that increasing the land tax will place restraints on big holdings. Whether tax is raised to 4, 5 or 6 per cent of assessed value, rich landlords have other sources of income and will remain quite unperturbed. The increased tax will fall most heavily on medium and small farmers; they will be forced to sell land, become tenants, or even to give up farming altogether and seek employment in the metropolitan cities or provincial towns. The German expert Paul Mayet calculated in the early 1880s that over a period of five years some 200,000 farmers quit to seek jobs in commerce or industry.

As for the land itself, we all know that Japan produces forty million *koku* of rice a year. Variations in production have an immediate effect on the economy. Only 13 per cent of Japan is arable land. Other nations are more fortunate: France with 54 per cent, Spain around 40 per cent, and European Russia 21 per cent, though some experts calculate that this could double or treble. Holland with a small land area profits from a splendid dairy industry, exporting to Britain. The bunch of academic bootlickers who compare land tax in Japan with these nations have no idea what they are talking about.

Rural indebtedness is another grave problem. I am told that it amounts to ¥341 million. Many farmers have pawned their houses, and are hard put to borrow even a few *yen*. Rates of interest in Tokyo are a little over 10 per cent; in the countryside borrowers must pay 25 per cent. We should set up Hypothec Banks like those of Europe to protect small farmers and reduce these very high rates of interest. It is senseless to say that tenant farmers will not suffer if the land tax is raised, and that this will only strip big landlords of their outrageous profits. Between big landlords and tenants there is a large class of superb, independent farmers. If the people who run the government today do not know this they will end up treating the farmers like beasts of burden as in feudal days, heaping levies on them until they die.

I am sorry to have tired you out with this long speech. I could go on for two or three days, but feel I must end now. It makes me gasp with astonishment when people who spend up to ¥100 for a week's holiday in the hot springs at Atami get together to demand that land tax be increased. A household of five people can subsist on half this sum for a whole year. The only way to put government finance on a sound footing is to prevent the value of paper money from falling;

that requires strict retrenchment and frugality. Government leaders should reflect on this, and realize that taxes must be reduced as much as possible in order to foster undertakings vital for national development. I wish I could say more, but that is enough for today and I plead with you to reject these bills outright.[27]

After this long tirade, President Konoe called upon Imperial Nominee Kaneko Kentarō to speak, as the Member most qualified to put the case for approving the bills. Educated at Harvard University, Kaneko had risen as a secretarial official in the Council of State, making his name as one of the brilliant legal specialists Itō Hirobumi employed to help draft the Constitution. Appointed Chief Secretary of the House of Peers in 1890, and always listed as an Independent, he remained an Imperial Nominee until 1906, while twice a minister in Itō cabinets, then became a Baron and Privy Councillor. Kaneko:

I have just listened with great respect to the speech of our most amiable and renowned Tani: his detailed investigations and zealous sincerity command my deepest admiration. While I support the bills to increase the land tax and disagree with most of Tani's arguments, I would not for a moment decry him and other opponents as 'rebels' or 'disloyal'. On the other hand, I must reprove him for saying that people like myself think farmers are rich because we know nothing about their sufferings. I was born in a farming village and memories of such hardships are still vivid in my mind today. Let me assure you that I do not support the bills because I think Japan's farmers have a ready surplus to pay taxes, as if I were some pasty-faced young student ignorant of their hard lot. Nor am I enthralled by academic theories of direct and indirect taxation. These matters are much disputed among economists in Europe and America.

My view is that after the 1894–95 war with China, government finance and the people's livelihood became constricted; cabinets conducted various negotiations and dissolved the Diet several times, while confidence both at home and abroad plummeted to the depths. The only remedy for this and the one sure source of revenue is, unavoidably, to increase land tax. So with regret for the farmers' hardships and swallowing my tears, I support these bills in order to maintain the dignity of our Imperial government both in Japan and overseas. I am just as sincere on my side of the argument as Tani is on his.

I have thought hard about the matter. When peace returned in 1895 I urged the government and people to keep in mind the financial problems that followed the Franco-Prussian conflict and the civil war in America. But our victory over China unleashed a mood of feverish euphoria; as if Japan at one swift leap had joined the powerful Western nations, a reckless expansion ensued with new undertakings mushrooming everywhere. Just three years later, we are now forced to squeeze the farmers, a most regrettable event.

Today, government revenue is drawn from the following taxes: land ¥38 million; customs ¥16 million; business, medicine sales and stamp duty on financial transactions ¥7 million; *sake* and soy ¥35 million, income tax ¥2 million. The present cabinet's budget proposed to increase land tax to ¥75 million, *sake* and soy taxes to ¥50 million. There is no way to increase the ¥7 million now being paid by commerce and industry; this simply cannot be stretched any further. As you know, companies with a capital of ¥500,000 pay tax on this, then are taxed again when they raise loans to buy land, put up buildings and install machinery. Finally they pay tax for employing workers and labourers. In effect, they pay taxes threefold. Delegations from commerce and industry arrive at the Diet gates one after another, petitioning for the total abolition of business tax or for its reduction. By very great efforts, *sake* and soy taxes can be raised to ¥50 million, but customs duties are fixed by treaty. That makes an increase in the land tax the government's only real resource.

In the 1870s land tax was fixed at 2.5 per cent of assessed value. Even if prefectural, town and village taxes have increased, the fact remains that as a national tax it provides the only way to maintain confidence at home and abroad, enabling government finance to make further advances.

The cabinet sought an increase to 4 per cent of assessed value, but the House of Representatives cut this to 3.3 per cent for a term of five years; despite all its efforts, the cabinet had to accept this, destroying any prospect for long-term stability. The resulting loss in government revenue for 1899 and 1900 will total over ¥16 million, while the reduction in land prices will cost nearly ¥4 million a year. I very much doubt that a firm foundation for government finance can be achieved by this.

Finance Minister Watanabe Kunitake in 1895 put forward a ten-year plan for postwar development, stressing the need for a concerted effort to promote industry, commerce and agriculture. Our colleague Tani worries about runaway military expansion, as I do myself. For a ten-year plan to collapse after just three years is not a good thing. To put it in practical terms, what use is it to build a steamship if one does not have coal? I would prefer a plan that provided for resources, not just construction. As US Admiral Mahan once said, a navy's power does not lie in mere numbers of ships, guns, crew or reserves: it lies in the wholehearted support of the nation. This is just as applicable to armies. The nation must be made rich enough to provide for the twelve army divisions envisaged by the postwar plan. While supporting the bills to increase land tax, I hope the government will also draw up proposals to promote commerce and industry, foster the national wealth, and expand knowledge among the people as a necessary foundation for these policies. We must frame a far-sighted plan for Japan's future development.[28]

At this point Tani interjected, asking Kaneko to explain how these objectives could possibly be attained if agriculture was taxed ten times more heavily than industry and commerce. He and Kaneko then argued the matter a little further. When Kaneko reiterated the need for long-term promotion of the national wealth and asked Tani in weary despair, 'Do you understand?', Tani replied that he did not, but that they might as well let the matter rest there.

President Konoe next called on High Taxpayer Kamata Katsutarō to speak. A member of Tani's *Konwakai* group, Kamata was a native of Kagawa Prefecture; a large landowner also engaged in salt production, his business activities extended to local spinning, banking and railway companies. He had been chairman of the Kagawa prefectural assembly and head of the local Education Society. Kamata:

I agree with Tani, but after his speech lasting two hours I will stick to essentials. On the issue of increasing land tax, two Diet dissolutions and three cabinet changes have already taken place in the last two years. Public opinion is clearly against it, yet the present cabinet has the obstinacy to put up further bills of this kind. Methods used to get them through the House of Representatives were dirty in the extreme; the majority disapproved but gradually succumbed to talk of negotiations, coalitions, etc., until the final result was a cut from 4 per cent to 3.3 per cent for five years, reducing the government's proposed increase in yearly revenue from ¥18 million to ¥7 million. The vote was, of course, by secret ballot. If the government raises ¥7 million per annum from these bills, after five years it will gain only ¥35 million, hardly a firm basis for national finance. With the reduction of ¥3,750,000 per annum by land price revision, the gain is even less. I suspect that even before the next five years expire, the government will tamper with land tax again. I questioned the Finance Minister about this in committee, and he said that within the next five years a new plan would be drawn up and submitted to the Diet. So what we have before us now is just a temporizing expedient. To put national finance on a sound footing we need to keep up the value of government bonds and to prevent an imbalance of trade. For the last two years imports have exceeded exports by about ¥76 million per annum, while the huge indemnity of ¥360 million Japan received from China in 1895 is almost exhausted. If the farmers, well over half the population, are now forced to suffer, all others will be adversely affected. Local development is a top priority, and these bills will bring national progress to a halt.

The lot of the farmers remains very hard. It has perhaps improved a little in the last ten years, but nothing like the gains made by people in commerce and industry; just a few extra home comforts, like better quality tea, floor mats and blinds.

Confronted by a deficit of ¥37 million, the cabinet wants to make it up from land tax. In the ninth Diet of 1895, when I held a seat in the House of Representatives, I opposed the ten-year plan but the majority blindly followed the cabinet. Now these bills to increase land tax, despite all my objections, have been passed by the Representatives and approved by a large majority of the House of Peers' special committee, to my profound grief. I believe that in the menacing conditions of east Asia today we must have a strong military establishment. Nobody denies this. But government finance must rest on a secure base; if not, an army of one million soldiers and a navy of 500,000 tons provide no security for the nation.

People like myself are not opposed to an increase in the land tax for selfish reasons; we do not seek to obstruct the government. For the sake of the nation we would suffer any tax, however harsh, selling our family heirlooms and capital goods if necessary. But with government finance in its present state, assenting to this tax increase is like dousing a fire with oil, quite ineffective and the cause of even more damage. I cannot approve any bills to increase the land tax unless fundamental improvements are made in government finance. After careful reflection you will all, I hope, agree with my opinion.[29]

By now, the House had clearly had enough. Baron Nishi Tsutsuji, a court noble, former secretary in the Imperial palace and member of the moderate *Mokuyōkai* group, stood up to propose that the debate should end. Many Members shouted 'Agreed! Agreed!', but before the motion could be put Imperial Nominee Miura Yasushi interjected. He had some advice for Kamata, he said, as voices still resounded for a closure. Kamata had declared that the House of Representatives had passed the bills by secret ballot, so they were therefore invalid. Miura demanded that this remark should be deleted from the stenographic record, as an unwarranted intrusion on the business of the other House likely to cause bad feelings. Kamata stuck to his words, and amidst further shouts and confusion President Konoe called for a show of support for Nishi Tsutsuji's motion. When all those in favour stood up, they were clearly a majority. A vote was then held on whether the bills should be regarded as having passed a second reading. When counted, Konoe announced that of 218 Members present, 159 had voted for, 55 against, with 4 votes invalid. After more desultory questions, Nishi Tsutsuji proposed that the third reading should proceed at once, despite attempts by some Members to continue with the second reading or to amend specific clauses. Once again Konoe asked all those in favour to stand; when a clear majority did so, the bills were declared to have passed, and the sitting closed.

In conclusion, one might ask, who were the real winners and losers? Yamagata had got his bills passed, yet so cut that the gain was less than half of the ¥18 million per annum he had originally hoped for. On the other hand, his successful manipulation of the Diet and outside forces to achieve what had seemed so impossible earlier in the year confirmed his reputation as a masterful political strategist. After his failure in June 1898, Itō Hirobumi maintained that the Diet could be controlled only if he formed a political party of his own. Yamagata had opposed him on this issue and ostensibly at any rate proved his point. But Itō went ahead anyway, launching the *Seiyūkai* in 1900 backed by much the same Representatives that Yamagata had used to pass his bill for land tax increase. The political parties, now confirmed in their role as partners in government, had their own reasons to celebrate, though the luckless Hoshi did not have long to savour his victory. He was stabbed to death in 1901 by an outraged opponent of his corrupt manipulations in Tokyo City government.

The losers were firstly all those with hopes that Diet politics could be kept clean and principled. But above all the masses of Japan, for Yamagata made up the shortfall of ¥7 million per annum early next year by a steep increase in *sake* tax that the House of Representatives approved with little opposition. The net result was that in 1900 the chief sources of government revenue had shifted to: consumer tax 37 per cent, land tax 30 per cent, business tax 8 per cent, customs duties 6 per cent.

Rural landlords must be adjudged winners, although forced to accept a measure of defeat in 1898, and even when their predominance in the House of Representatives was diminished after 1900 by a new electoral system making cities separate constituencies, increasing the number of

Representatives engaged in commerce and industry. For whatever specific individuals or prefectures gained or lost after the bills passed,[30] rural landlords as a class remained a powerful force in Diet politics; over subsequent decades land tax as a percentage of government revenue continued to fall: to 20 per cent in 1917, 10 per cent in 1925, until virtually abolished as a national tax in 1940.

Were the Diet debates on land tax anything more than theatrical outpourings? Not entirely; at least they enabled views for and against the increase to be put at length by informed and able speakers. Even if the outcome was never in doubt, the losers had their full say. The ideal of parliamentary government, vitiated though it often was by bribery, violence and manipulation both inside and outside the Diet, somehow seems to shine forth in such debates, with their touching appeals to the best in Japan's past and passionate concern for its future.

NOTES

1 Ario Yoshishige (1914: 49–50). For this edict (*jōyu*) and the Land Tax Regulations (*chiso jōrei*), see Naikaku Insatsukyoku, *Hōrei zensho* (Tokyo, 1885–), 28 July 1873. Meiji Japan adopted the German system of land tax; all agricultural holdings were classified according to average profit, and tax was assessed as a percentage of this.
2 Fukushima Masao (1962: 487–91). Azuma Tōsaku (1936: 54–5).
3 For the complexities surrounding this issue see, for example, Hara Monjo Kenkyūkai (1986), vol. 5: 566–7, 571–2, quoting *Dai Nihon nōkai gogai*, 25 December 1890; Ogura Takekazu (1951: 109); *The Japan Weekly Mail*, 17 December 1898, p. 608.
4 Banno Junji (1973: 46–7, 51–2).
5 Enjōji Kiyoshi, 'Chiso zōka hantai oyobi hantai undō no temmatsu', 12 January 1899, item 165 in *Kyūkizokuin gōjūnenshi hensan shūshū monjo*, MS (Kenseishiryōshitsu, National Diet Library, Tokyo). For Ōkuma's views on taxation, see *The Japan Weekly Mail*, 17, 24 December 1898.
6 Meiji Hennenshi Hensankai (1936), vol. 10: 325. Masumi Junnosuke (1966), vol. 2: 314.
7 Takizawa Naoshichi (1968: 998–9); Terabe Tetsuji (1953: 157–8); Shidō Motokazu (1954: 38–40).
8 Shinobu Seisaburō (1980), vol. 3: 320.
9 *Shinagawa Yajirō kankei monjo mokuroku, shorui no bu*, item 919 (Kenseishiryōshitsu, National Diet Library, Tokyo). Ario, p. 99.
10 For land prices and values, see Nobukane Kazunosuke (1969: 1973); Fukushima Masao, *Chiso kaisei* (1971: 283–4); Maejima Shōzō (1964: 149).
11 Araki Moriaki (1964: 10–20). Ōyama Hironari (1956: 29–30).
12 *Tokushima nichinichi shimbun*, 16 December 1898.
13 Masumi, pp. 88–90.
14 Ibid., p. 311. Hattori Shisō (1961), vol. 1: 186–9; vol. 2: 91–3.
15 *Shimbun shūsei*, vol. 10: 329.
16 Masumi, p. 317. Kuruma Yasushi (1931: 72–4).

17 Masumi, p. 317.
18 Dai Nihon Teikoku Gikai Shi Kankōkai, *Dai Nihon teikoku gikai shi* (1926: 1650–61), (hereafter DNTGS).
19 Kawai Yahachi (1954: 26–7).
20 For Tanaka, see Watanabe Ikujirō (1944: 373–9).
21 *Shimbun shūsei*, vol. 10: 327.
22 DNTGS: 1685.
23 Ibid., p. 1686.
24 Ibid., pp. 1689–93. Speeches translated in this chapter have many gaps and are much condensed in places, but follow the argument and aim to convey the tone of quite lengthy originals.
25 Ibid., pp. 1694–6.
26 Meiji Nyūsu Hensan Iinkai (1984), vol. 6: 467–8.
27 DNTGS: 1202–6.
28 Ibid., pp. 1206–7.
29 Ibid., pp. 1208–9.
30 Banno (1973: 54–5); Banno Junji (1971: 216); Sakeda Masatoshi (1978: 149).

3   The debate on poor relief, 1890

R. H. P. Mason

While poverty is presumably as old as mankind, poor relief has a respectable antiquity of its own. Organized religion, private philanthropy, local communities and state aid have all played a part in trying to mitigate the worst effects of destitution in Japan as elsewhere; and although governmental responsibility was comparatively slight until recent times, it has a history which began with entries (Snellen 1934: 172–3) in the eighth-century chronicle, the *Shoku-Nihongi*, recording the despatch by the Nara Court of food and medicine to famine- or plague-stricken provinces. Another entry describes the founding of a free dispensary (*seyaku-in*) in 730 by the consort of Emperor Shōmu, and charity asylums (*hiden-in*) were associated with this. In the Middle Ages, the Regent and effective head of the Kamakura shogunate, Hōjō Yasutoki (1183–1242), did what he could to alleviate popular distress during a series of lean years from 1225 to 1232 (Sansom 1958: 393–4). Among the measures he adopted at that time was a *tokusei* (virtuous rule) decree cancelling debts, a device the later Ashikaga *shōgun* frequently used to escape troubles caused not so much by nature as by themselves. During the Tokugawa period (1600–1868), both the shogunate and the fief governments recognized from time to time a special obligation to the infirm, the famished, and the orphaned (Sansom 1963: 133, 164; and Oda 1929: 589–633). However, the major responsibility was unquestionably carried by the village and urban ward authorities, as part of a generally enforced and accepted pattern of local self-help and autonomy, and this, in turn constituted a historical circumstance that lay behind much of the Meiji debate on poor relief. The question of efficacy of these various attempts at poor relief need not concern us here. Clearly, they should be thought of as creditable efforts, rather than as outright victories over sickness or want. The only point to establish is that there was at any rate a tradition of public help for certain kinds of private misfortune.

Following the Restoration of 1868, the initial steps were taken in transforming what had been essentially a small-scale and occasional system of relief into one that was national and permanent. During the first half of the Meiji era, the government issued a small number of separate regulations to assist persons for whom existence (or non-existence) was more of a problem than usual. The most important of these were: the Regulations for the Up-bringing of Foundlings (20 June 1871), the Relief Regulations (8 December 1874), the Famine Relief Fund Law (15 June 1880), and the Regulations for the Disposal of Dead Travellers (30 September 1882). Following this, development of poor relief in Japan became caught up in the far newer processes of constitutional rule. After the first Diet had been formally opened by the Emperor on 29 November 1890, the House of Representatives began its legislative sitting on the afternoon of Saturday 6 December 1890, by giving a first reading to, first, a bill submitted by the government and entitled Destitute Persons Relief Law (DNTGS: 471–2).

This bill had for its three cardinal principles (1) comprehensiveness; (2) subsistence; and (3) municipal autonomy. Under its terms, relief would be given to all adults, together with their dependent children, rendered destitute by sickness, old age or 'some other misfortune' (Art. 1), as well as to children without anyone to look after them. Persons qualifying for relief would receive 'a dwelling-place which will give shelter from the elements' and 'food and clothing necessary for existence' (Art. 6). Paupers falling ill were to have medical treatment at no cost to themselves, similarly, those who died would be buried at public expense. In addition, Article 8 of the bill stated that: 'Children who are receiving relief shall as far as possible be trained for an appropriate occupation'. In seeking to provide for all, and not just some, destitutes, as well as in its attempt to prescribe standards of relief in fairly precise detail, the government was breaking new ground. On the other hand, the provisions, in accordance with which the recently reorganized city, town and village authorities were made almost completely responsible for the financing and administration of the law, conformed more closely to traditional and existing practices. Several of these new municipalities were already undertaking relief work.

Other integral but, in a sense, subsidiary items in the bill urged local authorities to find work for employable paupers (Art. 7); strictly forbade the granting of relief in the form of cash payments (Art. 9); curtailed private charity to the extent that money or goods collected from philanthropists would be handed over to local authorities for use in a municipal programme of relief (Art. 21); and threatened anybody who obtained relief by means of fraud with a prison sentence of one month to two years (Art. 23). The new law was to be enforced from 1 April 1891 in all areas where the Municipal Code and the Town and Village Code, both of which had been promulgated in April 1888, were in operation. In effect, this meant that it would soon be applicable to virtually the entire country outside Hokkaidō and Okinawa. The enforcement of this law would nullify earlier regulations of the same general kind, with the exception of the Famine Relief Fund Law (Art. 24).

Since poor relief lay within the purview of the Home Office, the bill had been drafted in that department, and a senior member of it, Shirane Senichi attended the sitting as government-delegate. He had come down to the House ready to make out a case for the bill as a whole by way of introducing it to Members, and to reply to questions on it of a general nature. As government-delegate, he was entitled to speak first in the debate.

In his opening speech, and in the subsequent discussion (DNTGS: 472–6), Shirane carried out his assignment with a very fair degree of success. He was not long-winded, because the government had already supplied Members with a written memorandum on the bill, and, as he said, he would have an opportunity in the committee stage to explain its ideas in full. The arguments he adduced in favour of the proposed legislation will be discussed later. Certain Members insisted that they had a right to inquire there and then about specific items in the various sections of the bill, if they so desired. Shirane demurred, and repeated his request that such matters be left to the committee stage or second reading. A sudden altercation developed, with some Members taking strong exception to what they chose to regard as an attitude of contempt for the Diet, while others supported Shirane. The dispute reached its climax when Kikuchi Kanji moved that the House ask the government for a more co-operative delegate. The Speaker, Nakajima Nobuyuki then intervened, and, directing a number of placatory remarks to both sides, managed to put a quiet end to the quarrel. Shirane agreed to answer on points of detail, which he did; and Kikuchi eventually withdrew his motion.

Shortly after this, the Speaker, having calmed one storm, himself raised another when he sought to terminate the debate by introducing the second item on the order paper. This was the election of a special committee to consider the bill. The procedure which the House had adopted for electing these special committees was excessively time-consuming. There were nine places to be filled by election from within the House. Each Member wrote up to nine names on a ballot paper which he dropped in a box on a table in front of the Speaker after he had been called forward by a clerk reading the roll. At the same time, he put his visiting card into another box to show that he had voted. As the House had a total of three hundred Members, there could be as many as three hundred cards and 2,700 votes to check before the election was concluded.

Members who had already had enough of the delays entailed in this system objected vociferously to the Speaker's announcement that he would proceed with the election. Four separate motions were proposed and seconded, each of which was designed to simplify the procedure. A short but lively discussion ensued. The Speaker put each motion in turn to the House which rejected them all. Nakajima therefore ordered the clerks to conduct the election as usual; but when the actual balloting was drawing to an end, he indicated the growing pile of sick reports on the clerks' table, and relented to the point of suggesting that the boxes should be sealed in the presence of the House and the counting of votes deferred to the next sitting. The House promptly accepted this, and rose a few minutes after 5 p.m.

Sunday being a holiday, the House did not meet again until 1.15 p.m. on Monday 8 December. There was no discussion on the bill during this sitting (DNTGS: 479–81); simply a statement from the Chair that 271 Members had voted in the election of the special committee, followed by the checking and counting of ballots. This took three and three-quarter hours. When the deputy Speaker, Tsuda Mamichi, who was in the Chair, read out the results of the election, it transpired that Suehiro Shigeyasu, having received most (99) votes, would be chairman of the committee. Its eight other members were Koretsune Sadakaji, Tateiri Ki'ichi, Imai Isoichirō, Yasuda Isao, Tamura Koremasa, Kitagawa Norikazu, Amaharu Bumpei, and Inoue Kakugorō.

During the next ten days, this committee met on six occasions, at three of which Shirane and another official were present to give any explanations required. These investigations bore fruit in the shape of a completely new bill prepared by the committee to replace that originally tabled by the government. While it is apparent that the work of the committee was not held up in any way by incompetence or obstruction from the government side, internal disagreements must have loomed large. Only five of its nine members approved of the revised bill; the remaining four wished to reject both it and the Home Office proposals outright.

The majority view, as argued by Suehiro when the House resumed its debate on poor relief in the afternoon of Monday 22 December, was that a need for new pauper legislation existed, but the ministers had erred in being rather too generous and much too authoritarian. The revised bill would curb public expenditure by making adult relief available only on grounds of ill-health or decrepitude and not because of 'some other misfortune'. Moreover, the committee had lowered from thirteen to ten the maximum age at which children would be eligible for relief together with their parents, in the belief that boys and girls older than this had in the past 'been able to start on life's path, at any rate as temple apprentices or weeding the paddy fields' (DNTGS: 580). These two alterations were also expected to discourage the poor from becoming idle – an objective that attracted parliamentary support almost as readily as any prospect of a reduction in taxes.

Another series of amendments swept away *in toto* those articles in the government bill defining the quantity and quality of relief. The committee wanted to leave these matters entirely to the discretion of the local authorities. Consequently the administration's concern with such things as adequate shelter, essential food and clothing, medical care, the supply of relief in the form of goods or services only, and employment or educational facilities was condemned as 'gross officiousness' (DNTGS: 580), and the clauses reflecting that concern all deleted. For similar reasons, the prohibition of direct private aid was also jettisoned.

In short, the general effect of the revised bill was negative; it sought to diminish both the scope and the force of the government draft. Its single constructive item of note was the provision it contained for dealing with sick, as opposed to dead, travellers; something that had been lacking in the original bill.

As soon as Suehiro had finished his summary of the committee's activities and formal recommendations, Koretsune Sadakaji, as spokesman for its minority group, was authorized by the Speaker to explain why he felt that there should be no further action on poor relief in the existing circumstances (DNTGS: 580–1). Thereafter the subject was thrown open for general debate. Three Members had spoken in support of one or other of the two bills, and four Members had adopted the same general position as Koretsune, before the closure motion was put and carried (DNTGS: 589). By far the longest speech came from Suzuki Manjirō who strongly urged his fellow legislators to endorse the government's proposals. However, when the Speaker divided the House on the question of whether the bill should be read for a second time, the 'Noes' won.

On this occasion, therefore, and for some two to three decades afterwards, parliamentary performance did not match governmental promise – at least in this single matter of poor relief. Moreover, the performance was that of a chamber dominated by Liberal and Progressive interests eager to substitute popular or party rule for a system of bureaucratic and 'transcendental' cabinets. Why did this situation arise? Should it cause any modification of ideas about the structure of Meiji politics in 1890 or during the period as a whole? A recapitulation of the principal arguments heard in the House, for and against the two sets of proposals for poor relief outlined above, will provide at any rate the beginning of an answer to these questions. It will also throw some light on the social and ideological milieu in terms of which, and in view of which, the men of affairs of that time formed their opinions concerning the country's actual and future condition.

Broadly speaking, the different supporters of both bills were at one in claiming that the existing regulations were inadequate; that society had a moral duty towards its poor; and that recent changes within society had intensified the problem of pauperism. There was a measure of agreement in principle only; when it came to concrete recommendations, individual Members by no means thought alike. It would be tedious to ascribe a particular view to a particular Member in favour of a particular bill in every case; but in what follows it should be remembered, firstly, that the government's bill was more mandatory than the committee's and, secondly, that Suzuki Manjirō had no qualms whatsoever about the former.

The continued enforcement of the Relief and associated regulations of the early years of the era threatened to lead to considerable legal and administrative inconvenience. Mere consolidation of them, without enlarging their scope at all, would have been an improvement; and the necessity for a routine tidying-up operation of this nature became even more apparent after the local government statutes of 1888 had given more independence to the various municipal authorities to which the care of the poor would in all logic have to be assigned. Besides, there were obvious omissions or defects in the wording and execution of the existing laws. For example, a government and society bent on modernism and efficiency could hardly afford indefinitely to deal with sick travellers on the basis that they were legally already dead. Another anomaly, to which Members had their attention drawn, lay in the fact that the current existing residence qualifications for aid related to the pauper's registered domicile, and not his or her actual dwelling-place. The two were not necessarily the same; and the restriction deprived many indigents of relief, though, as far as one can judge, this was contrary to the original intention of the law. It was a case of the law having been seriously invalidated by movements of population. Similarly, although the current Relief Regulations allowed the various prefectures to apply for a national Treasury subsidy to defray part of the costs of their respective relief programmes, procedural hindrances deterred many of them from doing so. One result of this was that whereas Aomori Prefecture had set aside ¥7,153 for paupers in its budget for 1890, the corresponding figure for Iwate Prefecture was ¥7 (DNTGS: 586).

From thinking along these lines of minor amendment, it was but a short step to querying the general applicability of the old regulations. As Shirane said, perhaps the time had come to be 'mistrustful of their narrowness' (DNTGS: 472). He himself went on to cite two specific instances of what he meant. One was the stipulation that only solitary widows, widowers or orphans were entitled to assistance; households or family groups, no matter how poor, did not qualify. The other was the lack of any provision for a sudden emergency, resulting from, say, an earthquake or epidemic. Hence the insertion of the phrase 'or some other misfortune' in the first section of the government bill, an extension of eligibility which, as has been noted, the Representatives' committee took care to rescind.

However, the major divergence of opinion between the government together with the supporters of its bill, on the one hand, and the remaining Members on the other hand, stemmed from the question of municipal responsibility in all its aspects. Shirane made it clear that he did not believe that the town or village authorities could be trusted to carry out poor relief without some form of control from the centre. He, and those who shared his belief, argued that the chief merit of the Home Office draft was that it would impose a uniform standard of relief throughout the country.

In this, they seem to have had the state of the people on their side. There were in fact wide discrepancies in the way the destitute were treated, not only as from one region to another but also as from one district to another. Shirane described how in a few, more progressive, areas attempts had been made to organize public works for the unemployed, but, when the costs of such schemes outweighed their public benefit, it was a case of 'not being able to turn stomachs into backs' (or, as the English idiom would have it, 'near is my shirt but nearer is my skin'), and 'not being practicable to go on for ever in that way' (DNTGS: 472). Tateiri Ki'ichi, in the course of a short speech, remarked that 'it is evident that the matter would not be properly disposed of, if we entrusted this duty to the towns and villages, supposing that conditions remain the same as they have been up till now' (DNTGS: 588). Earlier, Suzuki Manjirō had made the same general point, but in an even more graphic fashion, when, talking about the difficulties created for more generous areas by an invasion of indigent applicants from elsewhere, he said:

Since it is laid down that Tokyo poor-houses will not help those who are not Tokyo people, there are cases of persons from Kanagawa Prefecture and elsewhere collapsing on the roadside, even though they have come to present themselves. When that happens, they have to be dealt with in accordance with the Regulations for Dead Travellers.

(DNTGS: 583)

This group in favour of the original bill directed similar criticisms at private charity as practised in mid-Meiji-era Japan. Philanthropists, the House was told, were numerous in the countryside but inactive in the cities (DNTGS: 586). The truth of this as a general description of prevailing conditions was not at all impaired by the existence of charitable institutions such as the orphanage run by the Fukuden-kai in the Hongō ward of Tokyo, where thirty-six children were looked after so well that Suzuki Manjirō came away from it feeling that he had 'just been washed in the compassion of Jizō in paradise' (DNTGS: 583). Tokyo in 1890 had a population of one and a half million; so the crux of the matter was not the thirty-six waifs comfortably housed and adequately educated by the Fukuden-kai, but that regiment of others 'who weep for hunger in a corner of some back-alley hovel'. Knowledge of this situation caused critics not only to deplore the disparities between districts in the scale of their philanthropic effort but also to ask whether society could expect philanthropists to go on bearing the brunt of the burden of poor relief. It is true that Shirane Senichi was alone in raising this question in so many words; but underlying all the speeches on the government side of the debate was the assumption that the time had come for thoroughgoing state and municipal intervention, either because the problem of pauperism had grown too big to be left to private individuals or else because the level of achievement of a previous age in this respect was no longer acceptable.

When people spoke of the 'evils of undiscriminating private charity', however, they chiefly meant that there was no way of ensuring that donations were restricted to the deserving poor, and were not a means whereby 'incorrigibly villainous and dissolute idlers' (DNTGS: 472) could live as parasites on the community. Nobody disputed the existence of such disreputable persons. Spurious beggars were seemingly not uncommon; and, according to Imai Isoichirō, something akin to gangs flourished in a number of places. He mentioned 'people who would appear to be spokesmen for these paupers', and said that they took advantage of any recession in economic conditions to 'use this as an excuse to threaten the rich and demand alms in an exorbitant way, and, having enrolled even those who have not yet entered the ranks of the indigent, usually distribute [the alms] to them' (DNTGS: 586). Thus, in connection with private charity, it was contended that the cabinet's bill on poor relief would kill two birds with one stone. They would make good its deficiencies, and by channelling philanthropic contributions into public funds would rid it of its more flagrant abuses. It may be noted here, in passing, that these Japanese strictures on uncontrolled philanthropy and unsupervized municipal or parish-type relief have their counterparts in the records of the enquiry into the operations of the English poor law at the beginning of the twentieth century (Bosanquet 1909: passim).

Very few of the participants in the debate were prepared to go so far as to disclaim in principle any kind of responsibility for the destitute. Suehiro declared while introducing the revised bill that 'From the first the deformed, the diseased, the decrepit, also abandoned or strayed children with no one to look after them, and the like, have somehow had to be helped as a matter of social and moral duty' (DNTGS: 580).

Takagi Masatoshi, who opposed both bills, spoke of 'special cases' (DNTGS: 588). Likewise, Koretsune Sadakaji admitted towards the end of his speech that he considered there was a *prima facie* need for new pauper legislation, though this did not make him any more appreciative of the proposals under discussion. Supporters of the bills generally expressed this sense of moral obligation in terms of the traditional concept of a family or household. Thus, we find Shirane at one point asserting that 'in a town or village intimate relationships prevail, just as if they were one household' (DNTGS: 475), and, in reply to a question, he explained that the new relief system would be enforced in conjunction with the Town and Village Code 'because it will be very much of a domestic matter for those towns and villages' (DNTGS: 474). This sentiment was most clearly voiced by Tateiri Ki'ichi who remarked: 'Local government is already in operation, and as we are coming to regard a town or village as one household, I think we should certainly do at least this much if there are poor people in this one village' (DNTGS: 588).

For Suzuki Manjirō, though the ideas were the same, their frame of reference was the national, and not the municipal, family. His is the oratory – impassioned and manifestly sincere – of the Liberal militant; in other words, it reveals an outlook so far to the Left in the context of mid-Meiji politics as to be indistinguishable in many ways from opinions on the radical Right:

It is argued that since the destitute are deformed, incapacitated, or vagrants, and virtually useless to the country, it is all right to leave such persons to die – that this would, on the contrary, be national economy. However, this is surely a most brutal argument. The nation is a nation of poor. By no means is it a nation of just the powerful alone. Why do the poor have to die for the sake of the powerful, and provide for the economy of the powerful? If we are warm-blooded animals, that is to say, human beings in any way at all, it is an argument that ought not to be voiced and is too disgusting to be mentioned even, I think.

(DNTGS: 582)

Similarly, he bitterly denounced the suggestion that a more generous system of relief would make the common people less thrifty. This he called a 'palace argument, and one that stems from ignorance of the conditions of the people' (DNTGS: 583). Those in dire need, he reminded the House, were also 'citizens of this Empire of Japan', and, no matter how much they themselves could be blamed for their hardships, they were entitled to help 'as a matter of moral principle' and because they were 'compatriots' (DNTGS: 582).

Practical reasons for favouring the legislation were also put forward to persuade those unmoved by appeals to altruism. On the grounds that poverty bred crime, it was urged that a nationwide system of subsistence relief would be of use in preserving law and order, not infrequently disturbed by small-scale pauper riots (newspaper files), and would reduce the number of prisoners (DNTGS: 582, 579–80). The latter had to be housed and fed at public expense anyway, so why not maintain the potential thief as a pauper? Again, poverty led to vagrancy, which in turn led to epidemics. If the destitute could be sure of getting sufficient food, clothes and shelter in their native districts, they would not have to take to the roads and the general danger of infection would be less (DNTGS: 582). This line of reasoning was not so far-fetched as one might think; there had been scattered outbreaks of cholera in the summer of 1890 (newspaper files; McClain 1976: 70). Statistics relating to poor-houses run by the Tokyo Prefecture authorities showed that nearly four in ten of their inmates were children (DNTGS: 583). Therefore approximately a third of any sum of money that the Diet chose to allocate to paupers would not be wasted in the sense of showing no material return, but rather could be regarded as an investment in 'the nation's agricultural and industrial enterprises in the future'. Moreover, by doing nothing to rescue its indigent the country ran the risk of losing the 'hands and feet of the expanding industrial enterprises', and the development of the 'gold nugget, Hokkaidō' would continue to be retarded (DNTGS: 582).

To recapitulate briefly, then, the main arguments enumerated so far for giving the bills force of law were: (1) the existing laws were inadequate in scope and inequitable in operation; (2) experience had shown that neither the local government bodies nor private charity could be relied on to provide everybody everywhere with the bare essentials of life, let alone medical care for the sick and occupational training for the young; (3) there was a moral duty to aid those unable to fend for themselves; (4) society could expect certain practical benefits from the legislation in the forms of an increase in production and a decrease in crime and disease. There was virtually no reference to the West and its system of poor relief in the course of the debate; and although Suehiro did mention them once as something of which a Westernizing Japan should take account (DNTGS: 579), it is obvious that the whole issue of whether or not to enact a new poor law was a domestic one to be discussed solely within the context of the nation's past performance and present requirements in this respect. The reason for this was that transcending but also substantiating all other pleas in his favour was the pauper himself.

He and his like probably numbered about 100,000 at that time. Answering a question, Shirane stated that between 1887 and 1889 an average of 20,000 persons a year received assistance under the current Relief and Foundling Regulations. The enactment of the government bill would inevitably cause this number to rise — he conjectured to somewhere in the region of 30,000 to 40,000 (DNTGS: 475). Suzuki's estimate was 30,000 (DNTGS: 584). Most other speakers thought these figures too low; but the upper limit, suggested by Takagi Masatoshi, was 100,000 to 150,000 (DNTGS: 588). Therefore, on the evidence, it appears that approximately 100,000 (or 0.25 per cent) of the country's inhabitants were somehow contriving to exist just at or just below the bread-line. Noting that 'even in normal times, there are many cases of hardship', Shirane said 'merely to be unemployed is to be threatened by starvation' (DNTGS: 472). Later, Suehiro Shigeyasu attributed this state of affairs to the rapidity of social change (DNTGS: 579).

In fact a small proportion of these 100,000 were killed by their poverty. Suzuki alleged that four thousand people a year were for one reason or another unaffected by the existing national, municipal or charitable palliatives for indigence, and so left to the final remedy of the grim reaper (DNTGS: 582). It would be helpful to have some verification of his four thousand – if that were possible. He based it on notifications to the police during the period 1883–88, and seems to have assumed, for example, that in every instance a dead traveller had expired for lack of something to eat. Nevertheless, though the exact number of such fatalities may have been as unknowable then as it certainly is now, the inference is plain: several thousand unfortunates were starving to death in the Japan of 1890. Suehiro's comment was curt but to the point – 'at the present time, the destitute in our midst are dying off' (DNTGS: 580).

It is not possible to conclude this brief account of the conditions of the poor without making some reference to Suzuki Manjirō's description of the public poor-house at Honjō, in Tokyo. This was one of the pauper institutions under the control of the city authorities; and Suzuki visited it on 10 December, that is the day following his inspection of the Fukuden-kai orphanage in Hongō. He found that the Honjō poor-house had a total of 467 inmates. Eighty of these were sick; 189 were children. There were two classrooms for those of school age among the latter. The other principal rooms in the establishment were a dining room, a communal living room and a work room. In the last, he saw paupers employed in the manufacture of charcoal balls, paper lanterns, rush or hemp ropes, envelopes and matchboxes. The profits accruing from the sale of these items were used partly to defray the institution's expenses, partly as pocket money for those who had to live there. In the dining room, paupers were consuming a meal of six parts wheat and four parts rice. Normal prison fare was seven parts wheat and three parts rice. 'As for the vegetables, they were with difficulty eating miserable shreds of radish leaves.' The living room had little more than eighteen square feet (i.e., one *tatami* mat) of space per occupant; he said that he was acquainted with conditions in prisons (*goku-ya*), but this place he felt to be 'an outpost of hell' (*jigoku-ya*) (DNTGS: 583).

Opponents of the bills frequently adopted the tactic of accepting the substance of what those in favour of them had said but belittling its importance. With this there went constant iteration of the idea that the central authorities had no business to be issuing nationwide regulations in this sphere at that time. It was true, they agreed, that the existing laws had their imperfections, but what of it? They worked tolerably well in practice, and it was stupidly officious of the government to frame new legislation simply to remedy technical faults and minor injustices (Koretsune Sadakaji, DNTGS: 581). This point could be made even more forcibly with regard to the revised bill, since its contents were only slightly different from the existing regulations. The same general line of argument was applied to the effects the government's proposals would have on municipal autonomy and private charity.

Municipal relief admittedly left much to be desired in a number of places, but, in the opposition view, local authorities could not be 'perfected' by a policy of interference and legal dictation from the centre (Yuasa Jirō, DNTGS: 585). It was stated, moreover, that the government bill, if enacted, would involve the municipalities in a great deal of legal expenditure. This would come about either because they would feel obliged to make use of the provision whereby they could sue other municipalities or responsible persons for the costs of relieving certain categories of paupers, or else because indigents would feel entitled to take legal action against the appropriate bodies if they had any cause for complaint in the way they had been treated. Also, the government was accused of saving the national Treasury at the expense of municipalities, by making the latter assume an unfair share of the financial responsibility for relief.

On the subject of philanthropy, these opposition speakers often excited themselves into a state of – not in every case credible – moral indignation. Suehiro's remarks to the effect that nobody could be sure that private charity would not develop eventually into a system of relief much superior to officialdom's programme for supervised municipal action (DNTGS: 580) were relatively mild, and interesting in themselves by reason of their evolutionary outlook. Another Member spoke of the natural right possessed by everybody 'to give his own goods or money to others', and continued: 'The bill, in regard to individual citizens of a charitable disposition . . . will restrict their charitable instincts, and so cannot but thwart their natures' (Yuasa Jirō, DNTGS: 585).

Even persons who strongly defended the philanthropist betrayed from time to time a certain amount of suspicion of charity – mainly on the grounds that it tended to foster laziness. Thus, Koretsune Sadakaji declared that the 'private work of philanthropists' was riddled with 'abuses'. Yet, in virtually the next breath, he asked 'if it is left to relief from the philanthropists, how many abuses will there really be?' and again, quite rhetorically: 'So far, no matter where it might be, have people been mere bystanders, if there are living in their town or village persons who are still more impoverished and threatened by starvation?' (DNTGS: 581).

Clearly, this self-righteous attitude was popular among critics of the bills. At the very least, it would have served to stifle doubts in their own and their listeners' minds. Moreover, it implied that proponents of the bills lacked a proper (i.e. patriotic) belief in the efficacy of traditional culture and institutions. For such reasons, the great majority of sympathizers on the opposition side of the debate would have doubtless been gratified by Horikoshi Kansuke's complacent assertion 'truly, our nation is rich in such kindness' (DNTGS: 587).

Naturally enough, the probable cost of the government's scheme for relief came in for hostile comment from those Members who objected to it. Using as his base his estimate of 30,000 paupers entitled to relief on the one hand, and the budget for the Tokyo municipal poor-houses on the other hand, Suzuki Manjirō had calculated that the bill would necessitate an annual expenditure of ¥600,000 – at a rate of ¥20 per person supported (DNTGS: 584). Takagi Masatoshi, assuming that there would be 100,000 to 150,000 recipients of relief, had inflated this to ¥2–3 million (DNTGS: 588): this was a sizeable sum, but not nearly so large as that which the Diet voted without hesitation for the war with China four years later.

However, in 1890, the House of Representatives was determined to do all in its power to reduce taxation, and so was not predisposed to agree to increases in administrative costs no matter whether these would be met out of national or out of local taxes, no matter how worthwhile the general objective, and no matter how marginal the total amount of money involved. The critics held, too, that to relieve the destitutes in the manner suggested by the government would make them as affluent as the normal run of ratepayers in a society where poverty was the lot of most, and local taxes were levied by a method of monthly apportion- ments. Takagi's way of putting this was to say that the poor would be 'eating each other' (DNTGS: 589).

The debate was not lacking in doleful predictions about what would happen to general morale in such circumstances. Horikoshi foresaw that:

> The people who pay relief taxes out of the sweat of their brows will not be at all thankful. And, on the other hand, the people for whom they are paid will also be ungrateful, thinking: – 'It is no more than is due. He is paying relief taxes for us only because the government has made it his duty'.
>
> (DNTGS: 587)

Again and again, it was claimed that the legislation would make the indigent more idle than ever. The virtues of enterprise and thrift would disappear from among the labouring classes, and in the end nobody at all would work if they had other means of keeping alive.

In many respects, the most interesting speech for the opposition was that given by Horikoshi Kansuke. (A young man of peasant origin, he was one of the first students at Waseda and a supporter of the Liberal Party.) The political Liberalism he expounded on this occasion was that fashionable in Europe in the mid-nineteenth century, and he had the full complement of *laissez-faire* economic principles. Nevertheless he did attempt to justify his arguments by basing them on general theory and principles. This is why his remarks are perhaps worth summarizing.

According to him, the proposed relief law was wrong because it rested on the fallacy that public funds could be used to assist private individuals. This was something that could not be allowed in theory, and should not be readily tolerated in practice. The misery of the destitutes was their own fault in all but a handful of instances. 'Are the poor made sick by society? Are they made idle by society? Are they made negligent by society?' he asked, before himself giving the answer that 'the poor eventually get themselves into trouble because they are negligent or because they are idle' (DNTGS: 586). Therefore, on this view, neither society nor the government had an *a priori* duty towards the poor, that is, a duty to protect individuals against themselves. To imagine otherwise was to assume that the state was an 'abstract person', and one might as well expect the authorities to legislate against over-eating, over-drinking, or other common but ultimately anti-social vices. This, incidentally, is a fairly strong refutation of the organic state concept which was at the centre of Meiji politics, in that it was not only the ideological stock-in-trade of the career bureaucrats but also commanded the support in one way or another of most party politicians.

Speaking as a village entrepreneur about to make good in the city, as well as a distant worshipper at the shrine of Manchester radicalism, Horikoshi had this to say: 'It [the bill] amounts to nothing more than robbing the diligent of their wealth. The law will steal money and give it to the lazy and careless.' As a result of this attack on capital, he thought, there would be a reduction in the demand for labour and a consequent falling-off of production. Talking of long-term possibilities, he was not frightened by the prospect that Socialism might easily develop from conditions of accelerating industrialization and growing class conflict, if nothing was done to improve the workers' lot beforehand. Socialism, he declared, was a problem for the future, and 'the fact is that laws are not drafted with an eye to the future . . . I think . . . the argument that we would enact a destitute persons' relief law because such conditions will appear in the future is fallacious.'

As for the more immediate outlook, he maintained that such a law would be warranted only if society were to be threatened by some imminent internal crisis. In other words, the sole justification for pauper legislation would be a state of affairs in which the problem of pauperism had grown so huge that it was about to undermine the entire structure of politics and society. Then, any money spent on relief could be viewed as some kind of unavoidable national defence expenditure and public funds would have been used for the general good. But the actual situation was not so critical at the end of 1890. 'Of course, there are destitutes; however I consider that we have not reached the stage when we have to relieve them by means of a special law' (DNTGS: 587).

Though Horikoshi was alone in mentioning a Socialist menace just over the political horizon, another Member who spoke against the bills agreed with him that pauperism was not sufficiently serious to merit a special act of parliament. Also a Liberal, Yuasa Jirō stated, firstly, that laws of this type should be enacted only when they were 'the inevitable outcome of the pressing needs of the times', and secondly:

> relying on the statistics given by Mr Suzuki and the government-delegate who introduced the bill, on the basis of these, I certainly do not think that paupers and others are numerous in proportion to our country's population of forty millions. This is the point, I think, at which those who approve part company from those who oppose. In short, the essence of my opposition is that there is no need to revise such a law as this in the circumstances [prevailing] in our country today.
>
> (DNTGS: 584)

This refusal to accept the government's, and Suehiro's and Suzuki's, protestations that actual social conditions cried out for a new poor law was the most damaging arrow in the opposition's quiver. By comparison, all other objections with regard to bureaucratic interference or fastidiousness, subsidizing laziness, and higher taxes were of secondary importance. The entire opposition case rested, in the end, on the pragmatic observation that the destitute in really desperate straits were not so numerous as to represent a major threat to society.

In a limited sense this opinion was correct. Some four thousand deaths a year as a result of starvation in a total population of forty million is not a particularly high wastage rate for a nineteenth-century (or twentieth-century) area of under-development. Indeed, the figure could have been several times larger, and still have been credible. It would follow from this, especially when deleterious consequences for farmers of bad seasons and the 'Matsukata deflation' in the early 1880s are taken into account, that the general standard of living before the Restoration, and in normal non-famine years, was some way above bare subsistence levels in the countryside as well as in the cities and towns. It is not possible to be dogmatic about this, because the whole subject of agricultural conditions after 1700 is complex. However, the statistics and relevant comment contained in the debate on poor relief in the first Meiji Diet appear to confirm the idea that in the first half of the nineteenth century the mass of Japanese peasants were not living all the time in a state of semi-starvation (Crawcour 1963: 40). So, too, does the fact that the higher authorities could contemplate legislation embodying the assumption that doctors were available to attend to the sick all over the country. Clearly, rural communities had long since been sufficiently wealthy to pay for the services of men like Suzuki Manjirō and his ancestors.

What other conclusions may be drawn from this abortive but not uninstructive debate? The relationship of the municipalities, or local town and village authorities, to the central administration lies at the heart of the discussions on poor relief. The government's obvious desire to use these bodies as essential but subordinate agents for its planned relief system is thoroughly in keeping with its general policy of financially painless (to itself) bureaucratic centralism. After the principles and broad outline of the system had been determined by officials of the Home Office, the requisite bill had been presented to the national legislature in order that they might receive the force of law applicable to the entire country. On the other hand, the execution and minor administrative details were entrusted to the local headmen and assemblies, and relief was to be paid for on a local community basis. This, to repeat, was the normal pattern of this aspect of the Meiji settlement; and it was one that held good also for the education, police and electoral systems, to cite other important instances (Fraser 1986: 119–23; McClain 1976: 64–9; Mason 1969: 27–58; Waters 1983: 73–5). In view of the extreme decentralization of large areas of national life before the Restoration, and in view of the fairly wide divergences in development and natural resources between one region and another, this attitude on the part of the Tokyo authorities is not altogether incomprehensible. The nation's business had to a great extent to be organized, and so imposed, from the centre if it were to progress at all.

Yet, however justifiable the Meiji trend towards centralization may have been in theory, and however successful it may have been in the long run, the fact is that it ran counter to much cherished practice and encountered stubborn short-term opposition from a populace by no means so docile as latter-day accounts would have us believe. In 1890, there still survived enough of the Tokugawa legacy of regionalism and village autonomy to provide something of a counterweight to the centralizing impulse of the new regime.

The opposition parties, without a single exception, had included in their respective election manifestos a promise to preserve and enlarge the independence of the local self-government bodies. This extract from the *Aikoku-kōtō* manifesto of 5 May 1890 is quite typical:

In the feudal era, our country went too far in the direction of regional

particularism and had an administration which was seriously weakened by decentralization. The system of every little corner of territory
maintaining its own independence was abolished at the time of the
Imperial Restoration; but there was an unexpected tendency for the
central government to enlarge its powers and the provinces gradually
grew weaker. Our party is determined to introduce a fair system of
local government, and to bring about a proper and reasonable division
of power.

(Hayashida 1927: vol. I, 273)

The various Liberal factions, together with the Progressive Party,
won a majority of seats in the first House of Representatives: and all
but thirty of the total of three hundred Members represented rural
constituencies. In other words, nearly every Member was – at least
locally – an important person who had been born in, and had often
continued to reside in, a small town or village. This was why Shirane
spoke defensively when trying to explain the coercive powers that the
government had written into its bill. This was why the amendments
committee had left these controls out of its bill. This was why objectors
to the proposals had talked of 'dictation', and this, no doubt, was one
of the reasons why the House as a whole rejected them.

Members were sensitive to anything likely to curtail the authority or
add to the obligations of the rural municipalities not only because of
their own provincial backgrounds and election pledges, but also because
most of them possessed first-hand experience of the problems and
responsibilities connected with local government. According to one
contemporary calculation (*Nippon shimbun* 15 July 1890), 158 of them
had been at some stage in their careers elected to the prefectural
assemblies, first set up in 1878. Many of these had sat in town or village
assemblies before making the prefectural grade. Other Members had
held the post of headman of a town or village. Some had achieved
preferment of three kinds, so to speak; that is, they had belonged to a
town or village assembly, they had been elected to a prefectural
assembly, and they had done duty as a local headman. It is only to be
expected, therefore, that they and their compeers in the gentry class,
whose votes had sustained them in the successive stages of their public
careers, would have felt a measure of personal commitment to the
general idea of at least preserving intact the rather limited freedom of
action allowed to municipalities by the Town and Village Code of 1888,
and concomitant powers over local taxation.

There is another facet of the functions and influence of the local
assemblies, as manifested in the debate as a whole, which merits

comment. The first debate in the first House of Representatives east of Suez was conducted in a purposeful, orderly and generally praiseworthy manner. The somewhat complicated arrangements for the seating of Members, as well as the procedures for voting within the House and obtaining permission to address the House, while perhaps not perfect in every respect, did provide an adequate institutional setting for serious deliberations. Moreover, there were no fights, no really unseemly interjections, and no embarrassing hiatuses; yet the debate never lacked qualities of vigour and precision. In short, the nation had nothing to be ashamed of in the initial effort of its first House of Representatives on the procedural side. This state of affairs reflected in part the high personal calibre of the majority of Members; again in part, it reflected the good sense and chairmanly skill of the Speaker who at earlier periods in his life had been both an important prefectural official and an eminent party politician; but it was also very much a reflection of the wide extent of Members' participation in the politics of organized discussion at the local government level before 1890.

The outcome of the debate on poor relief when considered in the general context of mid-Meiji political and social conditions is a different matter – or, rather, two different matters. The cabinet of the day was confronted by a hostile Liberal–Progressive majority in the House; but poor relief was not an issue on which the Representatives neatly divided themselves into a minority of government supporters and a majority of opposition party members. Of the eleven Members who had indicated that they wished to speak in support of one or other bill, Suzuki Manjirō and Amaharu Bumpei were Liberals, while Tateiri Ki'ichi and Ōtsu Junichirō were Progressives; in addition, Suehiro Shigeyasu was a Liberal leader. Conversely, six of the thirty-one declared opponents belonged to the *Taiseikai*, which was the name adopted by an intra-mural association of pro-government Members; and a seventh sat as an Independent. Nor will a crudely Marxist interpretation, along the lines that the rich landowners and bourgeois would as part of the class struggle automatically use their parliamentary power to oppress the poor, altogether fit the facts. At least two (Imai Isoichirō and Amaharu Bumpei) of those Members known to have been in favour of the proposed legislation were wealthy farmers, and all of them, by virtue of the high tax qualification for membership of the House, must have been persons of well above-average means.

Nevertheless, despite these reservations, it remains true as a generalization that the government's initiative in tabling a bill which, if it had been accepted by the Diet, would have led to a greatly improved relief system, was frustrated by an elected majority in the Lower House, consisting in the main of representatives of a politically Liberal but socially established village gentry. The Yuasa Jirōs and Takagi Masatoshis of the mid-Meiji world had won an easy victory in their first parliamentary trial of strength with the bureaucrats. In this, they were simply capitalizing on a series of gains made by them and their immediate forerunners in the political warfare of the Bakumatsu and early Meiji periods; at the same time, they were taking the first step in creating a tradition of rural landlord influence over the House of Representatives which was to last until 1945, and beyond in the form of a solid and enduring farmer-conservative governing party (LDP) alliance. In 1890, the position of this Liberal-landlord element, already strong if only because most Japanese still resided in country districts at that time, was further fortified by: the fact that its intra-mural association, the Yayoi Club, was by far the largest single group (130 members) inside the House; its great preponderance in an electorate which was limited to just over 450,000 adult males in a total population of forty million as a result of making the right to vote depend on the payment of at least ¥15 per year in direct national taxes; the importance of the land tax as the principal source of revenue for the state.

Of all the Meiji government's policies, it was to those relating to taxation that the Liberal supporters objected most strongly. They resented having to pay land tax at all at an annual rate of 3 per cent of the assessed value of their holdings; and they detested having to pay it so that the authorities could *inter alia* subsidize the new urban industries. Consequently discontent with the land tax had been one of the chief dynamics of the Liberal movement almost since its inception in 1874; and the promise to reduce it had been a major item in the Liberals' election campaigns. This was something to which they attached even more importance than either their animadversions on the bureaucrats' failure to secure revision of the unequal treaties or their pledge to safeguard the independence of local government. Certainly, neither the rural gentry nor the city industrialists were blind to the advantages of letting the poor shift for themselves, as this would make for high agricultural rents and low factory wages. However, the standing grievance felt by the landlords on the whole subject of taxation would have been sufficient by itself to destroy suggestions for measures like the Destitute Persons Relief Law in the first Diet, given the conditions of modest prosperity enjoyed at the time.

In that case, why did the government bother to table the bill if, as seems likely, the ministers could have foreseen that it would be rejected? This question does not admit of a simple, definitive answer. There is a possibility that, in the wake of popular excitement about the first general election and the opening of the Diet, the bureaucrats intended to lower the prestige of their political opponents by having them show at the outset that they put a higher value on sectional interests than on general welfare. In this way, the outcome of the debate could have been represented as a vindication of the claim that 'transcendental' (i.e. bureaucrat-led) cabinets were government for the whole people, while party cabinets would be rule by a fraction on behalf of its own supporters. However, this idea, which clothes the ministers' motives in an almost Machiavellian subtlety, is suspect if only because it is nothing more than conjecture; and the following considerations would seem to be more germane.

Firstly, nobody could be sure before the session began exactly how the government's relationship with the House of Representatives would work out in practice. As has been seen, party or pro-government ties were by no means absolutely binding on individual Members. Moreover, nobody pretended that the destiny of the Empire was at stake in this question of poor relief; the subject, though not unimportant, was clearly marginal in comparison with, say, the treaty problem, the forthcoming budget, or the Liberal–Progressive desire for party rule. Consequently, the government may have felt that this very quality of secondary importance in the context of the general political situation made its proposals for poor relief a useful trial balloon for testing the temper of the Lower House, and, at the same time, that this might secure their passage through the Diet without too much friction. In this context, it is worth remembering that the general notion that constitutional, Diet-centred politics would, and should, be stamped by compromise, rather than confrontation, was already in evidence as early as November 1890, even if it cannot be proved to have been an operative factor in the present instance (Akita 1967: 67–89).

Secondly, the influence of Yamagata Aritomo, who was Prime Minister in December 1890 and had been Home Minister until May of that year, should not be overlooked. During his term of office at the Home Office, Yamagata had been in charge of the drafting and promulgation of the local government statutes of April 1888. This was a task which he did not leave entirely to others, and the codes embodied many of his own ideas about government and popular participation in it. These ideas accorded perfectly with the notion that poor relief was primarily the responsibility of the local communities, and not that of the national government. The codes provided the towns and villages with the legal authority and institutional structure for carrying out precisely this kind of duty. Moreover, Yamagata had already put forward the view that if the more immediate, but in a sense trivial, problems of individual citizens could be taken care of by an efficient system of municipal self-government, the national legislature and ministers of state would be free to devote their energies to solving problems that beset the Empire as a whole (McLaren 1914: 420–1; Hackett 1971: 113–14).

Thirdly, the speeches (DNTGS: 469–70) delivered by Yamagata and the Minister for Finance, Matsukata Masayoshi, immediately before the commencement of the first reading of the Destitute Persons Relief Law, show that the government was fully aware of the difficulties it would encounter in obtaining the approval of the Lower House for its budget due in the first months of the new year. Therefore any legislation which removed increases in standard items of expenditure from the state revenues to the local rates, as the relief bill promised to do, would have been of help to the authorities in smoothing the way for the budget.

Fourthly, one cannot help feeling that the government deserved to succeed with its relief bill, and that the actual proposals submitted to the Diet in 1890 were but one stage in a continuous process whereby the state took over more and more of the obligation to assist the sick and destitute, an obligation which in the past had been chiefly associated with philanthropy and local community self-help. The 'modest prosperity' mentioned above really describes a state of affairs in which there was much poverty and some out-and-out destitution, resulting in crime and minor disorders. In these circumstances, the bureaucrats were behaving as responsible administrators in tabling the bill, and it was not such an extraordinary or unprecedented act on their part. Rather, it was simply a matter of a government trying to govern in a manner different in degree but hardly in kind from a traditional pattern of conduct and function; in the sense that, as mentioned at the beginning of this chapter, prior to 1868 both the shogunate and the feudal domains had started to add, to existing systems of local community support and private charity, official measures of care for the indigent, orphaned and other unfortunates.

This interpretation of the motivation draws strength from the evident failure of existing regulations and social institutions to keep all paupers alive in 1890, and also from the fact that the officials did not let the matter rest following their rebuff in that year. Although a general social security law (The Subsistence Protection Law (*Seikatsu Hogo Hō*) promulgated 1946) was not enacted until after the Second World War, piecemeal legislation, designed to control factory and mining conditions and to establish labour exchanges, unemployment payments for urban day-labourers and health insurance for industrial employees, was in force by the end of the 1920s, the initial Mining Act having passed the Diet in 1905. Successive ministries also used their ordinance powers to widen the scope of relief-type regulations, and encouraged local authorities to institute or improve their own systems of relief and labour inspection (ILO 1922: 137; Allen 1938: 159–84). All this was very much of an uphill battle against apathy and vested interests for the bureaucrats concerned. The difficulties of achieving anything at all in this field and the fact that most advances were made in the modernized, urban industrial sector of the economy stemmed in part from conditions in more developed countries where the poor law approach to pauperism was beginning to be superseded by a 'welfare state' outlook. However, the main cause was a national condition in which there was a heavy concentration of population in the traditional sector of the economy, composed of rural villages where tenant poverty underlay landlord prosperity and the response to indigence was at best paternalistic.

Nevertheless, the sequence of events implies that there were always some officials in the Home Office and elsewhere who were genuinely concerned about the plight of their poorest compatriots, either for reasons of compassionate altruism, or a concern with national strength, or because of a general enthusiasm for progress and equality with advanced Western countries in all aspects of material and social life. The political wisdom of the bureaucracy's introduction of the bill at that particular moment is questionable, but there are no grounds for impugning the good faith of at least some of its members, especially perhaps those who belonged to the second and third echelons of Meiji officialdom.

Two further points arise from this line of argument. One is that the essential business of the Meiji and later officials, as understood by themselves and usually admitted by their opponents, was to manage the nation's affairs. This managerial function they inherited from the samurai administrative class of the Tokugawa era. It had allowed then, and still allowed, for a good deal of arrogance, cupidity and conservatism, but in its essence it was the approach to politics of an empiricist with more than the rudiments of a sense of responsibility for the commonwealth. The second inference is that just as not everybody in Meiji public life who called himself a Liberal or Progressive was *ipso facto* a person of broad sympathies and enlightened views, so also is it true that not every bureaucrat was an unmitigated scoundrel of the worst reactionary kind.

In order to provide some concrete illustration of these last two points, it is necessary to quote once more from the transcript of the debate on poor relief. During the House's discussion on ways of improving the procedure for electing special committees, Suematsu Kenchō, permanent head of the local government section of the Home Office and one of the Representatives elected from Fukuoka Prefecture, had formally proposed that a quorum should no longer have to be present for the completion of these elections. In other words, he thought that there was no need to keep Members glued to their seats while their colleagues were voting and while the ballots were checked and counted; he also wished to change the rules of the House so that the Speaker could announce the results of these elections and read order papers in the absence of a quorum. Suematsu had spent several years in Europe, and in support of his motion he cited examples from Germany, France and England, 'though you are perpetually scolding me for citing precedents from elsewhere' (DNTGS: 476–7). When opposing this seemingly harmless and perhaps useful suggestion, Orita Kanetaka – a Liberal from Kagoshima, in itself something of an anomaly – poured this sort of scorn on it and its originator:

> If the West becomes our model, we can come to this House and eat oranges, we can smoke tobacco, or we can lie down on the tables and go to sleep. [The whole House laughs.] We may even be able to play cards. As for taking that kind or corruption as an example for the Imperial Japanese Diet – whatever may be the case with Mr Suematsu who has a good knowledge of Europe – I have never even visited Europe. Therefore . . . out of complete revulsion, I object to using it as an example for Japan.
>
> (DNTGS: 478)

There has been perhaps too much of a tendency to see Meiji politics in sharp contrasts of black and white. What is required now is an eye accustomed to various shades of grey.[1]

NOTE

1 Of course since this conclusion was first penned, much has been done to correct the imbalance. Articles and books by George Akita, Peter Duus, Roger Hackett, James McClain, Tetsuo Najita, William Steele, Neil Waters, and, for a later period, Gordon Berger immediately spring to mind. Also further research has shown that Orita Kanetaka was not such a 'red-neck' as he seems here.

4 Changing Diet attitudes to the Peace Preservation Ordinance, 1890–2

R. H. P. Mason

BACKGROUND

Unlike later legislation of the same general type, in particular the Peace Preservation Law (*Chian Ijihō*) of 1925, the Peace Preservation Ordinance (*Hoan Jōrei*) enforced by the Japanese government in December 1887 was pre-eminently a practical, non-ideological measure. It was put into effect at once; and its immediate goal and impact were to relieve the government of the day from some of the direct pressure currently being applied by its political opponents in the form of inflammatory newspaper articles, speech meetings, petitions and demonstrations, and personal harassment of ministers of state and other high officials.

In the second half of 1887, the always volatile Meiji political temperature rose sharply, though it did not reach the heights it had done, and was to do, on other occasions. The government (the first Itō cabinet) found itself on the defensive on a number of issues, some of its own making. Notably, its foreign policy had met with well publicized failure following the sudden termination by the Japanese side of a series of multilateral conferences. These had been convened in Tokyo to discuss revision of the numerous unequal and (in Japan) increasingly unpopular treaties that governed relations between the Asiatic state and the advanced imperialist and commercial powers of the West. The diplomatic rupture had taken place in July, and in August the Foreign Minister and Prime Minister Itō Hirobumi's closest political associate, Inoue Kaoru, resigned. Itō took over the foreign affairs portfolio himself, but for several months the cabinet had no fresh initiatives to offer either its counterparts overseas or its critics at home.

Further worry and uncertainty arose from the fact that the senior bureaucrats were heavily involved in preparations for a constitutional and parliamentary form of government. The drafts of the forthcoming

Constitution and related basic laws were being supervised by Itō, and the new arrangements would inevitably allow for far greater popular participation in government and more outspokenness about national affairs. Taking full advantage of this situation was a reinvigorated opposition, led by prominent political figures like Gotō Shōjirō, a former senior minister of Tosa *han* (feudal domain) and the national government, who since 1873 had been active in the quasi-democratic Liberty and Popular Rights Movement, and Tani Kanjō, a respected and very able Right-wing army general who until the summer of 1887 had been the incumbent Minister for Agriculture and Commerce.

In other words, in late 1887 the Meiji political scene was undergoing one of its recurrent periods of confrontation between a moderately conservative but entrenched bureaucratic government and a strong, wily and experienced 'popular' opposition. The latter proved all the more formidable on this particular occasion because it had managed to gather together into one body, the *Daidō Danketsu* or Unionist League, the usually disparate elements of the Liberals or *Jiyūtō* (under Gotō Shōjirō, Itagaki Taisuke *et al.*) the Progressives or *Kaishintō* (under Ōkuma Shigenobu *et al.*) and the small and scattered but vociferous bands of nationalists under the command of Generals Tani Kanjō and Torio Koyata. The Unionist League's leaders were actively appealing to the country, through newspapers and speech tours, for support for their demands which were chiefly for (1) reduction in the land tax; (2) greater freedom of speech and assembly; and (3) improvement in the country's foreign policy. For this reason, this particular wave of concerted agitation became known as the Petition on Three Serious Matters.

The government might reasonably have expected that in due course the opposition would break up as a result of internal differences, or at least that it would start running out of steam as people tired of the incessant disturbance. Moreover, opportunities for the government to reconcile itself with some of its opponents, or seduce them, would surely occur in the 'natural' course of political events, especially as the dawning of the day of constitutional power-sharing drew ever closer. In fact, all these things did come to pass. In the meantime, however, the government required a breathing space; relief from pressures it chose to find intolerable. Hence the Peace Preservation Ordinance of 25 December 1887 was promulgated the following day as Imperial Rescript No. 67 in a special edition of *Kampō* (the Official Gazette) on a bleak winter afternoon when, according to one commentator, a cold north wind was raising dust storms throughout the capital.

THE ORDINANCE AND ITS EFFECTS

The ordinance consisted of seven articles. (McLaren 1914: 502 is defective; see revised translation in Appendix I at end of this chapter.) These may be conveniently summarized as follows. Article I forbade secret societies and secret meetings. Article 2 gave the police full powers to halt meetings at their own discretion. Article 3 was mainly directed against the publication of books or pictures that were designed to disturb the public peace. Article 4, the most important at the time and the one most germane to this discussion, empowered the metropolitan police, with the prior approval of the Home Minister, to order known or alleged trouble-makers to remove themselves from the centre of Tokyo at short notice. The actual phrasing used to delimit the forbidden area was 'within a distance of three *ri* [12 km] radius around the Imperial Palace or around an Imperial place of resort'. Article 5 provided for specially stringent regulations to go into force in a particular province or district, whenever the situation in the authorities' eyes might warrant them. Article 6 listed penalties for infringements of these local emergency laws. Article 7 stated that the whole ordinance should take effect from the time of its gazettal.

The Peace Preservation Ordinance was extremely severe, not only in what it sought to regulate but also in the penalties imposed for infractions of its rules. In the case of Article 3 which deals with disruptive books and pictures, the offending objects, needless to say, would be impounded as well as the equipment used to produce them, and the persons responsible subjected to the punishments already prescribed in the Criminal Code and the Publications Regulations. Offenders against the other articles of the ordinance ran the risk of imprisonment, albeit 'minor confinement', i.e. not involving hard labour, for a period of one month to three years and a fine of anything between ¥10 and ¥100 (¥5 to ¥200 in connection with Article 5). For breaches of Article 4 a prison sentence of one to three years was mandatory, to be followed by up to five years of police surveillance in the offender's native district. It is also worth noting that the ordinance falls wholly within a tradition of administrative law. The police and the Home Minister had the whip hand in deciding who and what constituted a threat to the public peace.

There is no doubt that the Peace Preservation Ordinance was strikingly successful in its immediate goal of checking the activities of the opposition, particularly in Tokyo. Five hundred and seventy opposition politicians, mainly Liberals, several of whom were editors of influential newspapers, were forced to leave the central metropolitan district the morning after its publication. In many instances, it was alleged and remembered with great bitterness by the victims and their friends, the police behaved in a brutal and overbearing way in carrying out duties that were harsh enough in themselves. Some people (notably Kataoka Kenkichi from Kōchi Prefecture) were arrested and subsequently jailed for refusing to move. The opposition's activities outside Tokyo do not seem to have been greatly affected by the ordinance, however. Speech making and party gatherings went on up and down the country, and petitions continued to be drawn up and signed. Thus, the *Japan Weekly Mail* (hereafter cited as *JWM*) reported that 'It has now become the fashion for ministers, ex-ministers, and future ministers to place themselves in direct communication with the leading minds of the great provincial towns' (*JWM*: 21 July 1888, also 29 September 1888; also Ike 1960: 186). Also, many of the Liberals and Progressives banished by the ordinance simply withdrew no farther than Yokohama, where they could quite easily keep in touch with events in the capital and supervise the publication of their newspapers. It is difficult to find out how many people were actually punished for breaches of the Peace Preservation Ordinance, but they do not seem to have numbered more than about a dozen (*JWM*: 7 January 1888). This is not a very high figure in the circumstances of what must be regarded as a genuine threat to the public peace, even though the cabinet did exaggerate the seriousness of the situation for its own ends. Such evidence suggests that the government was largely content with the mere existence, and implicit menace, of the ordinance, together with the mass exodus of its enemies from Tokyo.

Moreover, the bureaucratic authorities were soon playing other, more conciliatory cards. In fact, immediately following the rigours of the Peace Preservation Ordinance, new and more liberal press and publications regulations were issued on 28 December 1887 (*JWM*: 21 January 1888). In April 1888, Itō Hirobumi who was originally from Chōshū *han* (later Yamaguchi Prefecture) resigned as Prime Minister; and his place was taken by a Satsuma (Kagoshima Prefecture) man, Kuroda Kiyotaka. The change over involved a new cabinet, and this in turn had made possible an invitation to Ōkuma Shigenobu, the founder and national leader of the Progressive Party, to be Foreign Minister.[1] The invitation was accepted, and the zeal for opposition among Ōkuma's Progressive supporters diminished accordingly. Furthermore, the new Constitution underwent a laborious process of ratification by the Privy Council through most of 1888, and was solemnly promulgated by the Emperor on 11 February 1889. To mark the happy occasion, the government released from prison many of its most determined opponents who had been put there during the past ten or twelve years, in some cases for what were clearly insurrectionist crimes, as well as those more recently incarcerated for breaches of the Peace Preservation Ordinance.[2] The ordinance itself was at this time allowed to lapse; and it appears that opposition leaders were once more freely residing and congregating in Tokyo from about the middle of 1889.[3] Most startling of all developments was the sudden entry of Gotō into the Kuroda government as its Minister for Communications in March 1889.[4]

Nevertheless, the ordinance had not been rescinded; it was simply not enforced. Moreover, while it is true to say that the impulse behind it was pragmatic and not ideological, its brunt had been borne by the Liberal and Progressive adherents of what had originally been a highly doctrinaire movement for a constitution and civil rights. For these men, whatever the genuflections and gyrations of their top rank leaders, the issue of the continued existence of the Peace Preservation Ordinance was real enough, and one they were prepared to pursue when the first Diet met in November 1890.

DIET DEBATE, DECEMBER 1890

Within the new legislature, which was to be summoned annually, the House of Peers was conservative, especially perhaps on social matters; but this does not mean that its Members were necessarily and always pro-government, despite their seemingly solid support for the authorities on the issue of retaining the Peace Preservation Ordinance. As for the first House of Representatives, it had a total membership of exactly three hundred. Of these, about 130 were affiliated with the Liberal Party; forty belonged to the Progressive Party; and the remainder consisted of a very small Right-wing National Liberal Party and fairly large grouping of Independents and government sympathizers (Mason 1969: 190–5). However, for various reasons, the system of monolithic, tightly controlled parties commanding the undivided allegiance of their parliamentary followings had not yet taken root in Japan; and for some purposes all Members of the first House of Representatives should be regarded as having been of an Independent turn of mind.[5]

From about 6 December, after the inaugural ceremonies and procedures had all been gone through, the Representatives were debating policy matters though not yet the government's budget proposals for 1891. These latter were by common consent the weightiest and most explosive item on their agenda, and the House had in fact on 6 December elected a special committee to consider them. On 18 December the order paper for the House of Representatives contained an announcement of the first reading of a bill to abolish the Peace Preservation Ordinance. The prime mover was Katō Heishirō; and the text simply read: 'That the Peace Preservation Ordinance, promulgated in Imperial Rescript No. 67 of December 1887, be abolished' (DNTGS: 542). The bill[6] actually came to the attention of the House towards the end of its customary afternoon sitting, after it had heard strong criticism by some angry Members of the Foreign Minister's performance the previous day when answering questions on notice (p. 144), and after it had given a first reading to a copyright bill.

Introducing his own bill, Katō made the following points (DNTGS: 542). His enquiries had shown that the overwhelming majority of Members were in favour of the bill, or at least not opposed to it. Some people argued that the ordinance was invalid because Article 22 of the Constitution guaranteed Japanese subjects freedom of residence within the law. On the other hand, the very last article (76) of the Constitution provided that all existing laws, ordinances, etc., should remain in force after it was promulgated. Consequently, in the view of Katō and his supporters, a special bill to get rid of the Peace Preservation Ordinance was in order. This part of Katō's speech reflects the general pre-occupation with the notorious 'expulsion' powers contained in Article 4 of the ordinance.

Turning to the ordinance itself, Katō attacked it for having been first of all drafted in far too much of a hurry and then, to make matters worse, enforced with indecent haste in a way that was 'unprecedented in the legal history of Japan'. He declared that such an ill-conceived piece of legislation was not 'worthy of the needful obedience of forty million subjects as the law of Japan'. The ordinance had clearly been issued as an emergency measure to counteract the situation prevailing in late 1887; but it was irresponsible of the authorities to try to cope with short-term crises by deploying laws that had a quality of permanence. The abnormal conditions that the Peace Preservation Ordinance had been conjured up to deal with three years previously could now be taken care of by other means. Standing administrative and police regulations would control small breaches of the peace; and for major disturbances, there were the martial law (Article 14) and special ordinance (Article 8) provisions of the Constitution. He believed that the government, too, secretly did not consider the ordinance to be any longer necessary.

With these remarks, Katō is really saying that, even though the Peace Preservation Ordinance was not being actively enforced at the time of speaking, there was something fundamentally wrong about leaving it in existence. In fact, he goes on to state explicitly that keeping the ordinance on the statute books was like 'plastering mud all over the fair face of Japan'. The mud 'must be wiped off [if only] for appearances' sake'. He drew an analogy between having such a law and requiring ministers of state to wear a bamboo wickerwork hat or a rickshaw-puller's 'jam-bun hat' (*manjūgasa*) over their formal Western attire when attending cabinet meetings. Of course, the ministers would angrily reject such a demand as beneath their dignity. Similarly, it was not humanly possible for the people of Japan to go on obeying an ordinance 'unprecedented even in savage countries'.

One other Member[7] spoke in support of Katō's bill, but did not really add much to the arguments he had adduced. And only one Member spoke against. This was Ōtsu Junichirō, a Liberal of unblemished credentials. Both at the beginning and at the end of his speech Ōtsu admitted that he was in a minority of virtually one, but claimed that he nevertheless wanted to air his views 'for future reference' (DNTGS: 542). With regard to the sponsors' claims that the ordinance was too harsh, an opinion with which he himself concurred, Ōtsu held the right course of action to be revision of the obnoxious parts, not complete abolition. Likewise, complaints that the ordinance was supposed to be only a temporary measure and that it had been enforced far too roughly in 1887 could best be dealt with by judicious amendment. One merit of this approach would be that the Diet would retain control over peace preservation legislation, which it would not have done if it encouraged the government to rely on the special ordinance power contained in Article 8 of the Constitution. The speaker was only half right on this point, as Article 8 empowered the Diet to disallow emergency ordinances when it next met, and it had to approve any the government wished to issue while it was actually in session.

Ōtsu also argued that the Peace Preservation Ordinance had some positive virtues; that it was actually responsible for the current state of tranquil domestic public order and the good name Japan thereby enjoyed overseas. This was in flat contradiction of the assertion of the bill's sponsors, contained in the written memorandum that went with their proposal, that the Peace Preservation Ordinance had served to 'disrupt the harmony of public opinion at home and to besmirch the national honour abroad'. As well, Ōtsu considered that it was wrong to imagine that the ordinance could work only in the interests of the cabinet. In words that soon turned out to be prophetic, he suggested that the safeguards embodied in this legislation might be required to protect Members and the constitutional processes if political and party strife, centred on the Diet, got out of hand, asking rhetorically what would happen 'if unruly persons banded together in this Diet'. After some considerable restiveness to begin with, the House heard out Ōtsu's short speech with a degree of patience; but when he had finished, it voted overwhelmingly, by Members standing in their places, for the bill. (Its Speaker by the way, Nakajima Nobuyuki, who was not in the Chair on this occasion, had been one of those expelled in December 1887; as was Nishiyama Shichō, a future Chief of Metropolitan Police.) Four days later, on 22 December 1890, the House of Representatives decided to omit the second and third readings of Katō Heishirō's bill; so the proposal to abolish the Peace Preservation Ordinance was sent on to the House of Peers, for that chamber's consideration.

SŌSHI VIOLENCE AND DIET DEBATES, JANUARY–MARCH 1891

When the House of Representatives reassembled on 8 January 1891 after a New Year break of thirteen days, it was in an atmosphere of deepening crisis. Five days later, on the evening of 13 January, the government re-issued Article 4 of the Peace Preservation Ordinance. This time, the law was not being used to expel uncongenial politicians from the capital but to evict between sixty and seventy common gangsters (sōshi) who had got themselves mixed up in politics. In other words, Ōtsu Junichirō's prediction of a few weeks earlier had proved true, and the authorities were acting with common consent, not out of selfish political interest but to protect individual Members of the Diet and the parliamentary process as a whole. Not all Members of the House of Representatives saw matters in this light, however, and on the morning of 14 January a Liberal Member, Suzuki Shōji, sought leave to interrupt discussions in the House on the budget, in order to introduce an urgency motion calling on the government to desist from enforcing the Peace Preservation Ordinance. Both House and government agreed that Suzuki's motion be put to the debate,[8] and after a short but animated discussion it was rejected. In effect, the House now seemed to be contradicting the nearly unanimous opinion it had expressed only a few short weeks previously that the Peace Preservation Ordinance should be abolished immediately. What had happened?

The root cause of the trouble lay with the budget. There existed a deadlock between the cabinet and the House of Representatives concerning provisions for the coming fiscal year, and growing feelings of confusion and panic about the immediate political outlook. The government had initially proposed a total expenditure of ¥83.32 million, and had continued to argue stoutly for this sum ever since the Diet first opened in November. However, in late December, just two days after the start of the Diet's New Year holiday, a special committee of the

House to consider the budget recommended a large cut of ¥8.88 million, over ten per cent of the government's figure. The latter wasted no time in saying that reductions of this order were quite unacceptable; nevertheless, it looked as if the House would follow its committee's suggestions. The opposition in the House to the original budget proposals was made up in the main of Progressives and Liberals who, apart from honouring promises to voters on the general subject of tax reduction, were using the issue to weaken their bureaucratic enemies' grip on the Executive power in order to pave the way for party cabinets. The Progressives were reasonably united and determined on the budget issue, but by mid-January a clear cleavage had occurred in the Liberal ranks between a 'hard-line' faction (*kōha*) and a compromising or 'soft' faction (*nampa*) with the latter ready to come to terms with the cabinet, on the basis of which the budget would be approved by the House (newspaper files; also Akita 1967: 79).

When the Diet re-opened, both factions were busy trying to consolidate and extend their influence in the days leading up to the House of Representatives' critical vote on whether or not to approve massive reductions in the budget; and both factions, or at any rate elements within them, were prepared to use *sōshi* to this end. The situation was rendered all the more volatile and difficult by the fact that the 'hards' and the 'softs' had almost equal support, if not among Liberal Members then in the House as a whole.[9] The *sōshi*, for their part, also seem to have been equally divided in their allegiance, and were only too ready to spring into action when called upon. Their most flagrant outrage took place on 7 January, when they broke up a meeting of Liberal hard-liners at the Yayoi Hall in Shiba Park. The following is a verbatim translation of the report of this affray published in the *Tokyo nichi nichi shimbun* the next day:

VIOLENCE AT THE YAYOI HALL: MESSRS UEKI AND YASUDA HURT
[*Yayoikan no sōdō, Ueki Yasuda Nichi no sōnan*]

The Yayoi Club [a Liberal faction] had arranged to hold a meeting from ten o'clock in the morning of 7 January in the Yayoi Hall at Shiba Park. About seventy people attended. Agenda items were to be: (1) policy with regard to the budget; (2) treaty revision; and (3) qualifications of Members of the House of Representatives. Mr Matsuda Masahisa was made chairman.

After dealing with some preliminary business, the meeting had just got down to discussing the budget, when more than twenty (some reports say thirty-six) *sōshi* suddenly entered, each waving a stick. They asked for an interview with Mr Suzuki Shōji, but since the meeting was in progress he refused to come out [and see them]. The *sōshi* then grew angry and, rudely pushing past the receptionist who tried to stop them, they marched into the hall, screaming 'The Liberals take bribes from the Progressives!' and so forth.

Advancing as far as the chairman's seat, they accosted Mr Ueki Emori, who was in the seat immediately to the chairman's right. 'Ueki, there is something we want to discuss with you. Come over here!', they said. [But] he scolded them, saying that he could not come and, as the meeting was a private one, they should take themselves off. Whereupon seven or eight of the *sōshi*, using the sticks they were carrying, began to hit him from both sides and from the front and rear. Surprised, he tried to stand on [his] chair, but somebody pulled him down by the hair from behind, and he fell. He then tried to get up a second time, protecting himself with his hands, and was subjected to [more] fierce blows. Since he had nothing in his hands, he attempted to ward off [the blows] by using his right hand and gradually struggled to his feet, receiving two [more] bad wounds the while. Blood gushed out and ran from his face to his chest. Mr Yasuda Yuitsu, who was nearby at the time, suffered a similar wild beating and was hurt.

Mr Hayashi Yūzō saw what was happening, and he led people from neighbouring seats in an attack on the *sōshi*, using their chairs as weapons. The *sōshi* got the worst of this encounter. Wounded on the hands, they all retreated into the lobby in considerable disorder. There, they were set on by the rickshaw-pullers retained by Members and other people [in the lobby] in a grand free-for-all. The *sōshi* got the worst of this engagement too, and were terribly beaten. One of them was taken prisoner; another was chased into a local police post. These two were taken to Atago-chō police station. Thereafter, the police kept a continuous and strict watch on the hall; and the Members, resuming their seats, went on with their discussions.

Other reports showed that Ueki Emori had indeed been badly wounded about the face and head, but Yasuda had got off more lightly. Damage to Yayoi Hall included twenty chairs smashed beyond repair, ditto one *hibachi* room-warmer, which a gangster had hurled at the chairman of the meeting only to have it miss the mark and end up embedded in a staircase. As for the captured *sōshi*, they turned out to be Yamada Kaneo and Okano Tadaaki, and were alleged to belong to the *Eishinsha* (Fulfilment Society?), an Ishikawa Prefecture organization under the control of a Liberal Representative from that area. The pair were initially released by the police after interrogation, but were re-arrested a few days later along with a number of others responsible for the fracas.

The accusation that Liberals took bribes from the Progressives reflects the anti-budget alliance between the Progressives and hard-line Liberals. It also indicates that this group of gangsters were acting in a sense as agents, self-appointed or otherwise, of the 'soft' faction Liberals. In another incident which caused considerable disquiet, the *sōshi* concerned were seemingly on the other side, acting for the 'hards' against the 'softs'. This affair took place on the evening of 10 January at the Imperial Hotel, where some members of the compromise party were holding a private meeting. Somebody came to the front desk of the hotel and requested to see one of the politicians involved, Toyoda Bunzaburō.

> When the conversation was over and he [i.e. Toyoda[10]] was about to get up and go, ten or so young men broke in and looked as if they were going to do Mr Toyoda a mischief. However, measures taken by the police to deal with the matter were effective, and they took the young men into custody before anything happened. Several of the eleven young men were carrying lethal weapons. Mr Toyoda was escorted home by the police.
>
> (*Yūbin-hōchi shimbun*, hereafter *YHS*: 12 January 1891)

Numerous other notices in the Tokyo press at the time show that *sōshi* had also adopted a favourite but thoroughly unwholesome tactic of making threatening visits to Members' homes and lodgings especially in outlying areas of the capital where police guards could not be supplied. One such encounter, reported at length, took place between Kudō Yukimoto (a Liberal hard-liner) and *sōshi* spokesman Urabe Keitarō. Kudō had refused to meet the entire deputation of 'five or six' rowdies who were pestering him, but at length consented to talk to Urabe alone. In the course of their conversation, he was accused of infringing the Imperial prerogative by favouring cuts in the budget, and at the same time of playing into the hands of 'Count Waseda' (Ōkuma Shigenobu, the leader of the Progressive Party) who, Urabe alleged, was hoping to profit from the political impasse and likely special general election to become Prime Minister. Kudō strongly denied both charges, causing Urabe, when concluding the interview, to warn him to take heed of the advice proffered or else it would be the worse for him. 'So saying, he [and his companions] bade farewell for the day. The next morning, they paid another visit, but Mr Kudō was not at home' (*Tokyo nichi nichi shimbun*, hereafter *TNNS*: 11 January 1891).

A possible key figure in the political discussions and imbroglio of the times was yet another, and better known, Liberal politician, Inoue Kakugorō. Inoue was of commoner (i.e. non-samurai) stock, and hailed from Hiroshima Prefecture. He graduated from Keiō University and while a student there, he had become very close with its founder and presiding genius, Fukuzawa Yukichi. Later, Inoue went to Korea to work as a journalist for the government of that country. At the same time, being a zealous Liberal activist at home and abroad, he was deeply involved in the abortive insurrection by the Korean Independence Party in Seoul in December 1884, and the so-called 'Ōsaka Incident' almost a year later. The latter is the name given to the activities of a group of Japanese Liberal revolutionaries who were planning to use force to liberate Korea. For his complicity in the second affair, Inoue was eventually imprisoned by the Japanese government, but later released – presumably under the amnesty to mark the Constitution.

After 1890, he pursued a successful career in business and politics in Japan, being returned to the House of Representatives no fewer than fourteen times. In January 1891, he was a declared leader of the compromise faction, and was about to resign from the Liberal Party on the budget issue. Furthermore, he seems to have long enjoyed the confidence of Gotō Shōjirō, former Liberal chief and now Minister of Communications; and this made him a likely mediator in any negotiations between the embattled bureaucratic cabinet and the political party opposition. Inoue was thus an object of interest, if only for his colourful past and personality, to both the *sōshi* and the press; and on 10 January it was reported that a completely innocent nocturnal visitor to his home had been waylaid by two ruffians who thought the man was Inoue and had cruelly beaten him until they realized their mistake.

A little earlier, Inoue's name had been linked with a visit, again in the evening, of two hard-line leaders, Suzuki Shōji and Ishida Kannosuke, to Gotō Shōjirō's residence in the Takanawa district of Tokyo on 7 January. The substance of the story was that, unknown to them, Suzuki and Ishida had been followed to Gotō's house by a 'house boy' *sōshi* in the service of Suzuki who for some reason suspected that his master might be heading for trouble. Sure enough, when the young man reached the minister's establishment, he found it well guarded by *sōshi*; even more disquieting, a number of people 'who looked like rickshaw-pullers' ran out of a nearby shop, and started whispering among themselves in a threatening way about Suzuki. Alarmed, Suzuki's follower boldly went up to the front door of the house and asked to see his master. This was refused, but he managed to hand in his name-card on which he had hastily scribbled an account of what was happening. When he had read this message, Suzuki showed it to Ishida and Gotō. The latter pressed his visitors to pass the night in the security of his home; and at the same time he arranged for the local police to be alerted.

A party of ten constables eventually arrived from Takanawa police station. The twenty or more *sōshi* surrounding Gotō's house were peacefully dispersed about 11 p.m., and Suzuki and Ishida returned home 'in the dead of night'. This was the bare bones of the story as published in the *Tokyo nichi nichi shimbun* under the caption 'The Night of the Seventh'; but of course various implications could be, and were, read into it. The *Yūbin-hōchi shimbun* used the heading 'Strange Goings-on in the Capital of a Constitutional Country!' (*Rikken Kokuno teito-ni kono koto ari ayashii*) for its account of the affair; while the *Kokumin shimbun* in an editorial openly accused Gotō of plotting to ambush Suzuki and Ishida, and was officially suspended from publication for a week for its pains (newspaper files: 9 January 1891).

Rebuffing and preventing *sōshi* attacks and threats not unnaturally became a major preoccupation of the politicians concerned, and of the metropolitan police. Following the incident detailed above, Suzuki Shōji was seen carrying a blanket into the Diet, presumably to cushion blows. Many of his colleagues equipped themselves with swordsticks, or formed mutual protection squads to keep each other company when outside the Diet premises; and there was a joke going round to the effect that Members were buying walking sticks for their rickshaw-pullers (*TNNS*: 8 January 1891, 9 January 1891; *YHS*: 9 January 1891).

As for the police, they faced almost insuperable difficulties. The area around the Diet building in Hibiya, once the session had resumed in January, was constantly and heavily guarded by mounted men as well as constables on foot, a total force which was reported to number at times as many as four or five hundred (*YHS*: 12 January 1891; *JWM*: 17 January 1891; *Nippon*: 13 January 1891). Diet Members were officially warned to be on the alert when not attending the sittings; and those considered to be in most danger of assault were assigned police bodyguards, sometimes in a ratio of five guards per Member (*YHS*: 11 January 1891; *Nippon*: 11 January 1891). Moreover, as mentioned earlier, Diet Members' places of residence, in the inner metropolitan districts at any rate, were watched, as were the *sōshi* who infested the same localities. It is not surprising, then, that the police attached to stations in these places (notably Atago chō, Azubu and Kyōbashi) were reported to be exceptionally busy and to have gone without sleep for three nights (*YHS*: 13 January 1891; *TNNS*: 11 January 1891; *Nippon*: 13 January 1891).

More portentously, other notices in the papers from about 10 January related to alleged discussions at Metropolitan Police Headquarters about instituting a 'Edo-*harai*'. These were in all probability deliberate leaks (*TNNS*: 10 January 1891, 11 January 1891; *YHS*: 10 January

1891). 'Edo-*harai*' means a 'sweeping' or 'purging' of Edo, and refers to a policy adopted from time to time by the old Tokugawa government for ridding their capital of undesirables. In mid-Meiji times the phrase could only denote application of the expulsion article of the Peace Preservation Ordinance, and if the preliminary newspaper reports were designed as counsel to the *sōshi* to take prompt steps to moderate their behaviour, they utterly failed to achieve this objective.

A day or two later, on 13 January, the blow fell. Expulsion orders signed by Viscount Tanaka Mitsuaki, the Chief Constable of Tokyo, invoking the Peace Preservation Ordinance, were issued to some sixty *sōshi* known to be actively involved in politics. Those affected were allowed ten hours in which to remove themselves to places more than the statutory three *ri* from the Imperial Palace for the duration of the current session of the Imperial Diet. Some gangsters were out when the police delivered the eviction notices; one was ill and granted a short reprieve. Most *sōshi*, however, complied with the orders without any fuss or argument, despite earlier shows of bravado and claims that they would risk death or imprisonment in order to stay put. Some, it seems, had already packed their bags when the police called, and put aside money for an extended stay out of town (*TNNS*: 15 January 1891).

Ten of the expellees travelled to Yokohama by various trains on the morning of 14 January. There, they were met at the two stations by a very strong show of police force and escorted to their various lodgings. The Chief Constable of Yokohama had been given some warning of what was afoot by the authorities in Tokyo, and had called out his men in the middle of the night in order to carry out his plan to overawe the *sōshi*. Before long, however, it was rumoured that the latter were planning a big get-together with their brethren who had gone to Kawasaki (even nearer Tokyo than Yokohama), Kanagawa and elsewhere in that general area. They intended also to invite *sōshi* who had escaped expulsion orders and were still living in Tokyo to the party, and hold a general debate on possible future courses of action from their point of view (*TNNS*: 15 January 1891).

Once again, the application of Article 4 of the Peace Preservation Ordinance had proved a remarkably effective way of tranquillizing the capital. Just over sixty out of a total of approximately 1,700 malefactors said to be in Tokyo had been expelled, but that was enough (*YHS*: 15 January 1891). *Sōshi*, their threats and their disturbances ceased to be a problem in the day-to-day running of Diet politics for the time being. Three had been discovered hiding in a drain near the Diet Building on the afternoon of 13 January, a few hours before the expulsion orders were issued. One more tried to slip into the Parliament on 14 January carrying offensive weapons, namely a dagger nine inches long and a large iron ball (*TNNS*: 14 January 1891; *YHS*: 15 January 1891). Nothing more happened to disturb the public peace; and the disastrous fire that completely razed the new Diet Building in the early hours of Tuesday 29 January 1891 was attributed to faulty electric wiring, not *sōshi* sabotage.

The metropolitan press, even papers consistently critical of the government, did not actually welcome, but at any rate strongly supported, the 'sweeping-out' of Edo, as the following excerpts from their editorials show.

> We certainly do not want [legislation] like the Peace Preservation Ordinance to remain on the statute book for ever. Yet, at times of social crisis when politically unprincipled ruffians and hooligans stalk round in broad daylight, we can only heartily approve the issuing of an emergency ordinance, which by bringing about the expulsion of the said ruffians and hooligans protects the liberties of the majority of honest and decent citizens.
>
> (*YHS*: 15 January 1891)

> It is a matter of profound regret to us that the government, the day before yesterday, enforced the Peace Preservation Ordinance. The Constitution took effect from November last year; and within two months of [starting to] operate the Constitution, which is supposed to make the people's liberties safer than ever, the authorities have been forced by circumstances to enforce this repressive law. This round of expulsions, unlike the previous one, is not designed to protect the government but, [rather] to protect the Diet. People who take part in politics must necessarily have courage. Moreover, physical strength is not unnecessary, and it is perfectly all right to use this in cases where it has to be used. However, when it comes to common gangsters who have no regular occupation and no fixed address making a living by threatening Members [of the House of Representatives] with swords and sticks, courage and physical strength are nothing more than a source of occasional bodily hurt and loss of reputation.
>
> (*Mainichi shimbun*: 15 January 1891)

A strongly dissentient view was put out by *Nippon*, however:

> Judging, it would seem, that a situation of plotting sedition or breaching the public peace exists, the Chief Constable the night before last, on the thirteenth, invoked Article 4 of the Peace Preservation Ordinance, and expelled from the capital several tens of

persons who had been harassing a number of Members of the House of Representatives. What a hateful misuse of power this is! Plotting sedition can only refer to people who amass weapons, prepare dangerous instruments and plan to subvert a whole province or more. Those who visit public figures in their homes in broad daylight and browbeat them with violent words cannot be held to be plotting sedition. Neither can those persons who waylay travellers on the roads in the dead of night and threaten them with intimidatory behaviour be thought of as plotting sedition. Such fellows can be controlled by the police and punished under the penal code, without there being any need to have recourse to the Peace Preservation Ordinance.

(*Nippon*: 15 January 1891)

In the House of Representatives, in the early afternoon of 14 January, debate on Suzuki Shōji's emergency motion to have expulsion orders against the *sōshi* disallowed was limited to a total of six speakers. The first three were for the motion; the others against (DNTGS: 693–4). Suzuki himself argued briefly that the House had already voted to abolish the Peace Preservation Ordinance and that it was consequently improper for the government to defy the Representatives' express wishes by enforcing the ordinance. Secondly, Members in danger of assault by *sōshi* were already under police protection. Thirdly, the *sōshi* were really 'patriots' (*shishi*) who should not be driven out of Tokyo but, rather, encouraged to come and occupy the public galleries in the Diet and listen to debates, so that they might understand the reasons for political decisions. Since Suzuki seemingly had already been a victim of *sōshi* attack and was in danger of suffering some further assault (*JWM*: 24 January 1891), it might be supposed that in tabling his motion on behalf of the gangsters, he was seeking to curry favour with them. No clear evidence for this line of thought has come to light, despite his allegedly friendly association with *sōshi* on occasions; and by reason of the wider implications of the whole budget issue and his own hard-line stand on it, Suzuki Shōji was likely to be in trouble whatever he did or did not do.

In what was perhaps his maiden speech in the House, a Member who was destined to sit in it for over forty years and to become Prime Minister of Japan, Inukai Tsuyoshi, gave general support to Suzuki, but bitterly condemned his calling the *sōshi* patriots. To him, they were 'lawless men' and 'ruffians' who should never be encouraged in their nefarious activities by anything said in the House. There is something more than a little sad and ironic in this, in view of Inukai's ultimate assassination by 'patriots' in army uniform.

Shioda Okuzō also spoke for the motion. After repeating even more strongly Suzuki's earlier point about enforcement of the Peace Preservation Ordinance at this juncture being tantamount to contempt on the part of the government for the resolution of the House on the matter, he went on to ask if the Representatives' ideas on other legislation, including the budget, would be treated in a similarly cavalier fashion. He also reiterated the argument that Members already had adequate protection by virtue of existing regulations and police watchfulness; and he added that the so-called *sōshi* 'outrages' had not been very serious (Ueki Emori and Yasuda Yuitsu might have had a different opinion on that!) and were mainly 'the outcome of the zeal with which arguments for and against are being pressed on individual Members'. Finally, Shioda, anticipating criticism of the motion, stated that those in favour of it were just as anxious to proceed with the budget discussions as anyone else. The three opposing speakers did indeed argue that Suzuki's motion was inopportune because it had interrupted debate on the budget. They also said that the Peace Preservation Ordinance was legally still in existence and perfectly well available to the authorities; as the House of Peers had not yet considered the Representatives' bill for abolition, still less had the latter gone to the Emperor for his assent. Moreover, in the opinion of these three Members, the government was quite justified in using the ordinance on this occasion, not only to protect the House but to safeguard the general peace of Japan. In short, the opponents of the motion stressed the priority of the budget, and rebuked Suzuki and his supporters for wanting the Legislature to 'poke its nose into' Executive matters.

After the closure motion was put and carried, and the results of a standing vote had been challenged, the Deputy Speaker ordered a secret ballot on Suzuki's motion. It was lost by 119 votes to 84. Approximately seven weeks later, on 7 March 1891, the House of Peers resolved to have Katō Heishirō's original bill for the abolition of the Peace Preservation Ordinance referred for consideration to a special committee (DNTGS: 413). This was within an hour of the House being prorogued for the first time, at the end of the first session of the first Diet on the same day.

DIET DEBATES, DECEMBER 1891

The second session of the first Diet opened on 26 November 1891, and lasted only until 25 December when the House of Representatives was dissolved. Once again, the budget was proving a source of difficulty between the bureaucratic cabinet (the first Matsukata cabinet) and the party opposition in control of the Lower House.

On 5 December, a second bill to abolish the Peace Preservation Ordinance was introduced into the House of Representatives by Andō Kyūka, who was a member of the generally pro-government group of Representatives known as the Great Accomplishment Society or *Taiseikai*.[11] It was necessary to go through all the formalities of a new bill, because, under Article 35 of the Law of the Houses, bills still under consideration at the end of a Diet session automatically lapsed. In proposing his bill, Andō rehearsed what were by now familiar arguments (DNTGS: 1300). He said that the ordinance was wrong in principle because it 'had a bearing on the civil liberties [*kenri*] of [all] Japanese subjects'; that it was 'full of imperfections' and 'excessively harsh'; that it had originally been drawn up to meet a general emergency, but the government had later taken to using it 'on account of temporary and trifling incidents'. His main plea, however, was that the House had already decided to do away with the ordinance, and he did not want to leave it 'half-dead' but proposed to 'kill it off'.

The leading spokesman for the government on this occasion was Shirane Senichi, a senior Home Office official, who was not a Member of the House but was entitled to attend it and speak in an official capacity by virtue of Article 54 of the Constitution. Shirane did not blindly oppose Andō's bill; but, in strongly advising caution, he effectively spoke against it. His principal contention was that it was still expedient to have the Peace Preservation Ordinance as a measure for dealing with certain situations, especially those that were serious to a point but did not really justify the use of martial law, and until the remnants of *sōshi* gangs had finally been eliminated. He reminded Members that on most recent occasions the ordinance had been used to protect them either in Tokyo or in the provinces, and that the House had tacitly acknowledged the validity of these enforcements when it rejected Suzuki Shōji's rescission motion earlier in the year. The Home Office had in fact been willing to go along with the House's wish for abolition in the previous December. However, events some weeks later had clearly necessitated re-activation of the ordinance. In his more sanguine moments, Shirane was ready to agree that the Peace Preservation Ordinance could probably be safely dispensed with, leaving major breaches of the peace to be taken care of by the imposition of martial law and the handling of minor contingencies to police regulations. Yet politics in Japan tended to be a rowdy and combustible business: 'just let there be a moment of political discussion, and immediately tobacco-trays fly and glasses take to the air'. He wanted Members to be sure that the underlying conditions which led to disturbances of the peace had been overcome before they moved to abolish the Peace Preservation Ordinance, and finished a good speech by saying that he hoped Members would 'reflect long and earnestly on the matter'.

Katsuki Yukitsune opposed the bill. According to him, too, the House had implicitly recognized the need for the ordinance when it rejected Suzuki's motion. On the other hand, if it passed the present bill for abolition and the public peace were endangered during the current session, the government would hardly dare enforce the Peace Preservation Ordinance without first obtaining the consent of the House, which might not be forthcoming for one reason or another. As for other emergency ordinances which the authorities might decide to issue when the Diet was not in session, these could well be disallowed by it when it next met, only to be re-issued once the session was over. Thus, the nation would be treated to the unedifying spectacle of alternating enforcement and cancellation of important legislation, and 'a game will be made of the so-called law'.

Hashiyama Chūzaemon asked that the bill be referred to a special committee, as he did not relish any more 'light hearted' abolitions of the ordinance such as had happened the previous year, and he felt in general that the House should consider seriously the effects on society at large of its powers under the Constitution to make and unmake laws. Disregarding this plea, the House voted forthwith for the bill as it stood. Moreover, following precedent, it resolved at the same time to omit the second and third readings.

Exactly a week later, on 12 December 1891, Andō Kyūka's bill to abolish the Peace Preservation Ordinance came up for a first reading (DNTGS: 1194) in the House of Peers. Shirane Senichi again spoke in favour of retaining the legislation. His speech was even more forceful on this occasion, perhaps because he could count on a sympathetic audience. This time, he linked *sōshi* violence with prostitution as well as politics, and insisted that the Peace Preservation Ordinance was the only suitable instrument the authorities had for containing such outbreaks. Furthermore, Shirane stoutly maintained that the ordinance was constitutional on the grounds that (1) all personal liberties were to some extent restricted by law and administrative constraints; (2) the House of Representatives itself had accepted the need for the ordinance and its enforcement earlier in the year; and (3) he could give a categorical assurance that the police and other officials would never abuse the provisions of the Peace Preservation Ordinance. One of his listeners, Andō Sokumei, clearly felt some disquiet on this last point and questioned Shirane about it, complaining that the police often used their powers under the ordinance to arrest people on the basis of conjecture only and without making proper enquiries, and that people affected had no right of appeal. Andō Sokumei also believed that the references in Article 4 of the ordinance to the Imperial Palace or an Imperial place of resort to be inappropriate, since the offenders punished under this section were quite guiltless of harbouring ill will to the Emperor and his family. Shirane attempted to reply to these comments, but seems to have missed the point of them. The Peers then decided to refer the matter to a special committee; but before this committee had a chance to report, the first Diet was brought to an end and with it Andō Kyūka's bill.

It is certain that the Peers would have rejected the bill anyway, even if the session had continued longer. This was to be the fate of all similar bills passed by the House of Representatives over the next few years – thrown out by, or lost on their way to or in the Peers.[12] Nevertheless, opponents of the Peace Preservation Ordinance persisted, and in the summer of 1898 they at last had their way. During the dying days of the third Itō cabinet and just before the brief tenure of office by the first Japanese party cabinet headed by Ōkuma Shigenobu and Itagaki Taisuke, the hated ordinance was undone as a result of votes for its repeal in both the Peers and the Representatives. Thus, what had been perpetrated eleven years earlier by administrative fiat was eventually annulled through a procedure of parliamentary bills, discussion and resolution.[13] This development is not only a minor index of the way Japanese public life was transformed in the second half of the nineteenth century by the promulgation of the Constitution and the setting up of the Diet. It is also a clue to certain important underlying conditions and trends.

CONCLUSIONS

In the first place, proper appreciation needs to be accorded to violence, and even more pertinently the ever present threat of violence, as significant elements in Japanese public life during these years. In general, Meiji politics were orderly, and the transition to a modern state correspondingly quick, as a result of such factors as authoritarianism, racial and cultural homogeneity and a widespread wish for compromise among the different elites. Yet, along with this quality of orderliness which proved dominant in the long run, there were other, violent aspects. After all, the era had been conceived during the 1860s in the scattered and persistent troubles of Bakumatsu, and had actually been born in a prolonged War of Restoration. Thereafter, much samurai dissidence had preceded the great Satsuma Rebellion of 1877; and there had been Liberal disturbances of one kind or another for the following ten years. Political assassination was another feature of the times, the most notorious instances being those of Ōkubo Toshimichi in 1878, Ōkuma Shigenobu (attempted) in October 1889 and Mori Arinori in February of the same year, on the morning of the promulgation of the constitution. All of these victims were important ministers of state at the time of the assaults. However much other factors like government panic or deviousness may have influenced the course of events, there can be little doubt that this raw and ugly circumstance of violence accounts for much of the history of the 1887 Peace Preservation Ordinance; in particular its creation by the cabinet in the dying days of that year, and the subsequent ambivalent and changeable press and parliamentary reactions to the legislation.[14] The same circumstance also helps explain the powers which are accorded to, and the duties devolving upon, the modern Japanese police.

Of course, most of the violence in this or any other age would not normally have been connected with politics at all, and the strength of the link in the early 1890s reflects the special circumstances of those years. Thus, the *sōshi*, though considered here mainly in a political guise, were, as stated earlier, basically common gangsters who found the new, liberal world of civil rights and elections to national and local assemblies vastly to their liking and full of easy pickings. Links between *sōshi* and politics other than of a sordid, remunerative kind no doubt did exist but only tenuously. The word *sōshi* means literally 'unruly samurai'; and it is quite possible that many of the mid-Meiji toughs who infested Tokyo and other large cities were former samurai who had failed to adjust to the wholesale abolition of their class in the 1870s. There is evidence of this in press reports on some of the individuals involved in incidents described in this chapter; and a scheme promoted by a group of leading Liberals to send *sōshi* as emigrants to America, Australia and Canada (*JWM*: 3 January 1891) may have stemmed from this feeling that they were displaced persons in their own society. However, by 1890 such *ci-devant* status did not really guide or vindicate the behaviour of the persons concerned. By then, gangsters were gangsters, however they came to be such. On other occasions, the papers (especially the *Japan Weekly Mail*) refer to the *sōshi* as 'schoolboys' or 'students', giving them a tincture of the political idealism often associated with youth. There could be something in this suggestion; after all, contemporaries presumably knew what they were talking about, even though they themselves appeared to be very confused at times as to exactly who the *sōshi* were and what they wanted (*JWM*: 10 January 1891).

Moreover, one can readily admit that individual strongmen, acting as bodyguards or houseboys, did render loyal and praiseworthy service to their politician employers. An instance of this is the way Suzuki Shōji was protected by one of his young male attendants. Nevertheless these further aspects of the situation, in so far as they existed at all, were really marginal to the main role of the *sōshi* as professional gangsters.

One somewhat paradoxical piece of logic – and ethics – will give the *sōshi* a kind of respectable political *persona* in spite of themselves. It can be argued that they were unwitting agents of a not unimportant familiarization process, so far as the new constitutional and parliamentary politics were concerned. In their swaggering, loud mouthed manner, in their small coteries, in their regional and 'water trade' (i.e. restaurant, brothel and general entertainment) affiliations, the *sōshi* belonged to traditional, 'majority' Japan; yet they were, when it came to the politics of 1890, immersed, body if not soul, in the new. Not uninteresting to write or read about, and not completely unattractive in a daredevil, mock heroic way, they proved good copy for the newspapers of the time. Invariably subject to heavy editorial censure and other criticism in some parts of a paper, they often found themselves treated far more lightly – even flippantly – elsewhere in the same issue. Given this aura, however slight, of folk heroes, the *sōshi* must have served to bring the remote and elitist operations of the national Diet down to the level and interests of the common (non-voting) man.

Quite apart from violence, plain uncertainty lay heavily over the Japanese political landscape in the second half of the 1880s. Everything was new; nothing had really been tested or tried. It could well be that the entire *Daidō Danketsu* campaign came to have as its prime objective the unseating of the first modern cabinet led by Itō; and that the Peace Preservation Ordinance was a resolute, heavy-handed response of the Prime Minister and his colleagues to that threat. Subsequently, throughout 1888, while the details of the new Constitution remained a fairly close secret, the newspapers forecast that it would allow for a separation of powers between an executive-bureaucratic cabinet and a legislative, 'popular' Diet; and, further, that these arrangements would lead to fresh initiatives by the political parties entrenched in the House of Representatives to win control of the cabinet. When all of this did in fact ensue, it naturally gave rise to immediate difficulties and made the future seem equally problematic. If we add to this grand constitutional uncertainty, the administrative and fiscal uncertainty of a stalled budget, and divisions of opinion in the cabinet and among the Liberals themselves, it paints a picture much less assured and monochrome than that usually afforded by a summary and hindsight view of Meiji political development.[15] This conglomerate uncertainty alone, would go some way to explaining people's varying attitudes to the Peace Preservation Ordinance over a period of time, as well as the promulgation of the ordinance in the first place. But, of course, uncertainty almost inevitably, as in this case, intertwines with violence, the one sustaining the other.

As well as aiding and abetting violence, uncertainty promoted, and itself reflected, a general fluidity in Japanese politics at that time. This in turn encouraged the pragmatic, consensual approach to the problems of government and political disputation, which after a few years became the hallmark of the Meiji constitutional order, and had been indeed a requirement from the time of the promulgation of the Constitution, if that document were to take effect. Issues and long-term goals were not forgotten, but made amenable to short-term bargaining and compromise. Already, in relation to what has been discussed in this chapter, it is possible to see disputes shaping up for resolution in this way. Particularly, it is clear that a sizeable and notable group among the Liberals were anxious from the outset to reach an agreement with the government on the matter of the budget; and consequently the question of whether any more of their number had to be bribed as a last resort to secure its passage is of little more than secondary importance. The fundamental process was government by compromise, and not government by corruption. George Akita is surely correct on this point; as he is when he states that the eventual resolution of the conflict over finances, whereby the first Yamagata cabinet submitted to a ¥6.5 million or 7.8 per cent cut in its budget, represented a genuine compromise, and not a sell-out by the Liberals (Akita 1967: 79–80, 84–5).

With regard to the Peace Preservation Ordinance, the same forces making for conciliation may mean that Shirane Senichi was sincere when he claimed that the authorities in December 1890 had been willing to go along with the decision of the House of Representatives in favour of abolishing the ordinance, though it is difficult to see how Shirane or anyone else could have persuaded the House of Peers to pass an abolition bill. Certainly, a lively sense of the ever-changing realities of politics, and an underlying desire not to push matters too far, must have influenced the House of Representatives against re-affirming its wishes in the matter when the ordinance was re-issued by the government in January 1891 in an effort to control the *sōshi*, even though abolition continued to be the long-term ideological aim of most Members.

The national Diet was by far the most important and most public forum for political argument and settlements. As such, it attracted and held the attention of statesman and politician, newspaper writer and newspaper reader, from the day it opened to the day it closed. From November 1890, Japanese politics, whatever else they were or were not, became Diet-centred politics. A number of reasons can be adduced for this state of affairs. Clearly, one was that the Constitution and Diet had fifteen or so years of struggle, anticipation and preparation behind them, all of which had been followed by a great deal of advance publicity at both official and non-official levels for the promulgation of the one and the opening of the other.

Another reason why the Diet commanded so much attention so early is that the Lower House contained many Members who were seasoned representatives and leaders at the local assembly level. This is a point made in the previous chapter, but it is worth reiterating. Of the sixteen who participated in the debates that are the subject of this chapter, nine had sat in their local prefectural assemblies, and several of them had served as chairmen of those bodies. Moreover, nine of the sixteen were elected more than twice to the Diet, and one (Inukai Tsuyoshi) was elected a total of nineteen times (below: Appendix III). What is true of this random sample is in fact applicable to succeeding Houses of Representatives. Many of their Members enjoyed established, widespread and continuous support in their local constituencies; and viewed in this light and in conjunction with local politics and local assemblies, the first House of Representatives and its successors to 1905 possessed a more genuinely representative and popular character than that indicated by the very limited franchise for national elections in those early years (Akita 1967: 82–4).

Thirdly, the Diet was important, and was felt to be important, by reason of its legislating and scrutinizing functions. The government of the day could no longer act entirely on its own. Its own proposals, notably the annual budget, had to be fought for and defended in the Diet; and criticism or bills emanating from that body countered and answered. Thus, the first Yamagata cabinet, through a senior spokesman, twice sought to justify its stand in favour of retaining the Peace Preservation Ordinance: once in the House of Representatives, and once in the House of Peers.

Finally, all this Diet debate and politicking, the thrust and counterthrust, the questions on notice and the questions without notice, government bills and private Members' bills – all of this was comprehensively and intelligently reported and commented on in the press of the time. The latter, in addition to the five or six major Tokyo dailies, included numerous and generally excellent regional and local publications. Between them, the metropolitan and local papers covered the country and the entire range of political opinion; and since they were mostly written in a lively and competent fashion and were technically well produced, they formed a kind of fifth estate of the realm, after the Emperor, bureaucrats, Peers and Representatives. The part played by the press in that already mentioned necessary familiarization process – the bringing of Diet politics downwards and out into the nation at large – must have been immense, and immensely valuable. Of course, such a role can only have been helped by fortuitous events like *sōshi* outrages and the great Diet fire; on the other hand, it must have been restricted to some extent by the size of the readership, which remained rather small during the 1890s. Yet this second point does not really negate either the great influence of, or the considerable credit due to, the papers in the matter. Neither do considerations such as the allegiance of most papers to the Liberal–Progressive cause; the consistently Right-wing attitude of one respected journal (*Nippon*) or the fact that the best of them all (*Tokyo nichi nichi shimbun*) was pro-government.

It is interesting to note, however, that the newspapers did tend to concentrate their reporting and comments on what went on in the House of Representatives, though proceedings in the House of Peers were by no means ignored. Such emphasis is perfectly understandable. It both reflected and promoted the feeling that the Representatives was the 'people's' chamber; it was in keeping with the opposition sympathies of the majority of editors and journalists; and it was the outcome of the fact that the most showy political combat and drama, especially that relating to the budget, took place in the Lower House. Nevertheless, in doing things this way, the mid-Meiji press may have contributed, albeit unwittingly, to the historically misleading 'over overshadowing' of the Peers by the Representatives.

All in all, the mid-Meiji press – so interesting, so lively, so vigorous – was a good representative of, and lusty participant in, its own society and that society's politics. This was a political process of 'frictional dialogue' between what may be loosely called a bureaucratic camp and a popular party camp (Mason 1969: 200–2, 211–13). This was, and is, a fundamental Japanese political process, one which, along with the centrality of the Diet, has lasted to our own day. In mid-Meiji times, it was typified by the great struggle over the 1890 budget; and, in a lesser way, by the history of the 1887 Peace Preservation Ordinance.

APPENDIX I: PEACE PRESERVATION ORDINANCE

1 Secret associations and meetings are prohibited; offenders shall be punished by minor confinement of between one month and two years,

together with a fine of between ¥10 and ¥100; ringleaders and instigators [shall have the severity of their punishment] increased by two degrees. With regard to the said secret associations and meetings, and in order to suppress contact and communication between [different] associations as provided for in Article 8 of the Public Meetings Regulations, the Minister for Home Affairs is [hereby] empowered to take the necessary precautionary measures; and anybody who violates regulations that may be issued in connection with such [precautionary] measures shall be punished as above.

2 Open air meetings and gatherings may be closed at the discretion of the police, regardless of whether or not permission [to hold them] has been previously granted. Persons disobeying police orders [in this matter] shall, if they are ringleaders or instigators or have attended the meeting knowing the circumstances and as aiders and abettors, be punished by minor confinement of between three months and two years, together with a fine of between ¥10 and ¥100. Minor participants shall be fined between ¥2 and ¥20. Anyone who causes others to carry weapons to such a meeting or who carries [them] on his own person [shall be subject to] an increase of penalty by two degrees.

3 Persons who print or engrave writings and drawings with the object of plotting or instigating sedition or causing a breach of the peace shall, in addition to the penalties prescribed by the Penal Code and the Publications Regulations, have the [offending] items confiscated together with all the apparatus used to produce them.

4 The Chief of Metropolitan Police or Prefectural Governors may, with the permission of the Minister for Home Affairs, order the removal within a fixed period of days or hours of persons who are residing or lodging within a distance of 12 km around the Imperial Palace or an Imperial place of resort and whom they judge to be plotting sedition or breaching the public peace, and forbid them to enter, lodge or reside in the said area for a period of three years. Persons who receive an order to remove [themselves] and fail to do so within the stipulated time, or who, having gone, later breach the prohibition [order] shall be punished by minor confinement of between one and three years, and shall be further subject to police surveillance for up to five years. This surveillance will be carried out in the place of the [offender's] registered domicile.

5 In cases where cabinet recognizes that extraordinary measures are called for in a [particular] district where there is a risk of a breach of the public peace [either] because of popular unrest or as a result of preparations for civil disturbance or the hatching of plots, it may

order in the district concerned and for a specified period the enforcement of the following regulations in whole or in part:

(1) It shall be forbidden to hold any kind of public meeting, whether indoors or outside and no matter for what purpose, without prior police approval;
(2) It shall be forbidden to publish newspapers or other printed matter without prior police examination;
(3) It shall be forbidden to wear, transport or traffic in any kind of small arms, pistols, gunpowder, swords or sword canes, without obtaining the permission of the local authorities on special grounds;
(4) There shall be instituted a system of checks on travellers out of and into [the area concerned] and of travel permits.

6 Persons violating orders [issued] in connection with the foregoing article shall be sentenced to minor confinement for a period of one month to two years and shall be fined between ¥5 and ¥200. Those guilty shall be rigorously dealt with under both laws.
7 This ordinance shall go into effect from the day it is promulgated.

(Hayashida 1927: I, 249–51)

APPENDIX II: EXPLANATORY MEMORANDUM FOR KATŌ HEISHIRŌ'S BILL TO ABOLISH THE PEACE PRESERVATION ORDINANCE

Explanatory Memorandum: The present Peace Preservation Ordinance is excessively severe in all respects, and does not resemble other laws in striking a balance between leniency and severity. Moreover, the existence of such an ordinance must, contrary [to what is intended] disrupt the harmony of popular feeling [*minshin*] at home, and besmirch the national honour abroad; and [for these reasons] it is to be detested. In particular, when we recall the circumstances prevailing at the time when our government issued this [ordinance] we believe that the authorities, too, imagined it was only needed at that time, and that they did not issue it as a piece of sound legislation [*ryōhō*] to last for ever. Therefore, we are anxious to abolish completely this ordinance, for which we do not see any need in the conditions prevailing today.

(*TNNS*: 12 December 1890)

APPENDIX III: LOCAL ASSEMBLY AND IMPERIAL DIET SERVICE OF MEMBERS OF THE HOUSE OF REPRESENTATIVES MENTIONED

Key: − = no; + = yes

Name	Local assembly	Elected more than twice
Amano Jakuen	−	3
Andō Kyūka	−	3
Hashimoto Kyūtarō	+	10
Hashiyama Chūzaemon	+	−
Inukai Tsuyoshi	+	19
Ishida Kannosuke	+	6
Kanno Ryō	+	−
Katō Heishirō	−	4
Katsuki Yukitsune	−	−
Kudō Yukimoto	−	9
Ōtsu Junichirō	+	13
Shioda Okuzō	+	3
Suzuki Shōji	+	−
Toyoda Bunsaburō	+	−
Ueki Emori	−	−
Yasuda Yuitsu	−	−
Totals 16	9	9

Note: Most of those listed as not belonging to a prefectural assembly nevertheless had had a solid experience of working in local government; and premature death cut short the parliamentary careers of Ueki Emori and Suzuki Shōji.

NOTES

1 Ōkuma had actually joined the Itō cabinet in February as its Foreign Minister; but this was at Kuroda's urging, and Kuroda and Itō had already agreed on a change of government. Kuroda continued to give Ōkuma strong support throughout the twenty months' ministry which ended with the serious wounding of the Foreign Minister in an assassination attempt.

2 According to *JWM* (16 February 1889), the total number of political offenders affected by the 'Constitution amnesty' was 162. They included such important politicians as Arai Shōgo, Hoshi Tōru, Kataoka Kenkichi, Kobayashi Kusuo, Kōno Hironaka, Ōi Kentarō and Ōishi Masami who were all released from jail; while others – notably Hayashi Yūzō, Nakae Chōmin, Takenouchi Tsuna and Ozaki Yukio – were freed from the restrictions

imposed by the Peace Preservation Ordinance. The pardons were total, and those fresh from jail were allowed to stand for election to the House of Representatives the following year, despite Article 14, Clause 4, of the Law of Election, which stated that persons who had been imprisoned could neither vote nor stand for election until three full years had elapsed after the completion or pardon of their sentences.

3 For example, *JWM* (6 April 1889) reported that Kataoka Kenkichi, who had recently been released from imprisonment for breaches of the Peace Preservation Ordinance, was planning to visit Tokyo as a special emissary of the most eminent Liberal leader and founder of the party, Itagaki Taisuke.

4 Gotō was trenchantly criticized for his decision to enter the government. He defended himself at meetings of his erstwhile supporters by saying that (1) he was obeying an Imperial command; and (2) he would continue to be associated with the *Daidō Danketsu* and would now be working to achieve its aims from a position within the cabinet (*JWM*: 30 March 1889). In view of various hard-line Liberal parliamentary leaders' willingness to use Gotō as a go-between in discussions with other ministers over the 1890 budget there may in fact have been something in this second point, and my earlier evaluation of the Count's motives (Mason 1969: 61) should be softened accordingly.

5 Factors militating against strong, united parties at this stage in Japanese history included: persistent loyalty to region and locality; small, single-Member constituencies; tiny electorates; and an element of novelty. All these gave rise to an elitist and individualistic approach to elections and politics. Furthermore, there was considerable bureaucratic (i.e. cabinet) opposition to the formation of large parties; and 'mass'-based, monolithic parliamentary groupings were new even in the West.

6 It had twenty sponsors in addition to Katō, all Liberals, and its explanatory memorandum is translated at Appendix II.

7 He was Noguchi Kei (1858–1905), a Liberal from Saitama Prefecture.

8 The actual motion was: 'That a special committee be established for the purpose of making suggestions on the rescission of the Peace Preservation Ordinance'. It was necessary, under Article 26 of the Law of the Houses, that the government should approve any suspension of debate on bills it had sponsored.

9 For instance, *JWM* (10 January 1891) gave the 'hards' 120 Members (forty Progressives and eighty Liberals) and the 'softs' 120 (fifty Liberals and seventy *Taiseikai* or government party). This sum leaves unaccounted for sixty Members, most of whom it reckoned would side with the moderates.

10 Other reports say that it was Kobayashi Kusuo, and not Toyoda, who was interviewed.

11 For a discussion of, and a rather different view on, the general attitude of the *Taiseikai*, see p. 211.

12 The Peers did manage to hold a number of substantial debates on the measure between 1891 and 1898.

13 The 1898 abolition bill was mildly opposed in the House of Peers by the spokesman for the government of the day. The previous cabinet (second Matsukata), however, had actually moved for the abolition of the Peace Preservation Ordinance in the House of Representatives, only to be rebuffed by the Peers. What made the latter change their minds in 1898 is not

altogether clear. The chairman of the Peers' committee on the bill, Marquis Hosokawa Morishige, when recommending the bill, spoke of its inappropriateness to the times (i.e. 1898); its infringement of civil rights; and the government's intention to replace Articles 4 and 5 with more suitable legislation later in the year. However, Hosokawa admitted that he was in a minority of one on his own committee in thinking this way.

14 For information on the state of civil unrest just before the ordinance was issued, see Hayashida (1927), vol. 1: 248. Earlier, there had been major outbreaks of Liberal-led unrest, like the Fukushima and Chichibu incidents (Ike 1950: 150–1, 160–6). In 1883, the students at the newly formed Tokyo Imperial University had indulged in large-scale rioting (Ōmachi 1924: 202–5); and in 1880 there had been open warfare on the streets of Tokyo between soldiers and policemen (*JWM*: 4 September 1880).

15 On differences at government level, see Akita (1967: 77–9, 85–8 passim). For the rest, the evidence presented in this chapter makes it clear that there were differences or shades of opinion among Liberals and Progressives about both the budget and the Peace Preservation Ordinance.

5 Foreign affairs debates, 1890–1

R. H. P. Mason

INTRODUCTION

In most sovereign states, at any rate until well after the close of the nineteenth century, foreign affairs, even more than domestic affairs, were determined by the various elites forming the national leadership. These elites, as well as representing the dynastic interests of reigning monarchies, emanated from functional groups such as the civil bureaucracy, the armed services, political parties, the churches, and the worlds of business, learning and journalism. Japan has been no exception to this general rule; and one can only suppose that the great majority of its people in the years from 1890 to 1892 had neither the knowledge nor the leisure, neither the sense of public spirit nor the degree of personal involvement, to care deeply about their country's foreign policy. For the minority that did care, the issue of treaty revision came first in their thoughts on the subject. No doubt, it also came second and third. Along with it, however, must be mentioned a feeling of concern on the part of certain political publicists and ginger-group activists about what they took to be Japan's weak political, commercial and military position in east Asia. People who fell prey to such anxiety usually sought to assuage it by urging a more chauvinistic outlook on a government that seemed steadfastly wedded to caution.

The treaties which by 1890 the Japanese with justification considered to be in urgent need of revision, were diplomatic and commercial agreements concluded with 'the Powers' great and small in the aftermath of Commodore Matthew Perry's forcible opening of Japan to worldwide trade and intercourse in the years 1853–4. Of those still in force, some dated from just before the Meiji Restoration of 1868; others, notably those with Germany and Austria–Hungary, were made in the first years of the new regime. Between them, this array of agreements had destroyed formally and finally the two-hundred-year

Tokugawa *bakufu* policy of national seclusion (*sakoku*). However, it was not this rude shattering of their country's traditional and peaceful, if isolationist, diplomatic stance that the mid-Meiji era Japanese resented but rather certain obnoxious features of the treaties which made them, in the parlance of the time, definitely 'unequal'. Thus, although careful to preserve the form of a compact between two equally sovereign and independent states, each treaty contained provisions relating to the administration of justice and collection of customs duties that seriously infringed the sovereignty of Japan. One-sidedness of this kind had come to be the established custom whenever one of the 'advanced' countries of Europe or the Americas chose to enter into relations with the less powerful and culturally different nations of Asia and Africa. Very briefly, in 1890 Japan still found herself tied to a situation whereby all judicial cases involving foreigners, both of a criminal and of a civil kind, had to be dealt with in accordance with the law of the homeland of the foreigner concerned, and by the appropriate extra-territorial consular court. These consular courts were by their nature *ad hoc* bodies; the people who sat in judgement in them were not necessarily versed in the law; and the language in which their business was conducted could be anything but Japanese. To make matters worse, it proved to be very difficult in practice for Japanese caught up in the workings of this quaint system of justice to appeal against any decision it might hand down. For the two or three thousand foreign residents in Japan (DNTGS: 534), mainly traders, things of course could hardly have been better. Not only were they completely outside the law of the land; as a substitute, they had the familiar mercies of their own national codes, enforced by their own national, and frequently fellow-merchant, consuls speaking their own national tongue. *Vive la difference*!

Practically speaking, the effects of such judicial arrangements over the years on Japanese litigants and would-be litigants could scarcely have been less damaging than the general insult and irritation they gave to collective Japanese pride. On the other hand, the number of Japanese actually affected by extra-territorial jurisdiction must have been fairly small. Moreover, given the fact that international trade as developed by Europeans had come to stay, and in view of the discrepancies between Japanese legal institutions and their modern nineteenth-century counterparts, there was some reason for the Powers to impose upon Japan in this fashion (Jones 1970: 71). The case of the tariff was different again. Here, the Westerners acted in a blatantly exploitive and coercive manner to make sure that the Japanese government was forbidden by the treaties to levy more than a token 5 per cent *ad valorem* duty on foreign imports. Further, as will be seen – and unlike the encroachment on judicial sovereignty – the flow of cheap goods from abroad that resulted from this injunction affected everybody in the country. The price of many everyday articles plummeted, it is true, but this in turn apparently led to severe economic dislocation and distress. Also on the economic side, foreign steamships had been able under the terms of the treaties to take from the less efficient native sailing junks much of the coastal and inter-island trade within the Japanese archipelago.

In contrast to the palpable disadvantages and minor irritations embodied in the 'unequal' treaties, the Japanese could take some comfort from one or two points in connexion with them. In the first place, they had stopped short of reducing Japan outright to the status of a colony or protectorate. Formally, Japan remained a sovereign state, still legally able to press for revision on its own behalf. Secondly, the treaties specifically prevented the foreigners from living or carrying on business except in certain settlement areas of the five or six recognized treaty ports.[1] This meant that the Japanese authorities could in due course hold out the privilege of freer access to the rest of the country (or 'mixed residence in the interior', as it came to be called), in return for surrender of extra-territorial immunities. Finally, the treaties of 1858 with the United States, Britain, Russia, the Netherlands and France all contained an article allowing for revision in 1872 at the behest of either party.

Acting on this clause, one of the senior ministers in the early Meiji administration, Iwakura Tomomi, took a large embassy to America and Europe in the years 1871–3, at any rate partly with a view to initiating discussions for revision (Mayo 1966). However, though polite and helpful to the Japanese ambassadors in every other way, the Powers showed themselves to be quite unresponsive on this central issue, maintaining that Japan was judicially and generally still too backward for them to consider surrendering any of the rights and privileges they had won for their nationals there. From this point on, it became clear that the treaties had no effective fixed term, but could be taken as running indefinitely or until revised through a process of mutual consultation and consent.

As it turned out, negotiations for revision in the 1870s, after the return of the Iwakura mission, were desultory. Foreign governments remained uninterested; and the Japanese authorities were preoccupied with domestic reforms and revolts. By the beginning of the next decade, however, the Imperial government had strengthened itself militarily and politically, and had made clear its determination to go on acting as the mainspring of an extensive modernization which, it was hoped, would lead eventually to the attainment of full equality with the West. Under Inoue Kaoru as Foreign Minister, revision once more became a major goal of official Japanese policy, and at the same time a subject for an increasingly vocal, informed and disseminated Japanese public opinion. Inoue negotiated long and arduously in a series of general conferences with the foreign representatives in Tokyo, intending to recover both judicial and tariff rights. He at last admitted defeat in the summer of 1887, when he felt unable to recommend to the Emperor and cabinet acceptance of the final terms offered by the Powers.

The talks on the tariff had never really come to anything. With respect to extra-territorial jurisdiction, the Powers agreed to the abolition of the consular courts, provided that a fairly large number of foreign judges be appointed to the Japanese lower and higher courts to ensure that these bodies understood and acted on the principles of Western jurisprudence, and provided that the proposed new criminal and civil law codes of the Japanese Empire be submitted for Western scrutiny and comment before they were promulgated. Proposals to perpetuate foreign overlordship in the Japanese judiciary in this way, once they were revealed in the newspapers, greatly antagonized Japanese public opinion, as did a suggestion that the new treaties should allow foreigners to own land. Inoue resigned as Foreign Minister in July 1887, after adjourning indefinitely the discussions on treaty revision.

Inoue's resignation from the cabinet had been accompanied by that of Tani Kanjō. Tani, a former military man, had been Minister of Trade and Agriculture. He chose some technical grounds for his action, but his real reason seems to have been a desire to make a strong gesture of protest against what he regarded as excessive kowtowing to the West, alike in the conferences on treaty revision and in national life generally. All his life, Tani spoke for nationalist, but not irrationally nationalist, causes in Japanese politics. As a consequence, he frequently clashed with the considerably more diluted and flexible conservatism of the group of moderate bureaucrats from the former domains (*han*) of Chōshū and Satsuma, who by then fully controlled the national administration. Perhaps what motivated him, fundamentally, was a strong cultural antipathy to the West.

Not long after quitting the cabinet, the Right-winger Tani and his supporters joined forces with a revived Left-wing opposition to the government to form the *Daidō Danketsu* in the summer of 1887. This was led at first by Gotō Shōjirō, another former government minister who, like Tani himself, hailed from the former domain of Tosa. There can be little doubt that Gotō launched his campaign with a shrewd eye to the impending inauguration of a constitutional and parliamentary form of rule promised for the end of the decade. Nevertheless, the actual spark that set him and his many thousands of adherents alight had been the miserable failure of Inoue Kaoru to secure new treaties that would be favourable to Japan. Included among these adherents were members of the Progressive Party, a political party that had been founded in 1882 and had consistently argued for the adoption of Westminster-style politics in Japan, along with the Liberal Party of Itagaki Taisuke and Gotō. However, as explained in the previous chapter, Progressive enthusiasm for joining in the general attack on the government cooled early in the following year (1888) when the *doyen* of the party and a major national political figure in his own right, Ōkuma Shigenobu, accepted an invitation from the cabinet to assume the Foreign Affairs portfolio.

Ōkuma knew that his appointment was meant to signal a serious new attempt at treaty revision; he laboured mightily, and after twelve months of discreet negotiations was on the verge of success. He had reached the stage of being able to conclude draft agreements with three key countries: the United States, Russia and Germany. Moreover, talks with Britain and France were approaching a similar consummation. In substance, the new arrangements would have brought about the end of consular jurisdiction within a very few years, in return for having foreign judges sit on the Japanese Supreme Court only for an interval of twelve years. Under the new proposals, Japan could also expect to regain tariff autonomy after the same period of time had elapsed. All these bright hopes were to fade. Once again, secrets were somehow let out of the diplomatic bag and *The Times*, in London, published a fairly detailed account of the measures agreed upon. Discontent simmered once more in Japan against any kind of concession to the foreigners' desire to exercise some degree of supervision over the country's judicial system; and, while being driven in a carriage to the Ministry of Foreign Affairs one morning in October 1889, Ōkuma had a bomb thrown at him by a young Right-wing fanatic. Terribly wounded, he had to retire from public life for some time. The incident also caused the Kuroda cabinet to resign, and the Japanese side was once more obliged to suspend negotiations for treaty revision.

Viscount Aoki Shūzō, a gifted and hard-working Foreign Ministry official with a German noblewoman for a wife, took over as Foreign Minister in a new cabinet headed by Yamagata Aritomo. In 1890–1, Aoki and the cabinet as a whole spent a considerable amount of time on the problem of treaty revision, trying to devise a way of accomplishing this that would satisfy both foreign and domestic opinion. But, in view of the severe setbacks that had already been received in this matter, and in view also of the introduction of a completely new factor into the situation with the opening of the first Diet in November 1890, their initiatives were of an understandably tentative and exploratory nature. In fact, the first Yamagata cabinet never got to the stage of holding another series of formal discussions with the treaty Powers.

Aoki himself had but a brief spell as Foreign Minister, since he resigned in May 1891 as a gesture of responsibility for an attack made on the crown prince of Russia while on an official visit to Japan. His efforts during a period of barely eighteen months to regain some of the essential attributes of sovereignty for his country and to improve its general diplomatic position, meagre and unproductive though they appear on the surface, are of course central to this chapter. Moreover, even in the wider context of Japanese national history in the second half of the nineteenth century, they deserve some recognition. He had come to the task well trained and equipped for it, by virtue of his apparently gruelling experience as deputy Foreign Minister for Inoue Kaoru in the years 1886–7; and it is clear from what follows that during his term of supreme responsibility in 1890–1, he was already envisaging the kind of revision that eventually took place in 1894 with the signing in London of the appropriately named Aoki–Kimberley treaty. This was an agreement with Britain that restored to Japan all its lost judicial rights in 1899 and allowed it to regain full tariff autonomy in 1911. The other Powers quickly agreed to similar arrangements, with the result that by the end of the century the detested unequal treaties were virtually a thing of the past. Patience and prudence at long last reaped their rightful rewards.

In the east Asian area, in 1890, both official and popular Japanese interest was concentrated on Korea, a very backward and rather corrupt country towards which many of the island people had come to adopt attitudes that were a mixture of the cavalier and the patronizing, and reflected no doubt the treatment they themselves had received at the hands of the Western Powers. Early in the Meiji era, the Korean monarchy and government had haughtily refused to have anything to do with the new Japanese reformist regime, regarding it as a hopelessly renegade agent of European civilization. For their part, certain important Japanese political leaders, together with many disgruntled samurai, had wished to remedy this situation by applying a policy of 'chastisement', but plans for a major military expedition to the peninsula were called off by more moderate government elements in the summer of 1873 after the return from Europe of the Iwakura mission. Three years later, a minor show of force by the Japanese authorities secured the treaty of Kanghwa, which re-established diplomatic and commercial relations between the two countries.

Thereafter the main concern of ministers in Tokyo seems to have been to bring about an end to China's claims to exercise a protectorate over Korea. For reasons that must have had a basis in a historical need for self-assertion, as already exemplified by Tokugawa period diplomacy, as well as an awareness in 1894 of the novel opportunities offered by world conditions at the time, Meiji era Japanese readily subscribed to Western notions of a global order in which all states, large and small, enjoyed at any rate in theory the same amount of sovereignty and independence. This they preferred to the traditional Chinese-painted picture of an east Asia consisting of the 'middle kingdom' surrounded by a medley of small, respectful and tributary nations. Events on the whole seemed to be marching on the side of the Japanese in this as in other matters; and the skilfully negotiated Li–Itō convention of 1885 (the treaty of Tientsin) committed both Japan and China to recognize each other's commercial and strategic interests in Korea. Five years later, the Japanese government was still to all intents and purposes satisfied with this general situation. It had done something to loosen gently China's hold over the peninsula, thereby reducing any threat of an attack on the home islands from that quarter (Lone 1989: 22–4), and at the same time it had succeeded in opening up an obvious and important arena for future Japanese trade, and political and cultural influence. There was apparently no thought in the minds of cabinet members in Tokyo, either in 1890 or for some years after, of enlarging on these advantages in any sudden or drastic way. Matters, it was felt, could be safely left to take their peaceful course.

However, Japanese men of affairs to the political and cultural Right of ruling cabinets always lay in readiness to call for policies of national firmness and expansion, though the redoubtable Tani Kanjō himself cannot be completely characterized in this way; and on the 'Liberal' Left, too, there were many opponents of the government who adopted a similar attitude. In point of fact, the men who were to emerge as leaders of a campaign for a constitution and a national assembly in Japan after 1874 were among those who had favoured taking a strong line on Korea in 1873 and had resigned from the government following their defeat on this issue. In continuation of the same trend, the more radical section of the Japanese Liberal Party had been deeply implicated in Korean affairs during the 1880s. Some of this group, frustrated in their demands for immediate and revolutionary popular rule at home, conspired with a Korean progressive faction led by the charismatic Kim Ok-kiun to overthrow the reactionary and indelibly pro-Chinese monarchical administration in Korea. These radical plots were quickly detected and suppressed in both Japan and Korea. Yet the memory of them inevitably added fuel to the fires of political animosity between the Japanese government and one section of its opponents; and in the minds of the latter there remained a steady conviction that Japan could, and should, help her own cause by taking a more definite and fraternal interest in her nearest neighbour, with a view to putting her on the path to progress, Japanese-style. Indeed, the aim of the Japanese adventurers convicted in the Ōsaka Incident of 1885 was the forcible 'liberation' of Korea, in the interests of Liberalism and as a preliminary to a similar *coup d'état* in Japan (Conroy 1960: 124–68).

Behind these cross-currents and entanglements lay the broad truth that, in the first half of the Meiji era, Korea, and even in some ways the knotty problem of treaty revision, impinged more on Japanese domestic politics than they did on the country's foreign policy. Furthermore, during these same years, affairs at home were vastly more important and exciting than anything done, or not done, abroad. Apart from the enormous programme of technological and administrative reform and innovation embarked on after 1868, the quarter of a century following the Meiji Restoration saw the development of a more distinctively political and ideological struggle over the national destinies. It was this 'struggle', best thought of as a dialectical interaction between the governing bureaucrats from Satsuma and Chōshū and their Liberal and Progressive opponents, which culminated for the time being in the promulgation of the Constitution and the opening of the first Diet in November 1890.

The terms of the Constitution, it is always worth remembering, allowed the Sat–Chō clique of bureaucrats to retain a strong hold on power at the cabinet level and over the Executive generally. They could do this because the cabinet theoretically held office at the Emperor's pleasure, and its composition did not, at any rate at first, necessarily reflect the state of the parties in the Diet.

Moreover, although the most important right granted to the representatives of the people was that of approving or disallowing legislation, this did not cover foreign treaties. Their board of scrutiny was to be the far more cameral Privy Council. Beyond these constitutional inhibitions to Diet enquiry, foreign affairs were protected by their generally nebulous and 'delicate' nature. For 'reasons of State', no government, however democratic, welcomes interference in this area. Despite these forbidding circumstances, however, certain constitutional powers granted to the Diet were to come into play in its handling of the country's diplomacy. Both Houses were empowered to *initiate* legislation (rather than just approve or disapprove of government sponsored bills) and to make formal recommendations to the cabinet or Emperor; and Members could present written questions to the government, questions to which the appropriate minister of state would be under a heavy constitutional obligation to reply, usually verbally and in person but on occasions in writing or through a deputy.

A survey of what was said and done by the first Diet in respect to foreign affairs turns out to be more of an examination of Japan's virgin parliamentary history than an investigation into the country's diplomacy at the time. It also reinforces an awareness of the intimate connection then existing between national policy and domestic political differences, some of which were of long standing. Finally, one leaves the subject more than ever convinced that the Meiji experiment in constitutional and parliamentary forms was never a mere façade, intended to mollify Westerners abroad into granting treaty revision or to appease Liberal agitators at home. Rather, it was a carefully planned attempt to adapt what was in so many ways an exotic philosophy and practice of government to Japanese political traditions and existing realities.

Those responsible for the attempt had resolved that it should neither disrupt the national leadership as constituted at the time, nor interfere with the lines of national progress already laid down. On the other hand, the bureaucrats in the cabinet and other high places fully expected the Diet to have from the outset a political life and influence of its own. Aoki Shūzō admitted as much when, soon after he had taken over as Foreign Minister in Tokyo, he advised the British government that future discussions on the treaties would have to take into account impending constitutional changes in Japan and, in particular, the mood of the forthcoming Diet:

> The people, through their chosen representatives, will then have a voice in the legislation of the Empire, and then the Imperial government will not be in a position to pledge with the same degree of certainty as they would now be able to do the enactment of those numerous enabling laws which are absolutely essential to the proper and complete operation of the new treaties.

> (Jones 1970: 132)

THE HOUSE OF REPRESENTATIVES

The House of Representatives in the first Diet held only one major discussion on foreign affairs. This occurred in the afternoon of 17 December 1890. It arose from a number of written questions on treaty revision, submitted on 9 December by Arai Shōgo who sat as one of the two Liberal Members for the second constituency, Tochigi Prefecture. Arrangements had been made for Aoki Shūzō to make a statement in the House in reply to Arai's questions. Before the Foreign Minister spoke, however, Arai obtained the permission of the Speaker (Nakajima Nobuyuki) to comment on the circumstances that had prompted his questions (DNTGS: 529–30).

Arai was of wealthy peasant stock and still, in 1890, retained some of the militancy that had marked his early years as a Liberal. He gave a short, eloquent speech. Its principal theme amounted to an unabashed request that the Foreign Minister should take the Diet, and so the general public, into his confidence by telling Members exactly what he and the government were actually doing, or else planned to do, about treaty revision: 'What I want to do now is to enquire of the government what policy it has for getting rid of this great incubus, and whether or not it intends to accomplish a revision of these treaties.' Arai backed up his demand for, above all, pertinent and up-to-date information by arguing that treaty revision had been a matter of common concern to the government and the people for over ten years, and could be satisfactorily accomplished only if the authorities took full account of, and acted in harmony with, public opinion. Any new treaties that might be concluded between Japan and the Powers would, he felt, be 'bound to be less than perfect', unless both Japanese and foreign publics knew about the terms in advance and were prepared to accept them. At one point in his speech, Arai readily identified with 'public opinion' the Meiji Emperor whom he depicted as 'labouring for the happiness of his subjects'. In this way, Arai implied, though he was careful not to say as much, that reluctance on the part of the government to follow public opinion in this matter would not merely lead to further diplomatic setbacks and be in itself undemocratic; it would also look suspiciously like grave disloyalty to the throne.

As a sequel to this demand for full disclosure of the government's intentions with regard to treaty revision, Arai chose to assert from time to time the further right of the Diet and the people who had elected it to exercise some kind of final control over the Empire's foreign policy: 'It is my hope that, in dealing with such a weighty problem, the common people will be made fully aware of the issues, and that treaties will be concluded in accordance with their views.' The same principle of *de facto* popular sovereignty was voiced even more bluntly when he declared that: 'I consider it imperative that the ministers of state should first of all listen to the voice of the people and obey it.' No reasonable man could have remained in any doubt about the gravity of the country's general diplomatic situation after listening to Arai. At the beginning of his speech, he had claimed, firstly, that all attempts so far at revision ('the most difficult of all our most difficult problems') had ended in failure and vacillation; secondly, that by 1890, the matter was giving rise to sensational and conflicting rumours; and, thirdly, that failure to revise had become a matter of 'unspeakable ignominy', and one concerning which successive generations of Japanese would feel shame for many, many years to come. Mixed in with this had been the following emotional outburst:

> For this cause, perhaps, men will groan in prison. For this cause, perhaps, men will lose their lives. For this cause, perhaps, men will suffer wounds. Truly, it must be said that this problem of treaty revision is Japan's great problem. Certainly it is a business that will miscarry if government and people are not stirred into making a common effort.

In these dreadful, although mercifully as yet largely hypothetical, circumstances, it was all the more distressing for good Liberals and patriots to detect what could be construed as a tendency on the part of the government to 'disregard public opinion in favour of autocratic control'. Arai anticipated various arguments that might be advanced against his plea for open and democratic diplomacy, only of course to reject them. Objections based on the need for diplomatic secrecy as a matter of standing international convention could not, in his opinion, be sustained. This was so, because the treaty problem (unlike 'military secrets and so forth') involved 'the welfare of the whole nation', and could not be solved except by some process of national consensus.

Apart from the requirements of secret diplomacy as enforced by all the Powers at the time, a Japanese government in 1890, in view of what had befallen Ōkuma Shigenobu and his treaty policies the previous year, to say nothing of Inoue Kaoru's efforts earlier, might well have preferred to keep its own counsel on negotiations for revision, for fear that an informed Japanese public would turn out to be a turbulent Japanese public. Arai, himself, drew attention to this possibility, saying: 'should the details of treaty revision be made known, they would inevitably provoke a great deal of discussion; and everybody would be criticizing and telling you [the government], for instance, that you must not do this or you must do that.' He countered this difficulty, however, by claiming that refusal by the government to disclose diplomatic information, in order to avoid domestic upset, could hardly be reconciled with a constitutional system of politics, such as Japan was then enjoying. Moreover, if the ministers did not wish to consider anybody's views but their own, they would be all the more likely to make grievous mistakes, since not even members of the cabinet could pretend to be less fallible than the ordinary run of mortals.

Finally, there was a possible objection along the lines that if the Japanese government told its own people too much about its plans and hopes for treaty revision, the representatives of the Powers would gain a definite advantage in the negotiations. Arai took the line that damaging revelations of this kind were inevitable anyway and that foreigners would be able to find out whatever they wanted to find out. In an allusion to the Ōkuma debacle, he recalled how: 'At the very time when the people of Japan were being kept in ignorance, foreigners were publishing what they knew in the newspapers.' It was following this that he made his point about the need for treaties to be understood by foreign peoples, as well as the Japanese public, if they were to be a success. Arai finished his speech with a short recapitulation of his actual questions to the government:

> What are the salient points in the history of treaty revision from its beginnings to the present time? Next, what is being discussed with the foreign countries to-day? What progress is being made? What policy does our government have for effecting treaty revision? . . . Will extra-territorial rights ever be withdrawn? If so, when? Secondly, is it intended to regain tariff autonomy some day? If so, when? In last year's scheme for revision of treaties, it was proposed to employ foreign judges. I do not suppose for a minute that the present [i.e. projected new] treaties make provision for the employment of foreigners, but is that fact set down in black and white? If so, how? When will you allow foreigners to live in all parts of the country and mix with the natives? Finally, will you grant to foreigners the right to own immovable property or not? If you are going to allow this, when? . . . Last year our cabinet attempted to resign *en bloc* as a result of the treaty revision problem, but what became of that attempt? . . . Did they resign and never bother to withdraw their resignations; or did they resign, only to be re-appointed to office? I should like to hear what happened.

If the Liberal opposition had opened its attack with some fast bowling by the fiery Arai, the bureaucratic government had in its Foreign Minister, Aoki Shūzō, a batsman who was capable of playing a stolid, yet in its own fashion artful, innings. It was Aoki's maiden speech (DNTGS: 530–6) to the Diet, and he began it in an understandably tentative way by wondering aloud if he could give satisfaction. Yet within a few minutes he had flatly and clearly stated that, unlike domestic politics, foreign affairs required secrecy in 'very extensive fields' and he did not intend 'to deal with matters that have to remain secret, despite the renewed demands which Mr Arai Shōgo has just made'. Aoki then quickly hit one or two other balls into the out-field in a decisive fashion. Article 13 of the Constitution read, 'The Emperor declares war, makes peace, and concludes treaties'. This, he argued, vested general power over foreign policy in the Executive arm as opposed to the Legislative arm of government, and in particular in himself as the responsible minister. Nevertheless, he professed himself anxious to enter into some sort of dialogue with the elected representatives of the people. Using language that foreshadowed the devastating attack on the principle of 'transcendental' cabinets that was to be launched by Ozaki Yukio in the House of Representatives twenty-three years later,[2] Aoki disclaimed any desire to 'build a castle out of those words "executive" and "rescript" and be besieged therein by you without saying a thing. I, in my capacity as Foreign Minister, want to speak and, what is more, must speak'. This was followed by a strong rebuttal of suggestions that the Emperor and his ministers did not take full account of public opinion when considering policies. As for Arai's final question about the alleged resignation of the first Yamagata cabinet sometime in the previous year, Aoki curtly declared that such queries could not be properly directed to the Foreign Minister.

All the foregoing assertions and comments served simply as a preliminary to Aoki's discourse. His speech was to last for over two hours, and most of it was taken up with answering the first of Arai's questions, the request for information on the salient features of the history of treaty revision to 1890. Here the Foreign Minister made the most of the opportunity offered him. He could answer a question from the Diet at length and without giving anything away. In short, he found himself batting on an easy wicket, and must have secretly revelled in his task.

The first point of substance in Aoki's historical *résumé* was that it had been the treaties of 1866, concluded with Britain, France and Holland in the wake of the hostilities in Kagoshima Bay (1863) and the Shimonoseki Straits (1863 and 1864) (Beasley 1955: 64–77), together with the treaties signed with Germany and with Austria in 1870, that had really done the damage from the point of view of Japan. Earlier treaties had been mainly straightforward commercial agreements which had not raised the question of extra-territorial jurisdiction except as a reciprocal right, as in the case of the 1854 treaty with Russia, and any stipulations on tariffs contained in them had been quite favourable to Japan.

Aoki's account of Japanese diplomacy and the treaty question in the 1870s was cursory and unemotional, except for a digression on the matter of 'safeguards'. His words here were somewhat heated and are hard to follow, but he seems to have been saying that at no time could either foreigners or Japanese people rightly demand safeguards from the Japanese government, before agreeing to revision of the treaties. Revision was Japan's right in principle as a sovereign and independent nation, and not really contingent on the settlement of specific problems like, for instance, toleration of Christian missionary activity or permitting foreigners to reside outside the treaty ports. Careful always to weigh his words, as a competent diplomat should, Aoki also managed to indicate that there were two or even more sides to the question of revision. According to him, it had been, and remained, pointless to envisage unilateral denunciation of the treaties by Japan, since Japan, too, had acquired certain rights by virtue of them, and in any case was not in a position to settle her claims by recourse to war.

In fact, the Japanese government had relied on a clause in the treaties of 1858 which it interpreted as allowing it to press for revision in July 1872; and Aoki summed up the complete failure of the Iwakura mission so far as treaty revision was concerned by saying: 'Thus, they [the American government] treated our government with disdain.'

Terajima Munenori, the Japanese Foreign Minister from 1873 to 1879, had already spent some time living abroad, and he realized that until the Japanese judicial and administrative systems were remodelled along the lines of those operating in the West, it was not realistic to negotiate for the abolition of consular jurisdiction. Therefore Terajima concentrated on the tariff. His efforts in this quarter proved equally unavailing because, according to Aoki, the European Powers, captained by England, stoutly upheld the dogma of free trade, the practice of which was proving so lucrative for them, and suspected Japan of protectionist inclinations.

The only gleam of light for Japan in this dark decade of the 1870s — and even it turned out to be a will-o'-the-wisp — had been a treaty concluded with the United States in 1878. This accorded Japan tariff autonomy. However, this major concession was conditional on similar treaties being drawn up with the other Powers, and, as the latter failed to materialize, Aoki described the American treaty of 1878 as 'ineffective', a word which was later to be used by opponents of the government in the House of Peers as basis of further questions to the Foreign Minister. Coming to the decade of the 1880s and Inoue Kaoru's assumption of the post of Foreign Minister in 1880, Aoki was able to speak with greater assurance because he himself had served as Inoue's deputy. He explained how Inoue's strategy of negotiating on both the judicial and the commercial aspects of the treaties, all at once and in a series of general conferences with the representatives of some seventeen treaty Powers, had made the going hard for everybody. Another source of difficulty was described by Aoki as follows:

> People both here and abroad thought the [existing] treaties were to be of indefinite duration. Therefore what had been an exceptional state of affairs came to be normal custom, and any changes in these customs were regarded as violations of vested rights.

Inoue's place as Foreign Minister was taken by Itō Hirobumi, who was also Prime Minister at the time, and deeply involved in drafting the constitution that had been promised by the throne in 1881.[3] Itō, consequently, was far too busy to attend to the treaty question; indeed, Aoki said rather waspishly that in all probability 'his mind [was] bereft of any plan for dealing with the situation'; and negotiations for revision lapsed for the time being.[4]

Aoki's cordial comments on the Ōkuma series of negotiations that began in 1888 have been vindicated by historians.[5] The new Foreign Minister's policy of talking separately with a few major Powers had had results that 'were better than those we [i.e. Inoue and Aoki] would have obtained in July 1887'. However, hostility within Japan to the proposed new treaties, details of which had been illicitly divulged to the world's press, culminated in 'an affair too sad for words'. The focus of Japanese opposition to the Ōkuma drafts had been the provision that foreign judges should sit on the Japanese Supreme Court for twelve years. This explains why Arai sought specific assurances on this point.

Having brought his remembrance of things past virtually down to the time at which he was speaking and his own period of responsibility as Japan's Foreign Minister, Aoki Shūzō confessed that the authorities had so far failed to 'secure the extension of rights which is this country's due'. He emphasized the intractable nature of the problem, while re-affirming the government's and his own personal intention to come to grips with it once more in view of the 'national policy . . . embodied in the Charter Oath'. Mention of this epoch-making document allowed him to reiterate one of the standard contentions of the bureaucrats of the time in their general ideological and political confrontation with Liberal and assorted party opposition. 'The evolution of the constitutional regime, which in itself is the reason for our meeting together and staying together in this place as we are doing, is attributable to article one of the Charter Oath.'[6] The authorities' purpose in taking this line was to stress that the Constitution, together with all the administrative reforms leading up to it, had been granted freely and as an act of grace on the part of the throne, and did not in any way represent a surrender to the Liberty and Popular Rights agitation. The Oath had been solemnly sworn by the Emperor in April 1868, the third year of his reign; whereas the Liberal propaganda for a constitution and a national assembly did not commence until 1874, at the earliest. The official point of view on the origins of the Constitution was a tactical weapon of considerable value to the bureaucratic rulers of Japan, and has proved to be every bit as respectable as any other interpretation of the political history of the first half of the Meiji era (Mason 1969: 19–21).

The remainder of Aoki's long speech consisted of an assortment of loosely connected remarks. These did not deal so much with the actual topic of treaty revision itself as with its various contexts: diplomatic and national; political; journalistic; and legal. He was clearly forced to talk around the subject in this way, because of his determination not to speak about the government's current plans for revision. He did manage to mix in a bit of specific information here and there with his more generalized observations; and even the latter are not completely without interest to historians of the period, however tiresome and unwelcome they might have been to the parliamentary audience for which they were originally intended.

For instance, he stated dogmatically that the treaty Powers had been prepared to make fairly substantial concessions to Japan 'in the long run' since 1872, and 'in particular ever since 1881–2'. Speaking in 1890, and so thirteen years before the conclusion of the Anglo-Japanese alliance, he felt able to assure the House of Representatives that their country was 'on the point of becoming the most valued ally in the East . . . . I can assure you that it is a fact that every country takes the view that here is a nation to be conciliated'. The Foreign Minister may have just been putting a brave face on things in making these optimistic remarks. But his speech as a whole was sober and truthful, if fundamentally evasive; by virtue of his official post he was in a better position than anybody else to make such assertions; and the future was to prove him right. At the time of speaking, he himself attributed this auspicious state of affairs to Japan's steady progress in administration since 1868. Reverting to this topic later on in his speech, he claimed that the judicial and political reforms accompanying the development of constitutional government provided foreign residents with adequate safeguards in the event of their coming under Japanese jurisdiction, while acknowledging that the unequal treaties had had their beneficial side in that they had helped to bring about this improvement in domestic affairs.

These conciliatory comments were followed by a repetition of his earlier warning against precipitate action on the part of Japan, such as unilateral abrogation of the existing treaties:

Anything like a sudden alteration in the present state of affairs, features of which are the treaty Powers' compliance with our demands so far and the friendship they have shown us, would be generally regretted . . . . Therefore, in these matters the government has striven to find out the best way of preserving this new-found equilibrium, and how far it is advisable to press forward.

On the other hand, Aoki made no bones about saying that the existing system of consular jurisdiction in the treaty ports was a flagrant violation of the recently inaugurated Japanese Constitution. This document had vested sovereignty in Japan in the person of the Emperor. 'As a result of these abuses [of extra-territorial jurisdiction], there are at present several independent entities within our independent Empire.'

One rather long passage in the second half of Aoki's discourse was devoted, somewhat surprisingly, to playing down the whole issue of treaty revision. It began with the remarks that both the Japanese government and the Japanese public had become overly obsessed with the two words 'treaty revision', and that, as Foreign Minister, there were many other matters requiring his attention. Added to this was a strong personal belief in the Japanese nation's capacity for wellnigh infinite progress. Such thoughts prompted him to call on the general public, through its House of Representatives, to direct some of its energies away from the frustrating tangle of treaty revision into other channels.

In particular, there was a need to develop the nation's economic resources, especially the coalfields of northern Kyūshū, and to expand trade with China and other regions of Asia. The United States of America, he pointed out, were far away and had their 'back to Japan', in the sense that they had few ties with the Island Empire and lacked good ports on their west coast. The Yangtze basin, on the other hand, was conveniently close and inhabited by a vast population. 'Suppose these 270 million people were to take goods manufactured in this country, might we not expect their consumption to go on for ever?' In his endeavours to stir his countrymen to greater action and initiative, even within the limitations imposed by the treaties, Aoki went on to make a slightly unfortunate allusion to the medieval freebooters (*wakō*) of south-western Japan, who, disregarding the national diplomacy of their age and 'sailing in mere fishing boats, as it were', had harried the coasts of China in the fourteenth and fifteenth centuries. 'Such brave men, I am convinced, could hardly be described as having been somehow circumscribed by the two words "treaty revision".'

In advancing these views, Aoki was attempting to seize the initiative, or at any rate was executing a diversionary manoeuvre, in the political warfare of the time. According to this way of looking at things, treaty revision did not have the same intrinsic importance as problems of economic development and foreign trade. Nevertheless, as Aoki himself admitted, it loomed as a prerequisite for solving these other problems. For this reason, and because it had been the principal concern of the Japanese government and people for nearly twenty years, revision of the unequal treaties continued to be a major preoccupation into the 1890s.

The Foreign Minister stated several times that the government intended to pursue the business impartially and in the interests of forty million people. It was anxious to take account of public opinion as expressed in the Diet, and especially in the newspapers. With these reassurances went a repetition of his earlier refusal to give explicit or detailed information on the government's actual policies for revision. However, he did at any rate feel free to say that the government planned to 'enlarge our sovereign rights, and, in the economic sphere, to do all that it can in the national interest'. This seems to have been a definite hint that the authorities would aim first at regaining complete judicial sovereignty, and be content for the time being with only a partial restoration of tariff rights.

Aoki also read out extracts from contemporary newspapers, meaning thereby to give some slight indication of the government's stand on specific issues. Thus, an editor's suggestion that foreigners should not be permitted to reside outside the treaty ports so long as the system of consular jurisdiction lasted received his official endorsement; but he rejected another journalist's advice that the government should concentrate on regaining tariff autonomy first, and defer the matter of extraterritorial jurisdiction. His attitude on this second point, of course, reinforced the 'hint' given a minute or two previously. Other newspapers had warned against making promises to the Powers about the timing and cancellation of Japanese domestic legislation. On this, Aoki declared that Ōkuma had done it 'as a matter of necessity . . . these circumstances were approved by the cabinet at the behest of His Majesty'.

The Foreign Minister then finished his speech with a brief, but in the circumstances provocative, reference to royal prerogative. He cited a precedent from the British House of Lords, year 1802, for the view that treaties were made or re-made by virtue of the crown's prerogative, and were not things with which parliaments could legally concern themselves. At this point, Aoki was interrupted by Arai Shōgo, who clearly objected to him trying to justify his silences in this exotic and antiquarian way, and he discontinued speaking.

Arai, himself, then took over the rostrum for a few minutes to condemn scathingly the Foreign Minister's performance. No concrete replies had been given to the specific questions about the prospects of abolishing consular jurisdiction and regaining tariff autonomy, questions which he had incorporated in his written memorandum and had raised again that afternoon in his introductory speech. For the Foreign Minister simply to refer to some already published newspaper articles and utter platitudes about the government's determination to solve the problem in the long run, was not good enough. Moreover, he (Arai) had not come to the House to hear the Foreign Minister tell 'funny stories' about foreign countries, this being a hit at the citation from the House of Lords debate of 1802. Arai then concluded his denunciation with a renewed cry for the government to stop practising secret diplomacy, and for the Foreign Minister to give unequivocal replies to questions on future policy for treaty revision (DNTGS: 536).

At this stage, proceedings were briefly interrupted by Suematsu Kenchō, a senior member of the Home Office who sat as an Independent Member for his native district in north Kyūshū. Suematsu angrily repudiated a suggestion in the Foreign Minister's speech that he (Suematsu) was under the mistaken impression that the new Commercial Code had been introduced by the government as a concession to foreigners, rather than for the sake of the Japanese. Aoki had based his suggestion on some remarks made by Suematsu in the course of a debate on the draft Commercial Code held by the House of Representatives on the previous day.

Aoki Shūzō then spoke again. He half-apologized to Suematsu for having misinterpreted his words. On the other hand, he was absolutely firm in his handling of Arai Shōgo: 'if it is a question of stating it again plainly, the position is this: to give details of the matters under discussion, that is to say, of the matters under discussion with a foreign government, would be an abuse of international convention' (DNTGS: 536). A few minutes afterwards, it was suddenly discovered that Aoki was no longer on the battlefield. He had quietly slipped away from the House and the Diet building.

Since the Foreign Minister's speech had lasted for a full two hours, it was by then some time after three o'clock in the afternoon. Including a recess from 3.37 to 4.14 p.m., the debate continued for approximately another two-and-a-half hours. Discussion tended to be somewhat ragged, but revolved around two main issues with a total of thirty-three Members taking part. One source of contention, of course, was the Foreign Minister's sudden and unannounced departure from the House. The other problem that agitated Members concerned procedure, and derived from the Speaker's initial rulings on supplementary questions. After the Foreign Minister's brief reply to Arai Shōgo's comment on his speech, both Katsuki Yukitsune and Misaki Kamenosuke had wanted to ask questions on matters like the open ports which related to the general topic of treaty revision but were, strictly speaking, outside the scope of Arai's original written questions and accompanying memorandum. The Speaker ruled such questions out of order, and quickly got into trouble for doing so. Misaki himself objected fairly strenuously on his own behalf; but Utsunomiya Heiichi most cogently voiced the feelings of the House, when he said:

> This [i.e., the Speaker's ruling] has far reaching effects on the privileges of the Diet, and is a very important matter. Therefore, it cannot be left unattended. Since a ruling cannot [properly] be given on the basis of the Speaker's opinions, it would be as well to consult the House at once.

> (DNTGS: 538)

Sentiments of this kind soon prompted the Speaker, who had at first maintained that regulation of the House was his job, to beat a dignified retreat. He explained that his suspension of Misaki's speech had been due to a misunderstanding, and went on to say that he would 'never at any time stop Members from speaking, so long as they were in order'. Nakamura Eisuke then accepted the Speaker's assurances on behalf of the House, and the matter was dropped.

This altercation with the Chair, though sharp in its own way, took second place compared with the outburst of criticisms provoked by the Foreign Minister's long-winded but 'inadequate' reply to the original questions, and his even less satisfactory conduct in leaving the House as soon as the going got rough. Member after Member rose to condemn the minister's behaviour as 'outrageous', 'exceedingly remiss' and 'scandalous'. Yamada Tōji formally proposed that the Speaker send a written summons to the offender, requiring him to return at once to the House and answer supplementary questions on his speech (DNTGS: 538). Discussion ensued as to whether this demand should be based on No. 141 of the Rules of the House of Representatives or Article 50 of the Law of the Houses;[7] while Tanaka Gentarō demurred with respect to the intention of the motion, pointing out that the great majority of Members had not yet had a chance to see the written memorandum for

Arai's questions. These people, Tanaka argued, were not therefore in a position to judge for themselves in what ways, precisely, the Foreign Minister's speech could be considered wanting. However, the motion that 'In view of the inadequacy of the Foreign Minister's reply, we should request him in writing to come here again, and ask [him] for explanations' was soon put to the House and carried. The Speaker then promised to do what he could to implement the motion, but doubted if concrete results could be achieved that afternoon.

While awaiting further developments, Members continued, in the main, to cavil at the Foreign Minister and to embroil themselves in petty disputes about procedure. From time to time, they managed to throw in a few remarks about treaty revision for good measure.

Ishizaka Sennosuke who apparently specialized in raising procedural difficulties –

> my habit of addressing the Speaker on the subject of procedure does not stem from any feeling on my part that the Speaker is incompetent. After all, it is but a trifle, and the fact that matters have invariably gone satisfactorily [heretofore] as regards votes, voting and agendas augurs well in my opinion.
>
> (DNTGS: 539)

– persisted in doubting whether it had been proper to put the motion at all, as he interpreted Article 50 of the Law of the Houses as having to be taken in conjunction with Article 52. In that case, representations on ministerial replies required more than thirty sponsors. Other Members and the Speaker firmly rejected Ishizaka's opinions. Consequently, he subsided, though not without giving a dire warning that 'the House will run riot, and even the Speaker will not know what to do . . . [and] we shall come under attack from the newspapers', if scrupulous attention were not paid to matters of procedure.

Before this, Uozumi Itsuji had asked the Speaker if there was any rule obliging ministers of state or other government spokesmen to report to the Chair when they wished to withdraw from the chamber. The Speaker replied that no law or precedent existed to that effect, but he hoped that the dignitaries referred to would take to observing such a formality as a matter of courtesy to himself and the House (DNTGS: 539).

Earlier still, before the motion for recalling the Foreign Minister had been passed, Hashimoto Kyūtarō suggested that debate on Aoki's speech should not be continued into the evening but resumed the following afternoon (DNTGS: 538). Nakamura Eisuke and Arai Shōgo supported this proposal for deferment. On the other hand, Haseba Sumitaka, Inoue Kakugorō and Shimoiisaka Gonzaburō all expressed strong opposition to delay, and in a series of short, brisk speeches (DNTGS: 539–40) reproached their fellow Members with lack of zeal, as well as denouncing Aoki's unwillingness to submit himself for further questioning.

We believe that this business is so important that today is no time for counting the hours.

I am greatly enraged by the fact that there are Members who at intervals emit great shouts of laughter.

(Haseba)

To say, at the same time that we decide that the Foreign Minister's conduct in leaving before explanations are completed is reprehensible, that we should perhaps postpone these until tomorrow goes to show that this House itself does not value its rights over-much.

Generally speaking, once we have begun deliberations, we do not break off in the middle – come night, come dawn.

(Inoue)

If [the Foreign Minister] has caught a cold, or is suffering from a headache or has got colic, there is nothing we can do about it . . . but I hope that he will come here at once armed with explanations which will satisfy us.

(Shimoiisaka)

Ōtsu Junichirō then spoke in favour of postponement. He declared that the Foreign Minister's speech had been lengthy and at times inaudible. Ōtsu, too, had decided to ask supplementary questions, but felt that Members needed time to digest what Aoki had said and to prepare their interrogation. 'To lose our tempers like children because he has left the chamber is surely to belittle the significance of the problem', he argued. Tateishi Kanji and Amano Jakuen agreed with Ōtsu, the latter requesting a vote on the matter. The House then resolved to discontinue its debate on the treaty problem for the time being, and to summon Aoki for the following day (DNTGS: 540).

There followed a further ten or so minutes of tortuous procedural dispute on whether or not to defer the rest of the day's order paper. This had been proposed by Ueki Emori, who objected to 'squeezing our deliberations into the gap left by the Foreign Minister'. Several Members seconded Ueki's motion. Others opposed it on the general grounds that it would create a bad impression if the House were to rise an hour before its usual time. Suematsu Kenchō wondered what the procedural position would be if the Foreign Minister failed to put in an appearance on the following day. The Speaker, anxious as always to temper the authority of his office to the mood of the House, observed that it was his responsibility to determine the order paper, but that he had a greater responsibility to meet the wishes of the House. Nakajima thereupon asked the House if it wished to continue with the order paper. When it resolved not to continue, he said that he could not announce the following day's order paper and, further, that he would write 'now' to the Foreign Minister but could not guarantee his attendance (DNTGS: 540–1).

Yokobori Sanshi said that he opposed the decision just made in favour of terminating proceedings for the day. Referring to Suematsu's comments a few minutes previously, he asked if the House now had to delay its other business indefinitely until it had heard further from the Foreign Minister. Amano Jakuen and Itakura Chū urged the Speaker to reconsider his decision not to announce the order paper for the following day. They wanted it announced, so that the House could resume its business immediately after hearing Aoki's replies to supplementary questions. In that case, there would be no risk of 'idling time away' (DNTGS: 541).

Orita Kanetaka, in a few well-considered observations, pointed out that he had supported Ueki's motion for suspending proceedings altogether, but this did not mean that Members who took this line were in favour of endless delays. Postponement had been sought only to give time for the Speaker to write to the Foreign Minister and for the latter to make his replies. When Aoki's exact intentions towards it were known, the House could take appropriate action.

The Speaker then declared that once the Foreign Minister's reactions had been ascertained, he would carry on with debates on the Copyright Bill and the Peace Preservation Ordinance Abolition Bill. With that, the House rose at 5.35 p.m. When the House of Representatives met the following day, 18 December 1890, at 1.22 p.m., the deputy-Speaker, Tsuda Mamichi, took the Chair and ordered the Clerk, Sone Arasuke, to read out the following communication from the Foreign Minister:

> As a result of a vote in your House yesterday, you ask me to reply again; but I beg to inform you by way of an answer that I have already yesterday replied to the best of my ability, and therefore find it difficult to comply with your request.
>
> 8 December 1890 Aoki Shūzō, Foreign Minister

To: Nakajima Nobuyuki, Esq.,
Speaker of the House of Representatives.

(DNTGS: 542)

Tanaka Shōzō spoke first in the resumed debate. He argued that the spirit of constitutional government could be maintained only if ministers of state and their deputies came regularly to the House of Representatives and treated their speeches to it with due seriousness. He also put forward the view that Aoki's refusal to answer further questions was illegal, since his abrupt departure the day before had disturbed the good order of the House and so violated Article 90 of the Law of the Houses. Furthermore, Article 51 of the Constitution (Itō 1931: 201, 80) expressly allowed each House of the Diet to draw up its own procedural rules; therefore Article 141 of the House of Representatives Rules, allowing Members to recall ministers for further questioning when their prepared replies to written questions had been 'irrelevant', had the backing of the Constitution itself. Tanaka ended by claiming that even though ministers were in the habit of taking refuge in Article 67 of the Constitution[8] when they got into difficulties in the Diet, if the House paid close attention to procedural rules and detail, Aoki and any other minister who might be tempted to act in a similarly off-hand fashion could be brought to book and forced to accede to its demands.

The deputy-Speaker next called Misaki Kamenosuke to the rostrum. Misaki complained that the Foreign Minister's speech the day before had been long on words but short on substance, and implied that his behaviour since then had been thoroughly recalcitrant. Nevertheless, he thought it futile to keep on summoning 'someone who lies down and will not come', and that the wisest course for the House to follow would be to drop the matter for the moment and make a fresh start by preparing entirely new questions for submission to the government.

This idea did not please Arai Shōgo, the chief sponsor of the original set of questions to the government on its foreign policy. Not unnaturally, Arai felt distinctly aggrieved at the way things were going. He called the Foreign Minister a 'violator' of the Diet and, after declaring that the House could not possibly submit to his discourteous and illegal treatment of it, indicated that action might be taken on the basis of Article 142 of the House of Representatives Rules.[9]

A number of speakers expressed support either for Misaki's policy of tactical disengagement or for Arai's desire to persist in harrying the foe. Ishida Kannosuke put himself firmly in Misaki's camp. He agreed that the Foreign Minister's speech had been in many ways too general and unsatisfactory. However, scattered through it had been indications 'for astute Members' of what was likely to happen with treaty revision. Aoki, moreover, had virtually stated that Article 4 of the Constitution could not be deemed to be operative while the consular courts remained in existence. This, coming from the Foreign Minister of the Imperial government, should have been a cause for general rejoicing, as it was tantamount to saying that the authorities planned to work for the withdrawal of extra-territorial jurisdiction. Ishida also felt that to keep on pressing the Foreign Minister to make further replies at that juncture might lead to a major upheaval between the government and the Diet. The better course, in his opinion, lay in submitting new questions to which, it was quite clear, he would be legally bound to reply (DNTGS: 543–4).

Konishi Jinnosuke made the same point about Aoki being legally obliged to answer new questions. He also sought to support the case for disengagement by rejecting Arai's view that Article 142 of the House Rules could be used to compel the Foreign Minister to attend again. Rule 142, he claimed, applied only when Ministers had not given any answer to the Members' questions. Aoki had replied. Moreover, he maintained that he had replied to the best of his ability.

Arai Shōgo, speaking less coherently than usual, next chided the House for being less fervent about the matter than it had been the previous afternoon. Urging his fellow Members to rule the Foreign Minister's letter out of order, he held that if they failed to do so 'last night's decision will fade away entirely'.

During the succeeding few minutes, Members either raised points of order, or else briefly spoke in favour of one or other of the alternative lines of action open to the House. It was left to Orita Kanetaka, speaking once again admirably to the point, to put forward some of the basic arguments for Arai's standpoint in a more skilful fashion than Arai himself had done. Orita considered Misaki's suggestion that Members should prepare new questions to be 'over-indulgent' to the Foreign Minister and the government. The general opinion in the House on the previous evening had been that Aoki's reply be deemed inadequate, and that further explanations should be sought from him as soon as practicable. Ministers ought to answer questions to the satisfaction of all Members, and should be kept at it until they did. Information could not be left to a process of inference and guesswork. Finally, if the House were now to reverse its earlier decision to demand further explanations from the Foreign Minister, it could not expect the government or anyone else to take it seriously. The constitutional, and political, principle involved in the question of how the House of Representatives should react to Aoki's treatment of it was clearly an important one. In Orita's own words:

In the future, when the Diet demands further explanations from ministers of state and government spokesmen after they have given very brief replies in this place and have left without their explanations ever coming properly to the point, what will Members do if they refuse on the grounds that they have already said what they have to say?

(DNTGS: 544)

Despite such powerful pleading, the case for pursuing the Foreign Minister further at that stage was already lost. After Orita had finished speaking, Suzuki Shōji made a short speech advancing yet more reasons for allowing Misaki Kamenosuke and Members associated with him to go ahead with their scheme for new questions. Suzuki reminded the House that the Foreign Minister had clearly stated that some important trends in the negotiations he was currently conducting with the treaty Powers could not be divulged, because of the overriding need for diplomatic secrecy. Yet there were other matters, such as ownership of land and legal rights, which, though formally secret, could be safely discussed in the Diet and elsewhere. Suzuki counselled Misaki and his group to concentrate on these more humdrum, but less politically and diplomatically sensitive, topics when drawing up their questions (DNTGS: 545).

After Suzuki had made these comments, a group of Members led by Naitō Rihachi asked for the debate to be terminated. The deputy-Speaker called for a vote on this. The 'ayes' won, and the House turned at once to the next item on its order paper.

In this inconclusive and frustrating fashion the only attempt by the first House of Representatives to mount a major debate on foreign affairs came to an end. In no parliamentary system, however liberal or sophisticated, has it been easy to organize constructive, in the sense of immediately fruitful, discussions on foreign policy; and in Japan during the years 1890–2 domestic legislation, and above all the budget, took pride of place with government ministers and parliamentary politicians alike. In addition, the Diet was inexperienced, and the bureaucratic cabinet of the day resolved to do nothing that would in any way impair its Executive independence. In other words, the ministers did not wish, as a matter of political principle, to see the legislators in the Diet gain any degree of control of day-to-day policy over and above the minimum allowed them in the Constitution. Finally, the same ministers had become engaged in fairly high level diplomatic talks on the treaty problem. They could plausibly plead the need for strict diplomatic secrecy, as practised by all the Powers at the time and just recently breached in 1889 to the detriment of Japan and Ōkuma

Shigenobu, in justification of their refusal to say much about the actual nature of these discussions. For all these reasons, it is not too difficult to see why the anti-government Liberal and Progressive majority in the first House of Representatives should have failed to elicit the information they sought from the responsible authorities, and so found themselves unable to exert any immediately decisive influence on the nation's foreign policy.

On the other hand, as everybody agreed, treaty revision, or rather efforts to achieve treaty revision, had been going on for a long time; the problem was onerous, and one that would affect all Japanese, born and unborn, until it was settled. In these circumstances, the turn of events must have been a personally damaging and frustrating setback for those Members of the House of Representatives directly involved in the initial encounter with Aoki Shūzō in December 1890. Further-more, the outlook for constitutional government in Japan would have been bleak, if there had been no kind of dialogue at all established between Diet and cabinet, in foreign affairs as well as everything else. In fact, the furious criticism with which the House of Representatives reacted to his handling of it does seem to have led eventually to a certain change of heart on the part of the Foreign Minister. On several occasions during February and March 1891, Aoki went in person to the House of Peers to answer written questions submitted by Members of that chamber; what is more, he tried to be more explicit and genuinely informative in talking to the Peers than he had been when replying to Arai Shōgo's batch of questions in the House of Representatives. Internal evidence shows that the course of events in one House was not entirely unconnected with what had transpired in the other. Thus, in some ways, the House of Peers can be said to have come to the assistance of the Lower House in its endeavours to wrest from the country's Foreign Minister some idea of the current state of the country's diplomacy. Perhaps as a result of this unlooked-for and apparently unplanned collaboration between the two Houses of the Diet, Aoki was both less long-winded and less evasive when at length he appeared once more in the House of Representatives to answer Members' written questions (DNTGS: 1100–2). Above all, he showed himself ready to entertain supplementary questions on his statements.

The date was 5 March 1891, only a few days before the first session of the first Diet was due to finish, as Aoki himself admitted in the introductory remarks to his statement; the Speaker, Nakajima Nobuyuki, was in the Chair; and the question to which the Foreign Minister was about to reply had been submitted by Misaki Kamenosuke on 24 December 1890. Clearly, from the date of Misaki's question, it had followed on from the decision of the House on 18 December to accept his suggestion that new questions should be sent in to the government on the treaty problem. The gist of the question, as recounted by Aoki, was:

> With regard to the policy which is at present being followed by the government in connection with treaty revision; is it the intention to try to regain rights of jurisdiction and tariff rights in their entirety at one and the same time? Or will it try to regain part of them first, while looking forward to regaining them in full some day in the future?

This was aimed fairly and squarely at the sensitive topic of the government's current thinking and negotiations on treaty revision. Yet Aoki did not equivocate. His answer to the first part of the question was an unvarnished 'no'. The government like anybody else, he conceded, would be only too happy to see everything restored at one stroke. However, as an actual goal of short-term diplomacy, such a hope was 'not practicable'. Aoki then reverted to a metaphor he had already used in the House of Peers, and which he obviously thought suitable as a fairly concrete indication of the government's approach to revision. He likened the task confronting himself and his colleagues in the cabinet to building a bridge.

> [suppose] you are going across a plain and meet with a river, and it is impossible to walk across the river. Therefore you must build a bridge. The Imperial government has resolved to build a bridge and cross to the opposite bank. I shall confine myself to speaking only of the length of the bridge. Most certainly, we do not want to make it 200 or 400 yards long. We plan to make it as short as possible.

The import of these words was crystal-clear. The government would do what it could to hasten the day when Japan should be in possession of all her sovereign rights once again but, being realistic, it was actually negotiating for a staged or partial, rather than simultaneous and complete, restoration. All in all, Aoki could have hardly been more forthright in his reply.

The second part of Misaki's question to all intents and purposes duplicated the first, and Aoki might well have felt that he had already answered it. However, he went on to speak specifically on it for a moment or two more. He stated that so far as tariff rights were concerned, 'I intend to regain them in part, but it is a very hard task to regain them in full'. This meant that he was working for a treaty to be signed in the near future which would restore to Japan at any rate a greater degree of tariff autonomy than the existing agreements allowed her. There was also an important inference in what Aoki did not say on this occasion. Coupled with the tenor of some of the remarks he had made on newspaper comment on his December speech, his silence now on the subject of consular jurisdiction indicated that he planned to abolish that, in full and as soon as possible.

The Foreign Minister finished his statement by reiterating a point he had made on the previous occasion about the Powers, too, having interests which they regarded as being secured by the existing treaties: 'any rejection of these and immediate resumption [by Japan] of full sovereignty would grievously discredit the Imperial government, and would bring much odium on the head of the responsible official, who is myself'. Immediately after making this observation, Aoki remarked that that was all he would say about Misaki's question 'to begin with', and remained on the rostrum, obviously expecting and willing to deal with further queries from the floor of the House. His brief but trenchant reply so far had embraced three general considerations. These were: (1) complete restoration of both judicial and tariff rights in the not-too-distant future as the ultimate goal of government policy; (2) partial restoration as the working objective for the time being, especially perhaps in the negotiations on the tariff; and (3) respect for international law and convention.

When Tanaka Shōzō did rise to question the Foreign Minister and attempted to speak by his seat, Inoue Kakugorō and others were quick to point out that he could not be heard properly. Aoki, therefore, obligingly got down from the rostrum to let Tanaka speak from there. Incidentally, Tanaka's exchange with Inoue had consisted of fairly light-hearted banter:

INOUE: Please, the rostrum.
TANAKA: Our guest [i.e., Aoki] is on the rostrum. Try opening your
          eyes since it is a very simple matter!
          (laughter)

and he opened his speech with a flowery expression of gratitude to Inoue. 'As a result of Mr Inoue Kakugorō's election, I am fortunate enough to have the honour of mounting the rostrum' (laughter). The rest of what Tanaka had to say, however, amounted to a rather too sharp and bad-tempered attack on the Foreign Minister's personality and policies.

He began by complaining that the Foreign Minister had merely repeated, in a greatly condensed form, what he had already told the House in December, which was not altogether the case. Then he alleged quite erroneously that the Foreign Minister in his earlier speech had pictured himself as earnestly given over to the problem of treaty revision 'from the first day to the last day of the year'. Tanaka described how such 'diligence on the part of this leading official' had led him to expect that fully equal treaties would emerge from the current round of negotiations. The reply just given by the Foreign Minister to Misaki Kamenosuke that morning, however, had disillusioned him; and he felt that talk of 'making a long bridge short . . . is after all the same work, to all intents and purposes, as that carried out by the previous Foreign Ministers, Mr Inoue and Mr Ōkuma'.

Tanaka had the grace to acknowledge that many aspects of negotiations for revision had to remain confidential, and that Members should refrain from asking about these. However, he wanted reassurance on a couple of points. Would the Foreign Minister refuse to conclude treaties that were not equal, in other words, treaties that did not abolish extra-territorial jurisdiction outright and completely restore tariff autonomy? Secondly, in what precise ways did Aoki's policy for revision differ from that of his predecessors in office, Inoue Kaoru and Ōkuma Shigenobu? The final shot in Tanaka's locker was a barbed reminder that 'a reply full of conceit and contrariness will be of no use' (laughter).

In a brief but dignified rejoinder, Aoki promptly denied that he had ever said that treaty revision took up all his attention. The words at issue, which he had uttered on 17 December, had been precisely to the opposite effect. While correcting misapprehensions, he paused to explain also that when he had talked of America having 'its back to Japan', he had been speaking solely from the point of view of geography, for 'America has been favourably disposed to treaty revision with Japan for some time, and in other ways, too, they are a people who feel extremely friendly towards Japan'. He apologized for this and any other misunderstanding which might have arisen because 'my way of speaking is a bad one'.

With regard to the substance of Tanaka's two questions, he confessed himself puzzled by the first, presumably because he had just said that the government would settle for a partial restoration of rights for the time being. The second question concerning the differences between his approach and that of Inoue and Ōkuma he could not answer, since such matters still had to be kept secret.

> For me, it is a case of going on planning, going on negotiating. Those two ministers who preceded me in office have negotiated; in other words, for them it is a bygone tale. I am doing work reaching from now into the future. Therefore, regrettable as it is, I cannot reply to that here and now.

Aoki's words here seem to imply that his concern with secrecy sprang from a desire not to reveal too much of the Japanese government's strategy for negotiation to the treaty Powers, rather than from any fear of breaking any international convention.

Still on the same day, 5 March 1891, the House of Representatives had an hour's recess, for lunch presumably, and when it resumed sitting the Foreign Minister was again present. This time, he had come to answer a series of questions submitted by Inoue Kakugorō on Japan's relations with Korea and, by extension, China.

Inoue was one of the nationally celebrated of the Liberal Party, belonging at the time to its 'Left wing'. This meant that he was a stalwart defender of popular rights at home, opposing tooth and nail the bureaucratic fixations and pretensions to political leadership of the Sat–Chō ministers, while at the same time being something of a demagogic idealist and expansionist when it came to foreign affairs. In this, he resembled Arai Shōgo and, like Arai, Inoue considered that a liberal, 'progressive' Japan had a kind of 'divine mission' to impose its pattern of reforms on more backward Asian nations across the sea. Again, like Arai, Inoue had been eventually jailed by the Japanese authorities for complicity in the Ōsaka Incident of 1885. He was further qualified to talk about Korea by virtue of the experience he had gained during a short period of employment by the Korean government as one of its advisers on trade negotiations (Conroy 1960: 124–68).

Inevitably, Inoue had been one of the critics of the Foreign Minister's speech and subsequent conduct on the afternoon of 17 December, though not nearly so outspoken on that occasion as he might have been. A little later, he had had his own clash with Aoki when the latter, obviously still nettled by his relationships with the House of Representatives, had flatly refused to answer some questions submitted by Inoue. The Foreign Minister had attempted to justify his unwillingness to co-operate by referring to what he chose to take as the explicit rationale behind Inoue's questions, a rationale which he deprecated as going too far in the direction of ideas of popular sovereignty for his and the cabinet's liking. These feelings he conveyed to the House in the following formal and somewhat insulting letter, which the Speaker had had read out on 17 January 1891:

The memorandum on the questions submitted under the names of Representative Inoue Kakugorō and forty-two others, on 23 December last year, clearly stated that the people ought to be the judge of whether or not to trust the government. Well, the government are of the belief that they are under no obligation to leave these measures

to be decided by the trust, or lack of trust, of the people. Therefore,
I shall not reply to the aforementioned questions.

Viscount Aoki, Foreign Minister

To: Nakajima Nobuyuki, Esq.,
Speaker of the House of Representatives.

(DNTGS: 732)

In brushing this note, was the Foreign Minister simply being 'choosy'
about words? In which case, he must have been almost certainly looking
for any excuse not to answer; motivated, no doubt, by pique and
personal fatigue, as well as by considerations of work-a-day political
and diplomatic tactics. Or was he in all sincerity antagonized by a sense
of deep ideological differences between himself and his parliamentary
tormentors? It is impossible to know now which of these conjectures is
nearer the truth. A case could perhaps be made out, however, that
Aoki's coolness reflected a deep departmental hostility to Inoue on the
part of the Foreign Ministry. It can well be supposed that Inoue's ardent
meddling with Korean internal politics had made him very unpopular
with the officials responsible for Japanese foreign policy. They must
have regarded him as a particularly dangerous privateer, and no doubt
were delighted when he was sent to prison for a year in 1887. Especially
had Inoue fallen foul of his namesake, Inoue Kaoru. The latter had been
Foreign Minister for most of the 1880s, and so the official superior and
close colleague of Aoki himself. Loyalty to his former chief, as well as
a sense of his own and his department's dignity, no doubt sharpened
Aoki's reactions to anything Inoue Kakugorō might say or do.

Unfortunately, there is no definite indication in the Diet Record of
the actual topic of Inoue's question on 23 December 1890; but, coming
so soon after the House of Representatives' debate on treaty revision,
it may well have been on that subject and the Foreign Minister's speech
on Arai Shōgo's questions.

Coming to the matter of the questions on relations with Korea, which
Inoue had sent in on 9 February 1891 and to which Aoki was prepared
to reply, these were all of an apparently trivial, niggling nature. On the
other hand, one may suppose that they were fair and suitable enough as
small arms ammunition in the running battle between the government
and its parliamentary opposition. Moreover, they came at a time when,
quite apart from anything that had gone on in the not-so-distant past,
Japanese official relations with Korea were undergoing some strain, due
to irritants like an apparently malicious decision on the part of the
Korean authorities, or their Chinese mentors, to cut down on the export
of foodstuffs to Japan, and unreasonable delays in allowing Japanese

interests to build a telegraph line from Pusan to Seoul (Conroy 1960: 189). With his thirty co-sponsors, Inoue's purpose in submitting them seems to have been twofold: in the first place, to inflict an irksome chore on the Foreign Minister and those of his subordinates who had to dredge up the information needed to frame a reply; and, in the second place, to show up the Foreign Ministry, and the government as a whole, as being somehow pusillanimous in their defence of Japanese interests in Korea.

The first of the three questions related to the repayment by the Korean government of a loan of ¥170,000 in gold made to it in the early 1880s by the Yokohama Specie Bank, which was a Japanese government agency. A little later, the Korean government had borrowed a further 200,000 *ryō* in silver; this time from the China Merchants' Steam Navigation Company, which was a Chinese government agency. What Inoue was asking about was not so much the actual repayment of these loans as the arrangements entered into by the various governments to secure their repayment. According to Inoue, the Korean authorities had offered the receipts of the three customs houses at the ports of Pusan, Wonsan and Inchon as security in both cases. However, he alleged, the Chinese government was supervising these Korean customs houses at the time of speaking, on the grounds that their receipts were security for the loan made by the China Merchants' Steam Navigation Company, and 'regardless of the prior rights of the [Yokohama] Specie Bank'. Inoue wished to know whether the Japanese government intended to lodge any objections to this state of affairs.

Although it had been an underlying principle of Japanese policy since the Kanghwa treaty of 1876 that Korea was a fully independent and sovereign state, no longer in any way a protectorate of China, this axiom had tended to remain a piece of diplomatic theory only. In practice, the Japanese government had been obliged to live with a re-assertion of control over Korean affairs on the part of the Chinese, especially since the arrival of Yuan Shih-kai as Beijing's commissioner in Seoul after the disturbances of 1884. Thus, the idea behind Inoue's question was to embarrass Aoki and his fellow ministers in more ways than one. For not only did it throw doubt on the Imperial government's ability to look after its own immediate pecuniary interests, it also suggested that the authorities were complacent about the prospect of Korea slipping back under the tutelage of China, an eventuality which, it was commonly reckoned, could only have been to the detriment of Japan.

The same general intentions no doubt prompted Inoue's second question to the government; but here it must be noted that the controversy about the sale of Korean food to Japan had been simmering already for two or three years. This concerned the export from Korea of *kōsan*, a preparation made from dried carrot (*otane-ninjin*) which was widely held in east Asia to have certain medicinal virtues. Inoue claimed that Chinese merchants were readily allowed by the Korean authorities to export this commodity, especially from the city of Uiju (Heiandō), whereas Japanese merchants who tried to do this ran the risk of having their goods confiscated by the same Korean officials. He then referred to the existence of a treaty of amity and commerce between Korea and Japan which granted the latter country most-favoured-nation status. Clearly, the kind of discrimination alleged, between Chinese traders on the one hand and Japanese merchants on the other, was a breach of this treaty, as well as injurious to the interests of individual Japanese. Again, he desired to know the reactions of the Imperial government to this situation (DNTGS: 1105–6).

Aoki chose to reply (DNTGS: 1106) at some length to both these questions, and he spoke in terms of studied moderation with regard to both their international and their domestic contexts. Concerning Japanese loans to Korea and the supervision of Korean customs houses, he said, firstly, that the Japanese government did not believe that Korean customs house receipts had been pledged as security for the loan from the China Merchants' Steam Navigation Company; secondly, that the Koreans had been repaying the money borrowed from the Yokohama Specie Bank regularly, if a little belatedly; and, thirdly, that the Imperial government's understanding of the situation was that Korean officials, not Chinese, were in charge of Korean customs houses, 'even though there is no doubt that the people at present employed by the Korean government were formerly employed by the Chinese government'. For good measure, he added that, in the experience of the Foreign Ministry, all Korean administration, and not just the customs, was currently being managed by 'completely pure-Korean officials'.

On the question of the export of carrots (*otane-ninjin*) and *kōsan* from Korea to China and Japan, the gist of Aoki's answer was that, with the quantity available for export being so small and with Korean government regulations for the trade being so troublesome, the matter hardly seemed worth bothering about. Particularly was this so after the significant drop in demand in Japan for such goods, as a result of the growing popularity there of 'Dutch [i.e., Western-style] doctors'. Koreans could, apparently, take the carrots into China on payment of 15 per cent duty to the Korean government; similarly, Aoki agreed that 'some few' Chinese merchants living in Korea had received official permission to export the goods to China, again on payment of a 15 per cent duty. Any Chinese merchant who engaged in unlicensed traffic, on the other hand, would be just as liable to punishment as a Japanese 'secret' trader. Official confiscation of goods would follow detection in each case. The only comment in Aoki's whole reply that smacked of criticism of Korea came at this point, when he suggested that one of the reasons why the Korean authorities had so many regulations to control the export of *otane-ninjin* was that its cultivation 'had become an occupation of the officials of the Korean government'. Finally, although Inoue seemed to think that Japanese nationals had requested Korean permission to export only to be rebuffed, he, Aoki, was able to state categorically and officially as Foreign Minister that the Japanese government representatives in Korea had never been approached by any Japanese residing in the peninsula on this question.

The third of Inoue's questions to which the Foreign Minister was replying that afternoon differed somewhat from the previous two. The document on which it was based was not an international agreement or treaty, but a newspaper report. Its scope, moreover, was not so much the general and ongoing attitude of the Japanese government in its relations with Korea, although fishing rights, especially around Cheju Island, were becoming a standing issue between the two countries, as the alleged physical maltreatment of individual Japanese by individual Koreans. In other words, it raised the issue of the private, 'natural' so to speak, rights of Japanese subjects, and the duty of the government to protect them in foreign places. One important feature, however, Inoue's third question did have in common with his other two. Implicit in it was a demand that the Japanese authorities should be more assertive in their dealings with Korea. The report had appeared in mid-July 1890 issues of various Tokyo newspapers and, as repeated by Aoki, read as follows:

> On the third day of this month, Japanese fishermen went ashore in the district of Maengyong, Cheju Island, to draw water. When the son of a Korean named Yang Chong-sin spotted them, he violently refused to allow them to draw water, whereupon the fishermen got very angry and chased him away. When Yang Chong-sin came out of his house and turned on them, the fishermen were eventually forced to draw their swords, and in self-defence killed Chong-sin and forthwith took to their heels. We understand that on the fifth, the Cheju officials called together all the Japanese fishermen in the seas round that island and questioned each of them. In particular, a certain Mr Hashimoto, who is a native of Saga Prefecture, was imprisoned in the local jail. He obtained his release only after a number of days and after being examined a number of times in the District Office

garden, at the end of which he sealed his statements with a thumb-print. Moreover, on the nineteenth the [Korean] officials ordered the Japanese fishing-boats to leave the seas around the island and on the twenty-first they all moved away.

(DNTGS: 1106)

Inoue desired to know if this report were true and, if so, what action the Japanese government intended to take in connection with it. It may be noted, purely by the way, that neither the journalist originally responsible for the story, nor any of the government officials or Members of the House of Representatives subsequently concerned with it, seems to have thought it strange that Japanese fishermen should be going about their business armed with swords.

In his statement, the Foreign Minister in effect denied the truth of the report and argued that there was thus no case to take up with the Korean authorities. More than once he said that if the story had been accurate, the Japanese government would have made representations to its Korean counterpart, but, even in that case, it would have acted discreetly, and not indulged in 'open' or 'rigorous' recriminations. Nevertheless, information reaching the Japanese Foreign Ministry from the Korean government and private Japanese sources indicated that a Japanese fisherman, Hashimoto Gonzaburō, had been involved in a number of separate, and perhaps fairly trivial, incidents, which presumably had become merged into one bigger affair in the pages of the metropolitan press.

A Korean named Yang Chong-sin had been murdered in July of the previous year; and in the course of their investigations the local Korean officials had questioned groups of Japanese fishermen. One of these, Hashimoto Gonzaburō, whose boat was moored at the offshore isle of Piyang-do, had at first denied knowing anything about the matter. Later, however, when interrogated again by a Korean official at Maengyong, Hashimoto described how 'on that day' (of the killing, presumably), two other Japanese fishermen had come close to the spot where he was fishing and insisted that they urgently needed fresh water. These two men then went ashore, but the local peasants would not let them draw water. Returning to their boat, they persuaded Hashimoto to accompany them back to the well. This time the Japanese got what they wanted, apparently without further incident, and returned once again to their craft: 'Then we did not fish here any longer but, turning towards the south of Huksan Island and saying "we shall get away now", we left the spot' (DNTGS: 1106). 'With that', Aoki concluded, 'the whole incident came to an end.' In particular, he insisted, Hashimoto had never been subjected to imprisonment, or even unduly onerous questioning.

Inoue was given leave by the Speaker to comment (DNTGS: 1107) on Aoki's statement. There were really two parts to what he had to say. In the first section of his speech, even though he called the Foreign Minister's reply detailed and truthful, he attempted, rather lamely, to denigrate it as 'irresponsible'. It was irresponsible, so he claimed, because it differed in a number of very minor matters of fact or interpretation from what he, Inoue, believed to be the case. Perhaps the only telling point Inoue made at this juncture was on the vexed subject of the export of *otane-ninjin* from Korea. He argued that it was not really good enough for the Foreign Minister to put forward as an excuse for inaction in this matter diminishing demand in Japan. Japanese merchants, after all, might well be interested in the much bigger, and seemingly far more lucrative, market for the carrots in China, where 'Dutch' doctors were not so fashionable as in Japan:

> It is a matter of bringing them from Korea to Nagasaki, and from Nagasaki to Shanghai. If this is done, goods bought for ¥1 in Korea can be sold for ¥15 when they go to Shanghai. Generally speaking, trade is not [just] a matter of bringing from foreign countries articles which are deemed to be in demand in one's own country. So long as it is profitable, even though one does not bring them into one's own country, they may be taken anywhere.

With regard to the affair of the Japanese fishermen and boorish Korean peasants on Cheju Island, Inoue waxed indignant at what he claimed to be the Foreign Minister's, and the Japanese government's, attitude of polite indifference. 'He has said in effect, "I have not yet had any news of Cheju; because I have not had any, I know nothing about it".' Aoki, in fact, had made it clear that the Japanese authorities had learnt of the slaying of Yang and the alleged sufferings of Hashimoto, but their information had been substantially different from that purveyed in the columns of the press. Inoue chose to ignore this aspect of things, however, and stated that the government should always be ready to take action in cases like this, even if it had nothing better to go on than newspaper articles and other hearsay.

That evidence of this type did not altogether lend itself to such treatment became clear in the next few minutes of Inoue's expostulations when he disclosed that, according to his latest information, the principal Japanese involved had been a Hashimoto Ukichi, not Gonzaburō, and his father Kentarō and, further, that these Hashimotos were natives of

Saganoseki in Ōita Prefecture, not of Saga Prefecture. The source of Inoue's new revelations proved to be a private letter that he had only just received from a member of the staff of the Great Japan Marine Products Company, a Saganoseki concern. This gentleman wrote that he was communicating with Inoue after reading a notice of his parliamentary question in the *Jiji shimpō* newspaper, and went on:

> Well now, this person Hashimoto Ukichi was in the vicinity of Piyang-do Island when Korean officials came along, forcibly arrested him, surrounded the boat, and kept him under guard, day and night, without even letting him move. Then Ukichi's father, Kentarō, arrived to rescue his son and, although he made apologies he was repeatedly refused permission. Even though he tried going to a number of Korean government offices, he could not get permission at any of them. 'At last the climax came when about seven hundred Koreans gathered round, took hold of me and my son and after closely examining us, made us write out depositions saying this and that, and we sealed those depositions.'

The writer of the letter promised to forward copies of the depositions mentioned, if required. After announcing this latest turn of events in the fisherfolk's saga, Inoue summed up his criticism of what he considered the lackadaisical attitude of the Japanese government in this and other matters:

> When you try saying that even though this has taken place you will let sleeping dogs lie because the people concerned have made no appeal, and that you will do nothing because there is no information from the [Japanese] Minister and consuls [in Korea], then we are forced to ask why high-ranking Ministers are sent out to protect our nationals in foreign countries, and why consuls are sent out.

The second, and shorter, part of Inoue's speech consisted of an expression of concern about the broad pattern and trends of Japanese relations with Korea, and Japan's general standing in east Asia. His remarks on these topics were terse. On the other hand, they reflect a high degree of personal and emotional involvement. One may readily admit that the specific matters he had raised in the Diet did impinge on wider problems in Japanese–Korean relations at the time as well as being, from another point of view, perfectly good sticks for radical Liberals to apply to bureaucratic backs. Nevertheless, there can be little doubt that this concluding section of his speech indicates in terms of his own inner hopes and frustrations why he had bothered to bombard the authorities with a set of somewhat footling questions, based on allegations about minor discrepancies in the conduct of the nation's diplomacy and on unsubstantiated press reports.

Inoue declared that he had spent four years travelling in Korea, China and Russia between 1882 and 1886. Harking back to the celebrated Kim Ok-kiun and the attempted *coup* by the Korean Independence Party in 1884, he averred that this had drastically changed the Japanese government's attitude towards Korea and, by implication, east Asia generally. Before 1884, there were signs that it had decided to help Korea and make her independent. After 1884, however, the same government 'changes course and pretends that we know nothing of, and do not participate in, east Asian affairs'. Clearly, Inoue was pleading for a more positive, reformist-cum-interventionist policy *vis-à-vis* Korea. Apart from any long-term risks Japan might incur from the government's apparent indifference to conditions in Asia, he said that for it to vacillate between intervention and non-intervention as it had done in the previous decade created immediate short-term problems of the kind illustrated by his questions, problems that affected the civil rights and commercial opportunities of Japanese subjects.

The speech closed on a note of guarded optimism. Even the incumbent cabinet ministers, claimed Inoue, had acknowledged that the 'problem of east Asia' was 'much more important' than either treaty revision or any issue of domestic politics. Consequently, 'even today, provided that they have perceived their mistakes, I am hopeful that they will make it their absolutely unchanging duty to consolidate the independent supremacy of Japan in east Asia'.

The Foreign Minister made a very brief and, of course, impromptu reply to what Inoue Kakugorō had just said. In this, Aoki chose to concentrate on the problem of the wider aims of Japanese foreign policy, thus ignoring very largely the points at dispute in the specific questions raised by Inoue. With regard to these, however, he did spend a moment pointing out that 'since Representative Inoue has had the cheek to be always asking questions about my business of diplomacy, this time I thought I would really go into matters and tried to carry out a full investigation'. Something of the acerbity existing between the Foreign Ministry and 'Representative Inoue' can be gleaned from this.

Aoki then proceeded to explain that he had been living in Europe during the mid-1880s, and therefore had had nothing personally to do with the alleged change in Japanese official thinking about that time. With respect to existing Japanese policy towards Korea, that is, the policy currently being implemented by the cabinet of which he was a member, he intended 'to make as few alterations as possible in the future'. Aoki's summing up of the guidelines which the Japanese government wished in 1891 to follow in its dealings with east Asia is quite masterly. His words are predominantly, and properly, prudent; but they also have a definite undertone of firmness:

> above all, to leave things as they are . . . the government intends . . . to make as few mistakes as possible with regard to Korea, China or any other country. Provided that diplomacy is conducted in peace, that is how it is. Should troubles arise, however, it will cost money. Perhaps it will require blood and iron, and it will be serious. It is not possible to make declarations on the spur of the moment about what we shall do. However, the government is discreetly taking up its own position and rather than letting the dignity of Japan be impaired by one jot in the community of Asia, we shall widen the national powers of this country. Among those national powers we shall strive diligently to broaden the national power in terms of politics, together with the so-called national power in terms of trade, and to make this country shine forth in the community of Asia.
>
> (DNTGS: 1108)

Inoue Kakugorō, in one sentence, pronounced himself satisfied with these assurances.

THE HOUSE OF PEERS

The House of Peers discussed foreign affairs at one of its first routine working meetings held on Friday 19 December 1890 (DNTGS: 31–42). The debate centred on a written motion that had been tabled by Viscount Tani Kanjō and Tomita Tetsunosuke. This motion was similar to a private member's bill, and took the form of a gently remonstrative memorial to the government, concerning the general economic plight of the country and the urgent need to rectify this by regaining tariff autonomy and then imposing protective duties on imports. It was accompanied by a fairly lengthy explanatory memorandum and read as follows:

> The House of Peers of the Imperial Diet considers as matters of the utmost urgency the calculation of the optimum volume of merchandise to be imported from overseas in terms of the national interest, and the levy of customs duty in order to protect the Empire's industries and at the same time increase its national revenue. Therefore, and in conformity with the treaty between our government and the United States of America ratified in April 1889,[10] we earnestly hope and hereby recommend that the government undertake policies with a view to amending the various articles in the treaties at present in force

with foreign countries that relate to customs duties and are said to require the consent of the treaty Powers, and [with a view to] determining and implementing regulations for customs duty and foreign trade in each of the open ports, thereby restoring full national sovereignty to the Empire, and at the same time that the government lose little or no time in devising and enforcing suitable customs duties and general trade regulations.

Proposers: Viscount Tani Kanjō
Tomita Tetsunosuke

15 December 1890   Seconders: [62 names]
(DNTGS: 31–2)

The House met to discuss this recommendation at 10.30 a.m., under the supervision of its President, Count Itō Hirobumi.

Itō called on Tani Kanjō, as the leading sponsor of the motion, to open the debate. Tani, good soldier and staunch and learned Confucianist that he was, stood to the Right of the Japanese political spectrum at the time (Mason 1969: 112–18). As was to be expected, his views were firm, but they were by no means immoderately expressed. He pleaded for recognition both by Japanese and by foreign governments of the grave dislocation and distress overtaking Japanese agriculture and traditional manufacturing industries, as a result of the influx of cheap goods from abroad. He also made much of the fact that Japan had had an annual average deficit in its foreign trade of ¥6–7 million ever since the Restoration in 1868, and that the figure for 1890 alone approached ¥36 million; this sudden increase apparently being due, among other things, to emergency imports of rice.

Both these evils of chronic economic depression and mounting loss of gold reserves from the national treasury could be blamed on the existing treaties which had prevented Japan from raising the level of customs duty above a mere 5 per cent *ad valorem*, thereby making Western imports far too cheap and far too popular for the national good. These treaties, Tani declared quite correctly, had been forced on Japan when the country was in its 'infancy' and the people 'had no understanding of the nature of international relations'. Tani quickly explained that at first the Japanese alone were to blame for this state of affairs; what riled him and many others was the failure of the Powers to agree to treaty revision, even though the Japanese had made every effort to mend their ways:

Since then we have founded universities and primary schools and other kinds of colleges, and we are daily shifting to Western civilization. We have supplied facilities for marine transport; we have opened railways; we have provided postal and telegraphic services and so forth. Moreover, we have sent various officials overseas to foreign countries and not only have we cultivated diplomatic relations, but I think it can be said that we have done all we can to create friendship for foreign countries. Nevertheless, on the subject of the revision of these foreign treaties, they had, as you know, a fixed term – a limited duration – but that period has already been exceeded by almost twenty years and still nothing has been done.

The adverse foreign trade balance spoke for itself. The depressed industries which Tani mentioned by name were silk weaving, especially the traditional fine brocades of the Nishijin quarter of Kyōto; the new mechanized cotton spinning businesses; and, to a lesser extent, sugar cultivation. He alluded to another problem area in the national economy, domestic production of rape seed oil and traditional lamps, when, speaking of the loss of gold reserves, he said that Japan was like one of the imported Western 'contraptions' that used kerosene and were flooding the market. 'At length, there will be a time when there is no more [kerosene] oil.'

This picture of unrelieved economic woe attributable to foreign oppression compelled Tani and his supporters to urge the cabinet to concentrate on regaining tariff autonomy in any fresh negotiations for revision with the Powers. Moreover, the implied willingness to defer recovery of judicial rights for the time being was, of course, directly contrary to what the Foreign Minister, in his speech to the House of Representatives, had indicated would be the government's approach. It also followed, and indeed the motion explicitly stated, that the Japanese authorities should impose protective duties on most foreign imports, once diplomacy won them back the right to do so.

Tani based his case for these policies on a maxim of 'the ancients' – 'When food and clothing suffice, decorum is manifest' (*Kuan Tzu*: I). In other words, if a choice had to be made, the kind of economic welfare to be achieved through regaining the power to institute a protective tariff must take priority over judicial or other institutional reforms which were in the ultimate analysis mere 'refinements'. He felt that the Japanese government was inclined to busy itself with these secondary matters, and to take too much pride in its architectural achievements, Western-style. Even the modern army and navy would be useless without a properly prosperous economy to support them:

So long as things are left as they are, slowly but surely, as I said earlier, the Treasury's store of money will decrease, and the lamp has to go out when the oil is all used. In such an event, even though the Army and Navy Ministers have repeatedly called for expansions of armaments, what will become of these? If, in the end, Japan's seminal agriculture, industry and commerce were all to grow poverty-stricken, no matter how many warships the navy had and no matter how many soldiers were in the army, we would have done no more than dress a skeleton in helmet and armour, and it would be quite incapable of doing any work. Is this not truly an awful prospect?

(DNTGS: 33)

Public opinion, foreign as well as domestic, occupied a prominent place in Tani's speech, as, indeed, it did in the debate as a whole. Treaty revision, in particular an improvement in the economy through a higher tariff was, he claimed, the heartfelt desire of all Japanese; and the Diet had been set up, 'praise be,' to give expression to such general wishes. Hitherto, 'under a completely absolutist system of government, nobody apart from a few officials has had an opportunity to complain about these matters'.[11] A remonstrance or piece of 'advice to the government' took on especial force and cogency when the responsible authorities were still unable to secure revision after nearly twenty years of effort, and when it was still impossible to discern current official thinking on the problem even after the Foreign Minister had already spoken at length about it in the Diet. In this fashion, the chief sponsor of the motion frequently invoked domestic public opinion as mediated through the Diet in order to goad his former colleagues in the cabinet into taking more strenuous action along the lines he favoured.

The self-confessed champion of 'Japanism' (*Nihon-shūgi*) also took the trouble to include in his speech several appeals, notable for their courtesy, to humane and enlightened opinion in foreign lands to concede Japan's case as a matter of common justice. With this call to exotic altruism went a reminder that trade by its very nature was supposed to be equally beneficial to the parties engaged in it, and a warning that if Japan continued to suffer from economic dislocation and depletion of monetary reserves, popular distress would lead to a breakdown of law and order. In that case, foreign residents would find themselves exposed to a revival of the xenophobic terrorism (*jōi*) that had characterized the troubled years before the Restoration of 1868. 'Things are bound to go downhill; and when ruffians are at large will the fault be theirs [i.e. the foreigners'] or ours? Apart from petitioning our ancestral gods to decide, there will be nothing we can do' (DNTGS: 33).

A tariff policy that would at least be mildly protective was the ultimate aim of the supporters of the motion. Until Japan's new industries based on Western technology – in 1890, mechanized cotton spinning was the most obvious but there were, and would be, others – possessed sufficient capital and technical skill to survive competition from abroad, they should be sheltered behind a sort of protective dyke, though this need not be so high nor so massive as to exclude foreign goods entirely.

> Our aspirations do not lie in the direction of imposing unreasonable customs duties and excluding outsiders. The regrettable truth is that they [spring from] a compassionate desire to strike a balance somehow and generally even things up.
>
> (DNTGS: 33)

History on the whole, and subsequent Japanese experience, have certainly vindicated Tani in this matter. Economic development of the sort and on the scale he and many others have desired does not occur by some freak of nature. It needs to be planned and fostered with a whole battery of fiscal and administrative weapons, including judicious use of the tariff. Tani, like Aoki Shūzō, had an evident faith in the capacity of his countrymen to succeed in the modern industrial world, given a modicum of help from their government. 'Speaking of the attributes of our country's people, they are not only very rich in scholarship but also resourceful. Furthermore, they are specially proficient in the arts and crafts' (DNTGS: 33). This emphasis on the already abundant human resources of Japan, as opposed to its small territory and relative poverty in natural resources, led Tani to condemn as 'backward and foolish' any nation that exported minerals and largely unprocessed products, and imported finished manufactures. 'Wise' countries, he insisted, unless like Russia or China they happened to be exceptionally large and well endowed, did precisely the opposite. His long-term prescription for Japan in 1890 implied the acquisition of wealth and strength through the export of manufactures; and he looked to the steady growth of modern industry behind a tariff wall. Despite the ups-and-downs and notwithstanding the environmental and other, more serious, setbacks involved, this is the course that Japan has sought to follow with a well known degree of success. Tani, therefore, for all his political and ideological conservatism and even reactionary impulses, in economic matters spoke with great foresight and moderation, and as a man ready to welcome wholesale change and innovation. His words occasionally have a bite of humour, too, as with his earlier reference to 'dressing a skeleton in helmet and armour' when talking of the government's aspirations for the army and navy:

Finally . . . we shall have spent ¥5 million year after year and all we shall have to show for it will be those splendid government buildings of brick and stone; and, regardless of their numbers, a state of affairs in which scholars are simply dried vegetables[12] is bound to prevail in the long run.

(DNTGS: 33)

This gibe about scholars apparently did not offend Katō Hiroyuki to whom the President next gave the rostrum. Katō, a celebrated student of Western political thought and its possible applications to Japan, was president of Tokyo Imperial University at the time. He had proved to be a useful henchman of the governing Sat–Chō cliques since his conversion from radical Liberalism seventeen years previously. This change of intellectual allegiance had been consolidated by marriages between his children and those of ministers of state.

In his speech Katō expressed a deep and fervent sympathy with the broad aims of the motion and the underlying intentions of its sponsors, and said that these would be sure to win the approval of all Japanese, let alone all Members of the House of Peers. Nevertheless, he announced that he meant to oppose the motion on two grounds. In the first place, just because the problem was so generally recognized, and not least by the ministers in the cabinet, there was little point in tabling such a motion with the idea of 'presenting it pompously to the government' (DNTGS: 33). Behaviour of that kind would be unnecessarily solicitous; and Katō likened it to telling a man convalescing after a serious illness and meticulously obeying his doctors' instructions to take good care of himself. In the second place, Katō found the wording of the motion unacceptably vague, observing that if it were 'a recommendation about ways and means of regaining tariff autonomy' it would probably command his support. He admitted that this defect followed un-avoidably from the cabinet's refusal to divulge details of its plans for revising the treaties. However, as it stood, the proposal was bereft of any suggestion with regard to 'ways and means'. Therefore it should be rejected.

Katō also made the point, incidental to his arguments at the time but historically speaking sound and shrewd, that the public opinion so vaunted by Tani had existed prior to the inauguration of the Imperial Diet. The only difference was that what had been before 1890 'spasmodic' expression of popular feelings, through newspapers and private representations to the government and so forth, had now become 'regularized' with the setting up of representative institutions (DNTGS: 34).

Tomita Tetsunosuke, the other leading sponsor of the motion, spoke next. He began by observing, somewhat slyly, that those in favour did not think of the government of Japan as an invalid or convalescent. If Katō or other friends of the cabinet chose to see things in this way, that was their affair. What supporters of the motion did believe, however, was that the people of Japan were sick – economically sick, that is.

Tomita then went on to reiterate some of the arguments that Tani had already advanced. The motion deserved support not just because restoration of tariff autonomy, along with the other rights granted away in the past, would give back to Japan a proper measure of dignity and independence in a world of jealously sovereign nation states. There were other, more pressing practical considerations, namely, the state of the economy. Higher customs duties would enable the government to cut internal taxes 'which today are so very heavy', and to balance the country's foreign trade. In a moment of mild drama, Tomita gestured towards his fellows in the House of Peers and exclaimed:

> Well, as for the goods we buy from abroad . . . . They are in front of our eyes! How about the clothes I and all of you are wearing? I do not know where they were made, but I do know that the raw material in them was not produced in Japan. I know also that they were not manufactured by the people of Japan. The manufacturing tax on them was paid to foreign governments. The costs of manufacture have been paid to foreign peoples. The charges for shipping them have been paid to foreigners. That is how things are!
>
> (DNTGS: 34)

Despite the time spent on pointing up particular discrepancies and aberrations, the chief purpose of Tomita's speech was to underline the dogma that a country prospered to the extent that it took care of its 'human potential' and managed to import raw materials and export manufactures. 'By no manner of means does [a country] develop naturally. Every country takes care of itself by exploiting its human potential' (DNTGS: 34). In order to substantiate this contention, which he obviously regarded as basic to the whole argument for a protective tariff, Tomita referred at length to the history of England, 'the place which I hold in highest esteem. . . . None will ever surpass England in prosperity of trade and in prosperity of manufacturing industry.' England, he claimed in a knowledgeable disquisition on the subject, had for two or three centuries been implacably protectionist. It had used Navigation Acts and a host of laws and regulations to nurture its shipping and manufactures, to the great detriment of foreign seafarers like the Dutch, and foreign producers of textiles like the Indian makers of muslin and other fine cotton cloths. The English had only lately taken up the doctrines of Free Trade as if it were some kind of religion, after the loss of their American colonies, and just when it had suited their overall commercial and manufacturing interests to do so.[13]

Yamaguchi Naoyoshi followed Tomita with some further reasons for supporting the motion. Cheap imports damaged sugar and rape seed in the agricultural sector of the economy; silk weaving, cotton spinning and nail manufacture in the industrial sector. In addition, the Army Ministry purchased duck cloth in England for military uniforms, even though this was an article produced in Japan. Admittedly, native Japanese industries suffered from various deficiencies such as 'rushed work' and shortages of capital and skilled labour, but the most serious cause of the general economic distress was 'business competition' as a result of the enforced low tariff. 'If we let matters continue thus . . . our forty million countrymen will be forcibly deprived, no less, of half the handicrafts with which Heaven has chosen to endow them' (DNTGS: 35).

Yamaguchi had a liking for statistics. One calculation he had done showed that the nominal 5 per cent *ad valorem* duty allowed by the existing treaties boiled down in practice to approximately 3.5 per cent. The original treaty concluded by the Tokugawa *bakufu* with Commodore Perry had permitted a 35 per cent duty on manufactures and 20 per cent on other imports; in 1890, the nascent mechanized cotton spinning industry would be helped by a 10 per cent duty, and secured by 20 per cent. The loss sustained by the national treasury as a result of the compulsory re-negotiation of the treaties in 1866 amounted to an enormous sum. In gross terms, Yamaguchi reckoned it to be between ¥200 and ¥250 million. This money could have been available to spend on coastal defences, the navy, or internal reforms, all of which, again according to the general run of thinking in 1890, required considerable fiscal outlays. Moreover, calculated at ¥11 or ¥12 million a year, the loss in customs revenue equalled the total annual taxes collected from Shikoku and Kyūshū.

And so just one evening of negotiations resulted in the grabbing of Kyūshū and Shikoku. . . . Suppose that [these] two territories . . . were captured and held down by a fleet of ironclads, what would be the reaction of our government and forty million subjects? Certainly, we would sacrifice life and property seeking to regain them. Yet the damage arising from the treaties is disregarded. I consider this a truly deplorable state of affairs.

(DNTGS: 35)

At the time when commercial treaties were first signed with Perry and other Western envoys, the Japanese authorities had been assured that as trade grew so would their customs revenue. However, this had failed to happen. In part, the reason had been the naivety of the Japanese in economic matters:

> The hungry warrior played with a toothpick. Money did not concern him at all. To-day, we are still heirs to this out-moded custom; and the people of the entire country, in matters of economics, are like forlorn stars on a moonlit night.

> (DNTGS: 35)

The main reason, however, had been the iniquitously low 5 per cent rate of duty. As a result, customs receipts in 1890 amounted to just over ¥4 million, a sum that barely sufficed to pay the official costs of diplomacy.

Yamaguchi considered that 'our forty million people should bear in mind this line of reasoning and make enquiries about the suspension of treaty revision'. He also believed that the government and nation should unite to 'resolve on a policy to regain [tariff rights]'. Such a policy would have to suit foreign requirements; and any new – presumably, he was thinking in terms of not fully equal – treaties concluded between Japan and the Powers would have to be of strictly limited duration.

The debate on Tani Kanjō's and Tomita Tetsunosuke's motion on the tariff was suspended between 12.35 and 1.15 p.m., while the House had a short lunch-time break. When discussion resumed, the majority of speakers continued to be in favour of the motion. Two Members who did venture to join with Katō Hiroyuki in opposing it were Okauchi Shigetoshi and Ozaki Saburō.

Okauchi, like Katō before him, expressed complete agreement with the general intention of the motion, but objected to its emphasis on tariff matters. He believed restoration of full judicial sovereignty, impairment of which 'invalidates the Constitution,' to be the more vital objective in any renewed treaty negotiations. Therefore, while naturally not opposed to the idea of regaining tariff autonomy, he could not vote for the motion in its present form.

> There is no harm, [I agree], in increasing the tariff slightly and enlarging the national revenues. But I doubt very much if it can ever be preferable to regaining extra-territorial [judicial] rights and making the Constitution effective. I could not condone action by the House of Peers of the Imperial Diet [which would indicate that] we had an interest in the restoration of tariff autonomy alone.

> (DNTGS: 39)

Ozaki Saburō, who addressed the House immediately after the midday recess, made a longer and more closely argued speech against the motion. He, too, disagreed with it fundamentally on the grounds that abolition of consular jurisdiction should take precedence over recovery of sovereignty in customs matters. His main argument for this view was that it had been shortages of foreign capital and foreign technical skills, and not the low tariff, that had reduced the Japanese economy to desperate straits. Domestic industry could benefit from foreign money and foreign expertise only if aliens were allowed to live and work freely in the interior of the country. However, it would be dangerous for reasons of general civil administration to permit this, unless consular jurisdiction were abolished first and all foreign residents made subject to Japanese laws and criminal procedure.

Ozaki also poured cold water on the implication contained in many of the remarks of the supporters of the motion that customs revenue would grow in direct proportion to increases in the rate of duty. This suggestion he denounced as 'simply an exercise in arithmetic', because the price of imports would soon be beyond the purses of what was held to be an already seriously impoverished Japanese population. Moreover, overseas trade – and with it Japan's hopes of further economic progress – would dwindle as a result of any drastic rise in import duties:

> Some of you may feel that even if imports do decrease, it will be to the good. However, in that case it will be quite impossible to maintain the national economy. If imports were to decrease, exports also would be bound to decrease.
>
> (DNTGS: 36)

Finally, if Tomita Tetsunosuke had been able to cite the case of England as an example of a country that had followed a ruthless and highly successful policy of commercial and industrial protection over a period of centuries, Ozaki had his own European model. This was Imperial Russia which, he said quite correctly, had made significant economic advances since 1700 by doing just the opposite. Russia, that is to say, had welcomed foreign imports and capital and had encouraged merchants and artisans to settle within its borders.

> Of course, Russians, too . . . took part in opening up the country. There has been absolutely no cause for alarm in having Russians, Germans, French or English make industry prosper in this way, as these [other] nationals are all under the same laws as the Russian people and have an obligation to pay taxes.
>
> (DNTGS: 37)

Other participants in the debate, who were in favour of the motion, took it on themselves to answer the objections raised by Katō, Okauchi and Ozaki. They noted with satisfaction that all the objectors shared the feelings of patriotic fervour and concern that had prompted Tani and Tomita to table their motion. Speakers who wanted the House to pass this motion also made it clear that, in their opinion, Japan had seemingly found herself in the unenviable situation of having to rank the two great objectives of treaty revision in some order of priority. In that case, they favoured putting the need to regain tariff autonomy first, and recovery of judicial rights second. Another point of difference between supporters and opponents of the motion concerned the role of the Diet as a supreme organ of public opinion. Supporters stoutly maintained that the Diet and House of Peers, if they were to function as they should, had to be prepared to press their opinion on great national issues of the day on members of the cabinet in this formal way. For them, it was virtually a matter of constitutional principle. Opponents of the motion demurred for one reason or another. One last notable theme in the discussion is that all these afternoon speakers for the motion showed some degree of understandable impatience and truculence when reflecting on the whole sorry story of foreign political coercion and economic exploitation.

Wakao Ippei spoke hesitatingly and with a stammer; nevertheless he made a short and effective speech along these general lines. He countered the proposition put forward by Katō that the motion represented nothing more than a needless embarrassment to the government with the remark that 'with the opening of this Imperial Diet, we have to pass motions which represent the main trends of public opinion'. Equally, the suggestion from Ozaki and Okauchi that recovery of judicial rights should take precedence over regaining tariff autonomy did not carry much weight with Wakao. He declared that consular jurisdiction affected only a limited number of Japanese living in the treaty ports. Tariff problems, on the other hand, handicapped the whole nation. Wakao also asked the House to consider the heavy wastage of administrative costs, as a result of the Treasury being forced to collect in internal taxes sums of money that could be far more easily raised through imposing a higher tariff. As an example of such wastage, he gave the tax on confectionery. This brought in ¥600,000 a year to the government, but cost ¥300,000 to collect. A small duty on imported sugar passing through Yokohama would yield as much in revenue for a fraction of the cost. For these reasons, Wakao hoped that the House would approve of the motion, and that the government would accept it and hasten to re-open negotiations with the treaty Powers. Should the latter prove obdurate, 'it will indeed be a matter of life and death. Sacrificing both our fortunes and ourselves, I believe we shall labour to the utmost on behalf of the country' (DNTGS: 37).

Viscount Matsudaira Nobumasa, the son of a *bakufu* Great Councillor (*rojū*), did not add very much to the case for the motion, apart from mentioning that the United States had already agreed to the restoration of tariff autonomy in their abortive 1878 treaty with Japan. However, Matsudaira indulged in a moment or two of personal reminiscence; and first-hand memories, fleeting though they may be, are always of some interest to the historian. Moreover, the fact that he, the son of a famous father and a scion of the once mighty Tokugawa, could hold a seat and speak in the Imperial Diet is some small testimony to the 'national reconciliation' aspect of mid-Meiji politics.

following the conference held in 1866 we were about to lose Shikoku and Kyūshū. At that time, people like myself were only ten years old; and my father was one of the *bakufu*'s senior councillors. Diplomacy in those days was extraordinarily difficult, and it seemed as if negotiations would be broken off, and Edo castle burnt. When I recall those times, they were truly unbearably sad. Later on, in an attempt to redress the import-export imbalance, I formed a league; and about 1875 or 1876 under the name of the Anonymous Society (*Bōkai*) we pledged ourselves never to use Western goods. Our strength was too slight, however, to give us much chance of realizing our hopes.

Happily, an Imperial Diet has [now] been convened, people such as myself have been able to take seats in the House of Peers, and I have been given the opportunity to express my own views on the motion after more distinguished people [have expressed theirs]. All of which is highly gratifying. I earnestly hope that the entire House will approve the motion and pass it forthwith.

(DNTGS: 38–9)

Baron Watanabe Kiyoshi spoke at far greater length than either Wakao Ippei or Matsudaira Nobumasa, but covered much the same ground as earlier speakers. He condemned the treaty Powers for their 'arrogance', declaring that delay in securing revision had not been the fault of the Japanese: 'Have our Ministers been discourteous? Has there been anything wrong with our politics or laws? Have they had any cause to grumble and complain about our telegraph, mail and shipping services or lighthouses?' (DNTGS: 40). Watanabe considered that both judicial and tariff rights should be restored immediately and in full by means of new and completely equal treaties. However, if it did come to having to make choices, then the Japanese government should direct its diplomatic energies and skill to winning back control over the tariff, so that the country might 'at any rate be kept alive'.

By far the most reflective and persuasive of the second group of speeches for the motion was that made by Miura Yasushi. This speaker answered Katō's criticism of the motion as being too general to be of any use by saying that because of the exigencies of secret diplomacy 'there is absolutely nothing we can do about this objection' (DNTGS: 37–8).

Miura also made some specific comments on the points raised by Ozaki Saburō. In the first place, assuming that the government could negotiate either for full judicial sovereignty or for tariff rights but not for both at the same time, then it was in order for the Diet to press for the latter 'which are the basis of the national economy'. However, if the government had already definitely decided to work first for restoration of judicial rights, he, for one, would accept that decision without further cavil. In the second place, Miura stated that he too favoured in principle the introduction of foreign capital and skills to the hinterland of Japan, but felt that the native economy was in no position to hold its own against the even greater degree of competition that would result from such developments, while it still suffered from an average adverse trade balance of ¥6 million a year.

> Speaking generally, I would ask you to agree that the country cannot make good until a way is found out of the disastrous situation of having ¥6 million unfailingly drain away every year, like a consumptive or a diabetic losing blood or vital fluid day after day, night after night.
>
> (DNTGS: 38)

Miura mingled some fairly perceptive observations of his own with these replies to the critics of the motion. Commenting on the ruinously cheap prices of imported consumer goods in Japan, he said:

> Japanese people, too, have feelings of patriotism and loyalty; and they would doubtless be reluctant to buy foreign goods [simply] because they were foreign goods and regardless of the price. But people [are swayed by] private as well as public [interest], and it goes against the grain to buy goods which are all too evidently expensive. The feeling that one ought to buy even foreign goods if the price is low is ordinary human nature.
>
> (DNTGS: 38)

Other remarks dealt with the various rumours that were current concerning the probable course negotiations for treaty revision would take once they were resumed. According to some people, Miura said, revision could be obtained only by the Japanese government consenting to employ either 'a lot of' or 'only a few' – opinions differed as to the number contemplated – foreign officials in its judiciary and other administrative organs of direct concern to foreign residents. Had such a concession ever been made after 1889, it would, of course, have amounted to a reversion to Ōkuma Shigenobu's approach to the treaty problem. Another rumour discussed by Miura, which proved ultimately true, held that new treaties would be signed, and that these, although formally equal, would continue to deny Japan full autonomy in tariff matters for a fixed number of years, 'since the tariff is of special importance to the foreign merchants'. Miura cautioned against any willingness on the part of the Japanese government to do a deal along these lines, in view of the precarious state of the economy.

The section of this speech that is of most interest today is a passage where, stressing the fundamental obligation of the Diet to represent public opinion to the government and the corresponding duty of cabinet ministers to take note of such representations and act on them, Miura outlined a collectivist view of the state and its politics. Theories of this kind share something with more individualistic ideas of democracy and were certainly capable of being used to bolster and extend representative institutions in the Japanese context, by reason of their emphasis on the joint responsibility of governors and governed for the welfare of the state or commonwealth. Nevertheless, Miura's enunciation of them on this occasion stood close to the traditional, paternalistic 'family-state' norm of Japanese political thinking. His words also help to show how this norm, though generally endorsed by officialdom and soon to be known as *kokutai*, was not just foisted on the people below by the authorities from above. To a great extent, it sprang from the age-old experience and deep convictions of the nation at large, and could be used by the critics – Right-wing or Left-wing – as well as the friends of cabinets and their policies.

'Because there are plenty of nurses to look after the affliction and the method of nursing is beyond reproach, there is no need to worry.' That is what is meant by saying treaty revision can safely be left to the responsible authorities in the government. But this cannot be deemed kind; and it is to treat as strangers compatriots who have fallen sick, on the grounds that they in no way deserve our concern because they have friends and relatives. This state is the joint responsibility of our forty million compatriots. Accordingly, although the authorities may be fully concerned, if we also exert ourselves in various ways, worrying about shortcomings and taking note of what is badly done, the authorities, too, because of that, will take care where they have not taken care, and will come to regard as urgent what they have not [so far] regarded as urgent. Moreover, as the ancients said, 'office is apt to bewilder'; those in office are easily bewildered and so the opinions of bystanders are of some value.

Therefore, if forty million compatriots show deep concern, it is as brothers; and it is never better to keep quiet and let the government officials wear themselves out. If we do keep quiet, this betrays a lack of concern. Consequently what has been proposed to-day comes from feelings of loyalty and concern for the state for which we are jointly responsible. It is not possible to call it [i.e. the proposal] just, and then put it aside.

(DNTGS: 37)

The afternoon speakers so far had been Ozaki, Wakao, Miura, Matsudaira, Okauchi and Watanabe. After the last had finished, the President, Itō Hirobumi, announced that he was closing the debate, but relented when Toyama Masakazu said that he had some questions to put to the sponsors of the proposal. When allowed to take the rostrum, Toyama proceeded to make a rambling but thoughtful speech, which took the form of a set of serious and penetrating questions on the motion.

Toyama confessed to not being able to understand the constant assertion of those in favour of the motion that they represented a unanimous and settled 'public opinion'. He reminded the House that only twelve months earlier the Japanese people and press had been at odds among themselves on the whole treaty revision issue, with many voices crying that since it was still far too early to permit foreigners to reside and work in the interior of the country, the government should be chary about concluding fully equal treaties. Now, Toyama said, all this previous discord had apparently come to an end, and members of the House of Peers were being asked to believe that everybody in Japan was prepared for equal treaties and agreed that tariff autonomy, rather than abolition of consular jurisdiction, ought to be the prime aim in any renewed negotiations. Would public opinion, Toyama asked, definitely and unswervingly accept a possible ten, or even twenty, years' delay in the restoration of full judicial sovereignty?

Toyama also felt confused about the aim of the motion. On first reading it and the accompanying memorandum, and after listening to the speeches of its two sponsors, Tani and Tomita, he had been reasonably sure that its intention had been to put tariff autonomy ahead of full judicial sovereignty in importance. However, Watanabe Kiyoshi, a keen supporter, had appeared to be saying that both these 'rights' were of equal importance and that the government should negotiate for their simultaneous restoration. So what was the true aim of the motion?

Finally, still on the subject of ultimate aims, Toyama wished to know whether it was a motion simply urging a speedy recovery of tariff autonomy; or was it suggested that the government, once it had regained the power to do so, should proceed at once to impose import duties of an undeniably protective nature? The two things, he insisted, were rather different (DNTGS: 40–1).

Tani Kanjō was then asked by the President to reply to Toyama's queries. He avoided completely the one about public opinion; but, with respect to the motion's aims and intentions, Tani stated flatly that it arose from a concern with practical [i.e. economic] advantage, rather than arguing over 'empty [i.e. judicial] rights'. '[Our] chief ambition', he went on a moment or two later, 'has been to make quite clear to the authorities the hardships of the people and a state of affairs under which society in general daily disintegrates' (DNTGS: 41). Of course, recovery of judicial rights counted for a great deal; but a ¥6 million annual deficit in overseas trade would lead to certain destruction. This was the settled opinion of Tani and his associates. Rather mordantly and morbidly reverting to his own earlier metaphor of a skeleton, and applying it to Tomita's allusion to the dress of Members, he exclaimed 'You gentlemen in your Western clothes look almost like Westerners. But before long, your outward forms will be [made an empty sham] when death changes you into skeletons.' Aoki Shūzō's attempt to divert public attention away from treaty revision by impressing the House of Representatives with the glowing prospects awaiting Japanese trade and industry in China, came in for a similarly caustic comment or two: 'The speech sounded like an urgent appeal by the Minister for Agriculture and Commerce to make goods and take them to China for sale!' (DNTGS: 41). How could the Japanese economy ever take advantage of opportunities like this abroad, Tani asked indignantly, while it continued to suffer so catastrophically from the effects of cheap imports at home?

It was left to Viscount Torio Koyata, another 'political' army general and noted champion of ultra-conservatism to wind up the debate. He was in favour of the motion, albeit somewhat disingenuously, as the real purpose of his remarks was to ask the President to act on his earlier decision to terminate the proceedings.

Torio explained that he had expressed support for the motion when first approached by its sponsors. He approved of it in principle, and had considered it suitable material for the 'first utterance' of the House of

Peers. However, as he was at pains to point out, it had seemed suitable because he had expected nobody to disagree with it, and because treaty revision was the responsibility of neither the House of Peers nor the Imperial Diet as a whole. Further progress in the matter was not even the responsibility of the government of the Empire. Seldom can the real onus and blame for the economic and diplomatic impasse that thwarted Japan in 1890 have been put more firmly, or more deftly, on the shoulders of the offending foreigners!

Japanese opinion, in other words, was aroused and unified, yet powerless to achieve its demands. In this situation, Torio felt that protracted and 'meddlesome' discussion was not only futile, but possibly harmful to boot. 'If we adopt the motion simply as an expression of hope and sympathy with the government which at the moment is doing its utmost, I consider this will be enough' (DNTGS: 42). Hard diplomatic negotiations should be left to the responsible experts, in Torio's view. Since, he reminded his fellow Peers, 'we are not politicians or anything like that', it would be wrong for them or any other person not directly involved to submit detailed recommendations on the best way of achieving revision. In particular, he deplored the likely effect on foreign opinion of some of the more belligerent and, he hinted, vainglorious comments of previous speakers.

> people in the House of Peers have stated forcibly that . . . we must be ready to risk our bodies and our lives. . . . It is quite absurd. This sort of thing cannot be done. The various countries in the world have been established from long ago, but there is not one which has not on occasion fallen victim to attack from other countries. If one is to adopt that sort of unreasonable attitude, I myself was involved in the shooting at Shimonoseki and have not waited until now [to engage in military combat with the foreigners].
>
> (DNTGS: 41–2)

Torio's speech was full of paradox and irony, but its outlines are clear and it stands in the Diet record as a fitting finale to an animated and by no means uninteresting debate. Its principal demand was swiftly met. As soon as he had concluded, Baron Senke Takatomi requested that the closure motion be put. This was carried, as was a further suggestion, put by the President, that Tani's motion be passed by the Peers and presented to the government as a formal resolution of their House.

The debate, therefore, had come to an end, to be followed by a few minutes of altercation between some Members and the President on the latter's management of proceedings. Itō put these grumblers in their

place politely but firmly; and the House rose for the day at 3.30 p.m.
precisely.

On 13 February 1891, the House of Peers, with Prince Konoe Atsumaro
acting as its President, heard Aoki Shūzō reply to a question which had
been submitted to him by Tani Kanjō and Tomita Tetsunosuke on 20
December 1890 (DNTGS: 260). The question had arisen from a remark
about the 1878 commercial treaty with the United States made by Aoki
on 17 December in the course of his long speech to the House of
Representatives on the history of treaty revision. Aoki had said then
that the 1878 treaty had proved to be 'ineffective' (*mukō*). What
worried Tani and Tomita was that, for them, this same treaty possessed
considerable symbolic force as a worthy example of what could be
achieved in the field of tariff diplomacy. The agreement with America
had sanctioned in principle the restitution of full tariff rights to Japan;
so Tani and Tomita had explicitly referred to it in a thoroughly
approving fashion in their earlier proposals for action along these lines.
They now wished to know whether the Foreign Minister's dismissal of
the 1878 treaty as 'ineffective' meant that it had been annulled;
because, if so, this would signify the complete collapse of a major
bulwark in the case they were putting up for urgent re-negotiation of
the tariff.

In his reply, Aoki agreed that his words on the previous occasion
might have been 'a trifle misleading'; but he maintained that the phrase
in question needed to be read in the context of everything he had had
to say about the 1878 treaty. When speaking in the House of Representatives, he had mentioned a section of the agreement with the United
States which stated that it could come into force only after all the other
Powers had consented to the conclusion of similar treaties with Japan.
Since this condition had never been met, the 1878 treaty remained, for
all practical purposes, a dead letter. When thus replying to Tani and
Tomita in the House of Peers, Aoki took the trouble to read out the
relevant section (Article 10) of the treaty, and he explained that when
he had used the term 'ineffective' he had meant by this that it had never
been possible to put the treaty into effect. The word did not mean that
the treaty had been annulled; indeed it had been ratified in Washington
the following year, and still lived on as a matter of diplomatic form and,
perhaps, symbolic intent (DNTGS: 260).[14]

Tani Kanjō was given permission by the acting President to comment
on what Aoki had just said. Although his opening remark – 'The Foreign
Minister has replied today to a question which we submitted last year'
– might be taken as veiled criticism of a certain tardiness on the part of

that high official in attending to his parliamentary duties, the general tenor of Tani's speech was genial enough. He announced that Aoki's explanation confirmed what he and Tomita had thought to be the case all along, and so was 'reassuring' from their point of view. However, he felt that the real reasons for their questioning of 'ineffective' might not be clear from the necessarily condensed, and inevitably ambiguous wording of the memorandum that had accompanied their question.

The underlying motive, he was now at pains to tell the House, had been concern that the 1878 treaty had somehow lost validity. People like himself who thought recovery of tariff rights an urgent national priority attached great importance to the longstanding willingness of the United States to meet Japan's wishes in this matter. To discover that the treaty lacked validity was 'like seeing the motion which we had tabled turn into the discarded skin of a cicada, and the evidence we had so laboriously gathered reduced to nothing in a moment' (DNTGS: 261). Consequently, always bearing in mind the desperate state of the country's economy, they had felt compelled to obtain from the Foreign Minister some clarification of his remark.

Expanding for a moment or two on the general terms and circumstances of the 1878 treaty, Tani praised and thanked the United States for 'going to the trouble of framing a kind and considerate treaty with Japan', and expressed the hope that, even at this late stage, the other Powers would show themselves similarly well disposed. He also warned the Foreign Minister and anyone else who might be concerned in future negotiations for revision of the treaties 'to exercise the greatest care' with respect to this matter of the tariff, as it was vital to the well-being of the country.

Tani declared further that he and Tomita had not picked on these particular words of the Foreign Minister simply in order to quibble with him or to score cheap debating points. Moreover, if anybody but the Foreign Minister had talked of the American treaty as being 'ineffective', they would not have taken any notice at all. (The actual phrase Tani used to denote indifference was *baji-tōfu*, i.e. 'an east wind blowing in a horse's ear'. Horses were supposed to be unconcerned by the east wind because it heralded warmer weather.) However, in the overall economic and political circumstances, and taking into account the nature of the office of the person who had uttered the vexatious word, it had been a matter of legitimate patriotic concern to ask for further explanations. Tani's speech then, on this present occasion, had arisen from a desire to make it plain that the reasons for submitting the question about the epithet 'ineffective' had been serious and honourable. At the same time, he had intended to remedy some of the admitted deficiencies in the written memorandum for his and Tomita's question.

Some time after eight o'clock in the evening of 6 March 1891, Aoki came again to the House of Peers to answer Members' questions (DNTGS: 406–7). On this occasion, Itō Hirobumi was there to carry out his duties as President; and the questions had been submitted by Nishimura Shigeki and Marquis Saga Kintō on 23 February 1891. As summarized by Kudō Takeshige, they went as follows:-

1 Would foreigners be allowed to reside anywhere in the country?
2 Would foreigners be allowed to own land?
3 Would tariff autonomy be regained, and would the rates of duty be reformed?
4 Would foreigners or foreign ships be permitted to engage in coastal trade?
5 Would a law allowing for the naturalization of foreigners be enacted soon, or at some later date?

(Kudō 1901: I, 47–8)

After making his usual cautionary noises on the topic of diplomatic secrecy, which anyway his questioners had already made it clear they did not wish to see breached, Aoki replied to the effect that:

firstly, that as soon as fully equal treaties were concluded, these would by definition allow nationals of the parties involved to live anywhere in each other's territory [in other words, one of the Japanese government's aims in treaty revision was to secure the abolition of the system of treaty ports];

secondly, that foreigners would not be allowed to own land;

thirdly, that Japan could confidently look forward to regaining full tariff autonomy 'within a few years', but the sort of revisions the government was contemplating would not let it in the first instance do more than modify the existing tariff with a view to obtaining a modest increase in customs receipts [here Aoki was obviously thinking of the eventually successful strategy of settling for a full restoration of tariff rights after a fixed number of years];

fourthly, that neither foreigners nor foreign craft would be allowed to engage in coastal trade in Japanese waters under any new treaties [on this point, the Japanese were apparently prepared to stand firm and bring about a change in the existing situation, mainly at the expense of English interests];

fifthly, that since any regulations for the naturalization of foreigners had now to be approved by the Imperial Diet as a matter of constitutional procedure, this was not a matter on which the government could take independent action.

(see DNTGS: 407)

At the beginning of his speech which, in view of the lateness of the hour, was appropriately short as well as commendably factual and to the point, Aoki remarked that many members of the House of Peers had already gone home, but since what he had to say would be incorporated in the Diet Record, the absentees would be able to peruse his replies at their leisure. This comment is interesting as evidence that the Imperial Diet was well run from the technical point of view from the first. But what is even more gratifying to the historian is that this section of the Diet record reveals that before getting down to the substantive part of his reply, Aoki made a few highly pertinent and valuable general observations. This was the occasion on which he first spoke of treaty revision as a bridge which Japan must build and cross before she could make further progress. Progress in what direction, one might ask, only to discover that Aoki has dealt with this wider question also.

The circumstances were hardly less remarkable than what was actually said. Aoki was speaking half way through the Meiji era, and late one evening to a half-empty House of Peers on the very eve of the close of the first session of the first Imperial Diet. Moreover, although Foreign Minister at the time, Aoki was basically a second-rank official and politician, who never really rose to the commanding heights of Meiji political leadership. He managed nevertheless to give on this occasion a small gem of an exposition, the subject of which was Japan's recent and future progress. His words will stand as a monument to the moderate innovating policies of intelligent, 'conservative' bureaucrats, policies which more than any other single factor gave shape, colour and resonance to Japan's Meiji transformation:-

> Well now, at the beginning of the Meiji era, the government of our Empire, adopting the principles of Liberalism and destroying the old precept of 'closed country', established a policy of opening the country and has adhered to it down to the present day. Since that time, the Imperial government, when framing policy, has issued announcements about the old regulations and customs in all sorts of respects, and has sought to preserve what is good [in them] and to eradicate what is harmful. Moreover, apart from this, we have followed a policy until now of learning what we could wherever we could [lit., have taken stones from another mountain and polished them as if they were jewels]. To put matters in a different way, the institutions and culture of old Japan, which were already in a state of civilization, are

naturally advancing more and more. We are attempting to meet foreign institutions and culture half way, and by these means to make things in the new Japan as good as anywhere in the world. This, indeed, is what is meant by calling on the ministers and subjects of His Imperial Majesty to [look after] their liberty, which is a gift from the Emperor and is the greatest privilege humans can know . . . to look after it, no . . . rather, while preserving law and order, at the same time to develop more and more in freedom and gain ever-increasing happiness, thereby greatly strengthening the monarchy and enlarging our sovereign national rights.

And now, the Imperial government considers that our domestic institutions are generally in fairly good shape, and that the time has come for us to go further and turn our attention to [conditions] overseas. On the one hand, [we wish] to do as much as we can to ensure the protection and security of the lives, property and other concerns of our nationals overseas, be they businessmen or officials. And, on the other hand, politically speaking, we have become a factor in what is called world history and have entered the ranks of the advanced nations. [Accordingly] we want all these advanced nations to acknowledge the rights and interests pertaining to our Empire . . . .

Yet there is still one bridge to be crossed before this objective can be reached, and that bridge is also an essential means to making any further progress. I refer simply to the treaties at present existing with the Powers . . . . Revision of these treaties is the bridge or stairway to the objectives I spoke of earlier.

(DNTGS: 407)

CONCLUSIONS

The first session of the first Diet came to a close on 8 March 1891, to be followed in due course by a second session which ran from 26 November to 25 December 1891. On the last of these dates the House of Representatives was dissolved by the Emperor at the behest of the bureaucrats forming the cabinet, even though it had completed barely a quarter of its four-year term, because these same bureaucrats were desperately anxious to obtain a Lower House in which government supporters would be in the majority. Accordingly, preparations for a second and, as it turned out, bloody, general election were soon under way (Akita 1967: 98). During the short second session, there were no set debates or ministerial replies to Members' questions in the general field of foreign affairs. Kudō Takeshige notes that earlier, in the first session, Komuchi Tomotsune had tabled a motion in the House of

Representatives, which followed the lines of Tani Kanjō's recommendation in the House of Peers in requesting the government to set about the restoration of tariff rights as a matter of urgency. However, Kōmuchi's motion never came up for debate and so lapsed. Kudō also states that it was during these first two sessions of the Diet that petitions began to circulate among Members calling for strict enforcement of the existing treaties with regard to the residence and business activities of foreigners (Kudō 1901: I, 49).[15]

These demands for 'strict enforcement' later grew into a major campaign, both inside and outside the Diet, the aims of which were clearly to harass foreign governments, through their nationals living and working in Japan, into granting substantial diplomatic concessions, and simultaneously to arouse public hatred for the Sat–Chō cliques of bureaucrats who still determinedly stood in the path that led to the formation of party cabinets. Such tactics were in many ways shrewd; because over the years foreigners had been tacitly allowed by the Japanese authorities to ignore the letter of the treaties in some respects; because it was foreign residents and businessmen who gained most from the legal and tariff arrangements currently in force and who had up till then most strenuously opposed any modification of the system; and because foreign policy had always been the issue *par excellence* for forging the widest possible body of political sentiment hostile to the government. On the other hand, the vehemence of the Diet's agitation for 'strict enforcement,' together with the xenophobia it evoked, upset foreign governments, and gravely embarrassed a Japanese political leadership bent on gaining treaty revision through gentler means of persuasion. In the second half of 1891, however, it must be remembered that in the dying days of the first Diet most of this still lay in the future, and all that could be heard were the early rumblings that preceded the storm.

In addition to the brief duration of the second session, it is conceivable that cabinet changes after the first session ended in March 1891 had something to do with the apparent loss of interest in foreign affairs by the first Diet. Aoki Shūzō's abrupt departure from the post of Foreign Minister, as a result of the attack made on the Russian crown prince by a mad Japanese police sergeant at Ōtsu (Shiga Prefecture) on 11 May 1891, had come only a week or so after Yamagata Aritomo resigned as Prime Minister on grounds of ill health. The new cabinet was headed by Matsukata Masayoshi, who had Enomoto Takeaki appointed Foreign Minister in place of Aoki.

The first Matsukata cabinet lasted just over a year, and was in trouble from the outset. Unlike the preceding three strong cabinets led by Itō

Hirobumi, Kuroda Kiyotaka and Yamagata Aritomo, it was unduly subject to schisms, as vested interests or powerful out-of-office bureaucrats manipulated the cabinet for their own ends (Akita 1967: 90–105). Matsukata himself, though a very able administrator in his own special field of national finance, possessed scant experience of, or interest in, national diplomacy. His principal objective on taking office was to secure a pliable House of Representatives which would agree to his budget proposals, and to this end he and his colleagues planned the massive interference that marred the second general election.

As for Enomoto, he had served with success as ambassador in St Petersburg in the 1870s and had later been envoy in Beijing, but he lacked his predecessor's long record of personal involvement in the treaty revision problem. Indeed, throughout his career Enomoto remained something of a political *parvenu*, apt to be regarded with thinly veiled contempt (Iguro 1968: 383–4, 405). This hostility sprang partly from his being a renegade who had prospered to an outwardly remarkable degree in the service of his former enemies. Twenty-two years previously he had been the last active military opponent of the new Meiji regime to quit the field of battle, and his surrender of Hokkaidō in summer 1869 had brought to a close the War of the Restoration. In a society that, however perversely or pervertedly, still held by the 'feudal' principle of loyalty, such actions were not readily forgotten or forgiven. Further, Enomoto through no fault of his own had neglected to be born in the Sat–Chō purple. This sort of hereditary handicap alone tended to condemn anyone on the government side to a position some way below the top; and in Enomoto's case, it was accompanied by a reputation for personal pusillanimity, if nothing worse. Thus, in one way or another, the new Foreign Minister seems not to have appeared attractive game to the big bureaucrat hunters in the Diet.

Certainly, the first Matsukata cabinet (May 1891 to July 1892) did not greatly exert itself with regard either to treaty revision or to relations with Korea. Ministerial indifference doubtless led to a certain slackening of interest in the Diet. If nothing new was being done or envisaged in national diplomacy, there could be nothing new for Diet Members to say or object to. Finally, there is another aspect of the matter which should be mentioned here. By 1892, treaty revision had once more become tightly enmeshed in, and subordinate to, domestic politics. This was because in 1890 the government had published the drafts of new Commercial and Civil Codes. These represented a major element in the Western-style legal system that the ruling bureaucrats were resolved to introduce into Japan as part of their programme of enlightenment and civilization; they were also, of course, an essential preliminary to equal

treaties. However, largely for reasons of native and traditional sentiment, the draft codes were strongly opposed in, and in the end rejected
by, both houses of the Diet, despite the pleas of Enomoto among others
that they should be accepted subject to amendment at some later date.
Clearly, useful negotiations on the foreign treaties could not be resumed
until this problem of the Codes and their enactment by the Diet was
settled (Jones 1931: 141–3).

The sum and substance of all this, then, is that the foregoing is the
record of the first Diet's deliberation on foreign affairs – all two and
a bit days of it. Furthermore, notwithstanding the recriminations of
Arai Shōgo and those like him in the House of Representatives, the
bureaucrats in control of the cabinet in the main persisted in keeping
their own counsel about the timing and contents of their plans for treaty
revision; similarly, regardless of the pained insistence of Tani Kanjō
and his supporters in the House of Peers that the recovery of tariff
autonomy should precede the regaining of judicial rights, the terms
eventually worked out with the treaty Powers neatly reversed this order
of priorities. In these circumstances, it may be wondered if it is possible
to wrest from this subject any conclusions that are not strictly negative!

To reflect in this way is certainly sobering. On the other hand, while
the political and diplomatic context within which the Diet had to work
clearly limited and shaped its treatment of foreign affairs, this context
is itself so crucial a part of the history of the times that any fresh
information on it provided by the debates on national diplomacy,
however abortive they may have been, is of value. Briefly, the wider
context consisted of three separate but interrelated problems: diplomatic secrecy; transcendental, i.e. bureaucratic, cabinets; and the
putative role of the newly established Diet as a forum and engine of
public opinion. Before commenting further on these general problems,
however, there are one or two points of a more restricted kind to be
made. All of them arise from, or are relevant to, the debates and other
proceedings that have been reviewed.

For a start, attention should be drawn to the excellence of the Diet
Record as a source of information on Japanese history. Even small and
seemingly inconsequential sections of it have a way of conveying the
mood and preoccupations of the times, and often throw beams of light
on larger themes of the national history. It is easy enough to give some
concrete examples of what is meant by this; they also serve to amplify
the substance of this chapter.

When Tani Kanjō and his allies in the House of Peers went to the
trouble of enumerating particular industries harmed by imports and
publicly bewailing the outflow of bullion from the national treasury as

a result of an excess of imports over exports, nobody denied the accuracy of their facts and figures. It is clear, then, that a number of important occupations – mainly associated with the traditional economic structure of agriculture and rural handicrafts, but including also the new mechanized cotton spinning industry – were in poor shape. Indeed, the cultivation of sugar, cotton and vegetable oils for industrial or non-culinary use was destined to die out as an effective and significant part of the economy. The inference is that the Japanese economy, especially its rural sector which was still by far the biggest, suffered from dislocation and depression all through the 1880s. In the first half of the decade, the 'Matsukata deflation' and near-famine conditions in the north-east provinces had aggravated this but, later, the chief cause may well have been chronic inability to compete with cheap imports (Mason 1969: 81–2, 150).[16]

A related point emerging from Tani's strictures in the Diet is that unequal treaties did quite serious physical harm to Japanese society, and were not just blows to the national pride. The question of retrieving tariff autonomy tends to be the poor relation in Western accounts of the history of treaty revision, concentrating as they do on the more lively and better documented inroads of consular jurisdiction. On the other hand, one cannot help feeling that Tani was right in his basic ordering of priorities. Fundamentally right, that is; even though diplomatic exigencies coupled with, perhaps, the compulsions of an avowedly Imperial constitutional theory and jurisprudence, dictated that judicial sovereignty should be regained first.

Turning now to Aoki Shūzō's statements in the Diet, these indicate that treaty revision, when it did at length come in 1894 was not really a sudden *coup de théâtre* or rabbit pulled from a hat by Messrs Itō Hirobumi and Mutsu Munemitsu. Rather, the Aoki–Kimberley Agreement of 1894 should be considered as the crowning achievement of many years of diplomatic effort and cumulative experience for good and ill. Itō and Mutsu did not just succeed where everybody else had failed.[17] Their success was the apotheosis of the successes of the others, as well as a negation of the failures of the others. Thus, their winning strategy kept to the principle followed successively by Inoue Kaoru, Ōkuma Shigenobu, Aoki Shūzō and Enomoto Takeaki, of doing nothing that would smack of illegality or arbitrariness; it borrowed Ōkuma's approach of separate and private talks with one or other of the key treaty Powers; and it continued along the lines laid down by Ōkuma and Aoki of giving preference to the abolition of consular jurisdiction, even at the cost of postponing the recovery of tariff autonomy.

Finally, on the subject of Japanese relations with Korea, Aoki's comments in the Diet seem to be a true reflection of the government's viewpoint in 1890–1. Their tone of prudent and almost kindly, if watchful, moderation despite Chinese and Korean provocation sounds specially impressive when contrasted with Inoue Kakugorō's diatribe against official passivity. The whole tenor of this part of the Diet Record confirms the accuracy of Conroy's account of the period as a time, essentially, of 'wait and see'.

We are aware of course, that Japan did fight China in 1894 and oust Chinese influence from Korea, and that this even without Herod's speculations, could be taken as evidence presumptive that the Japanese government was planning the *coup de grace* many years before. But unfortunately for the theory, though perhaps fortunately for our faith in the human race (to 1893), it is not supported by evidence *minutus*; the pattern of Japanese activity in Korea during these eight years is much too inconsistent and, yes, blundering to be part of an evil plan.

(Conroy 1960: 185–6)

The dispute between Inoue Kakugorō and Aoki Shūzō about Korea also reveals something of the tension and inordinate difficulty underlying Japanese foreign policy at the time. After all, there is an appreciable disparity of aim and approach between what Aoki said, even when speaking extempore and endeavouring to placate his critic, about making 'this country shine forth in the community of Asia', and Inoue's desire to secure 'the independent supremacy of Japan in east Asia'.

From here it is but a short step to the first of our 'big' problems: the need for diplomatic secrecy. It is hardly necessary to repeat that, throughout the nineteenth century, diplomacy was something carried out largely in secret between one national government and another. This was the traditional way of doing things among the great Western Powers; and since Japan hoped to treat with these countries with a view to getting full acceptance by them as part of their world, it behoved her to observe the convention. But respect for international rules was not the only reason why Japan found it necessary, and indeed advantageous, to follow the practice of diplomatic secrecy during treaty revision negotiations. Passionate concern about their country's standing in the world had been the hallmark of Japanese political activists ever since the days of *jōi* ('Expel the barbarian!') in the 1860s, and *seikan* ('Conquer Korea') in the early 1870s. The speeches of Arai Shōgo and Inoue Kakugorō, to say nothing of their pre-parliamentary activities, are testimony of this. So, too, are some of the remarks made by Tani Kanjō in the House of Peers, not to mention his well-heeled colleagues' declarations of personal willingness to sacrifice life and fortune in the sacred cause of treaty revision. And Ōkuma Shigenobu's wooden leg was yet another kind of testimony. In fact, that statesman's personal misfortune and the diplomatic miscarriage it precipitated were the result of serious breaches of diplomatic secrecy in the form of press revelations; while the bomb that was meant to kill him was supplied by Ōi Kentarō, a leading Liberal radical and close associate of Arai and Inoue (Conroy 1960: 218–19).

Treaty revision could only be feasible if the Japanese government were successful in maintaining an atmosphere of calm and politeness for their talks with the Powers. Open antagonism or an itch for hasty solutions, in other words the kind of approach likely to find favour in the Diet, would seriously weaken the prospects for revision. Similarly, with regard to Korea, firebrands like Arai and Inoue had probably done enough damage to the cause of Japanese-style progress already, almost certainly assisting the resurgence of Chinese and traditional influences there in the second half of the 1880s. The Japanese authorities were right to adopt a posture of non-involvement. Yet, however correct and opportune official policies on treaty revision or Korea might be in conception, to succeed in practice the government had to have the privilege of conducting diplomacy in its own way, free from too much prying, open interference, or carping criticism.

In short, the Japanese public that mattered could not be trusted with too great a knowledge of, or domination over, the country's foreign policy. Moreover, because so much of the politics of the first half of the Meiji era had been conducted in a spirit of activism and confrontation in domestic as well as foreign policy, the first Diet, and especially the first House of Representatives, contained an unusually large number of declared, stop-at-nothing opponents of the Sat–Chō administrators and all their works. Cabinets at the time needed every weapon they had if they were to maintain control and continuity in diplomacy, let alone find satisfactory solutions to standing problems.

To this end, not only was the practice of diplomatic secrecy a help; so also were the various constitutional barriers which militated against the Diet exercising a direct influence on foreign affairs. For, as the Meiji Constitution was understood and operated during those early years, foreign policy remained a matter formally for the Emperor to determine with the assistance of his cabinet ministers and the advice, if necessary, of his Privy Council. Consequently, the Diet had little or no legal authority to obtrude its own wishes into this area. Thus, Tani's recommendation on the tariff, though approved by the Peers as a formal resolution of their House, had no power to bind the government;

likewise, views aired in the House of Representatives, no matter how forceful or popular they might be, did not necessarily affect official policies.

These 'safeguards' of diplomatic secrecy and constitutional bias in favour of the Executive were only on balance advantageous to the government, and only on balance beneficial in the domestic and international situation of 1890 and 1891. In other words, they carried with them certain limitations and constraints which meant that they could not be crudely used as blunt instruments for crushing attack from the Diet; or, if they were so employed, further and more serious troubles would very likely ensue. To give a practical example, as Arai Shōgo had pointed out in his introductory speech to the House of Representatives, the implementation of any new treaties would depend on the approval and co-operation of the Japanese general public. Lifting restrictions on the residence of foreigners in the interior of the country comes at once to mind here. In the same vein, as Aoki Shūzō himself had recognized in his correspondence with the English government, there was the problem of the enabling legislation which would certainly be required in connection with new treaties, and which the Japanese cabinet would have to steer through the Diet. The fate of the draft Civil and Commercial Codes is an indication of the sort of difficulties that could be encountered in this respect.

Most important of all as an inhibiting factor, however, was the impossibility of separating foreign affairs from the great domestic and constitutional problems of the day, which centred on 'transcendental cabinets' and their degree of responsibility or accountability to the Diet. These weighty matters were far from resolved even at the end of the first Diet. But some things were palpable and certain even before it opened. Cabinet would have to win the consent of the Diet for all new legislation, including an annual budget; and ministers or their spokesmen would be obliged to answer Members' questions submitted in the prescribed manner. Like it or not, government and Diet would need to establish some kind of working relationship, and whatever their bureaucratic and autocratic (in a word, transcendental) inclinations, there is no doubt that, with the inauguration of representative institutions, management of the Diet came to be a primary concern of the Sat–Chō group of statesmen.

In these circumstances, it would have been almost unimaginable folly for the Minister or any other official responsible for foreign affairs to take such an uncommunicative and unyielding stand on the grounds of diplomatic secrecy or Executive privilege that the Diet, and in particular the opposition-controlled Lower House, would be stung into a frenzy of absolute non-co-operation with the cabinet in all spheres of national politics. Political quarrelling, however acrimonious, which was conducted with reference to a sense of common purpose and within the framework laid down by the Constitution and its associated laws and procedural rules, was one thing. Open political warfare, with no holds barred and neither side even talking to the other, was something else again and far more disastrous and deadly. This is why Aoki's action in walking out of the House of Representatives on 17 December 1890 was not just bad-mannered. It was suspiciously like bad politics. Yet, Aoki, although he did remove himself on that occasion, came back to the House of Representatives on others to reply to questions in quite a full and fair fashion: and he never shirked his responsibilities to the House of Peers. Moreover, despite his talismanic use of the phrase 'diplomatic secrecy', he had by the end of the first session of the Diet intimated a good deal of what was passing through his and his colleagues' minds, as they were preparing once again to take up the business of treaty revision.

It could also be argued in Aoki's defence that foreign affairs was a particularly difficult portfolio at that stage in Japanese history. If the general accountability of the cabinet to the Diet had been an accepted convention of political life, parliamentary politicians, even those with a career to foster, might have been more ready to allow the diplomats to wear their cloak of discretion in peace; but, of course, in 1890 this precondition did not obtain. Rather, if anything, the reverse was true and foreign affairs, to say nothing of successive Foreign Ministers, suffered unduly from the atmosphere of neurosis and power-testing that pervaded the domestic political scene. Furthermore, as has been abundantly pointed out already, the two great problems of foreign policy at the time – treaty revision and the situation in Korea – were both fraught with all kinds of difficulties and liable to turn critical in any one of a number of different ways. It was probably beyond human wit in the situation prevailing in the early 1890s to allow the Diet an effective voice in diplomacy and at the same time maintain a foreign policy that was civilized and consistent.

Linked with this is the question of consensus as a major factor in both traditional and modern Japanese politics, especially as a means for resolving conflict. Purely domestic disputes, for instance over the financing or location of railway lines, could be settled by time-honoured methods of conciliation and compromise. Because the issues and parties involved all lay within the same society, such fights were within the family, so to speak. Foreign affairs, and above all the treaty problem, were quite different. Independent foreign governments and other powerful but alien entities (e.g. trading houses) were beyond customary Japanese techniques for harmonizing dissimilar points of view or differing interests.

For all its 'foreign' complexity, treaty revision had technically speaking revolved around a few well understood points of international law and convention; and, in this restricted form, was an issue first and foremost for the professional diplomats in the corridors of power, and one with which they were well able to cope. In contrast to all this, affairs Korean had a wayward and ongoing logic of their own. This logic made them susceptible to such powerful and unpredictable forces as Chinese and Russian, as well as Japanese, imperialism, and was itself determined to a large extent by pervasive and persistent Korean venality and incorrigibility.

It cannot be really imagined that in July 1894 the Japanese government looked back four or five years into the past and said, 'Ah yes, Inoue Kakugorō was right all along'. The suggestion that forcing, and seeming to resolve, the issue in Korea made life easier and happier at home in Japan, in the Diet or elsewhere, is likewise historically suspect. Just as the Korean problem was haphazardly diverse in its origins, so was it essentially 'open-ended' in relation to the future. In these fluid circumstances, seasoned Japanese bureaucrat and virtuous Japanese party politician alike were going to help each other pile mistake on irretrievable mistake.

A good deal of the blame for the kind of situation that could so easily bedevil Japanese relations with other countries in Europe or in Asia must rest on the first and subsequent Diets. Criticisms made in the legislature of the official foreign policy obtaining over the years from 1890, no matter whether directed at the government's halting progress with treaty revision or at its acquiescent attitude towards Korea, were often ill-founded. Moreover, if not ill-founded, they could be unhelpful and even damaging.

This finding raises the last major question to be touched on in these 'Conclusions': the role of the Diet as a forum and engine of public opinion. At a minimum, it might be pointed out that it was hardly feasible to have a national assembly which did not discuss foreign affairs in any shape or form. Therefore the choice was not really between having the Diet extend its purview to the country's diplomacy or restrict itself rigidly to domestic matters, but between having or not having a Diet at all; and, whatever the dangers or discomforts for the government's foreign policy-makers arising from the actual course of events between 1890 and 1894, there can be no doubt that it was better for the general political development of Japan to have the Diet open when it did. Any time would have been a bad time from one point of view or another to embark on the momentous experiment with constitutional and parliamentary forms of rule. Moreover, it is highly unlikely that the treaty Powers would ever have consented to revision if Japan had not adopted representative institutions.

But there is more to be said for the first Diet than just this. On the assumption that any new treaties, to say nothing of existing arrangements for foreigners, would have to pass the test of public acceptance, it was not altogether a bad thing to have the issues involved aired and thrashed out in the form of a parliamentary debate. General discussion of this kind would quickly indicate to the Japanese authorities what points in particular were regarded as important by whatever public it was that cared to have an opinion about such matters. Furthermore, the expression of these predominant interests and concerns in a gathering such as the national Diet would have been noted by foreign governments, making them realize more clearly than before the position beyond which the Japanese negotiators could not be pressed in view of their domestic 'public opinion'. Thus, if Aoki were to tell the ambassadors of the treaty Powers that, for example, foreign ownership of land in Japan would be extremely unpopular or that there could be no question of reviving the idea of appointing foreign judges to the Supreme Court, the whole tenor of the Diet Record would bear him out.

In the same vein, by adroit use of his obligation to reply to Members' questions, the incumbent Foreign Minister could hope, if not to convince the hostile majority in the House of Representatives of the rightness of the government's policies, at any rate to give them cause to think again. At the same time, he would be affording valuable aid and comfort to the substantial minority of government supporters in the House.

Even more importantly, in view of the fact that their statements would be included in the Diet Record and reported in the metropolitan and local press, Aoki and his successors could plan, when speaking to the Representatives, to speak also beyond them to the electors and the general public. Of course, Aoki was moved at times to deny explicitly and in writing that the government was constitutionally bound by public opinion in determining its policies for treaty revision or any other area of foreign relations, and this line of defence must have always been somewhere in the back of his mind. Yet, on other occasions, he insisted that he and the other ministers were not swayed by 'partisan considerations' when contemplating the issue, but were intent on acting for the good of all the 'forty million inhabitants of the country'; and that he had both a desire and a duty to speak out in the Diet. He even managed at one point to ask the people through their Representatives to lessen their enthusiasm for treaty revision a little, in favour of turning some of their attention and energies to the prospects for foreign trade with the Asian mainland. In short, it is fairly obvious that both the cabinet bureaucrats and their parliamentary opponents either took their stand on, or sought to appeal to, something they called public opinion when disputing the great foreign policy issues of the day.

In this connection, it is worth considering some of the ways in which the first Diet could be held to represent public opinion, and how it set about asserting such a claim, apart, that is, from the obvious tactic of questioning and criticizing the ministers of state. There is no doubt, for example, that the three hundred Members of the first House of Representatives formed an impressive and representative sample of an educated, lively and extremely influential middle and upper-middle class composed of small landlords, industrialists, civil servants of the sub-prefect rank or higher, pedagogues and members of new professions like journalism or law (Mason 1969: 27, 31, 133–44, 198).

In one way or another, then, the first House of Representatives could fairly claim to represent middle-class public opinion; that is, virtually the public opinion of the times and, most certainly, a public opinion that mattered. The House as a whole and many individual Members discharged this obligation competently and at times brilliantly, always remembering the rather severe constitutional constraints within which they had to operate. Moreover, on foreign affairs especially, the Lower House could be regarded as representing a national, and not just a sectional, public opinion, since there is no evidence whatsoever that the people at large were in principle less opposed to the unequal treaties than the Members of the Diet and the section of the educated, well-to-do middle class they directly represented. Certainly, governments at the time never attempted to play down the basic right of the House of Representatives to represent the nation as a whole on this or any other issue.

Turning to the House of Peers, it is gratifying to note that it, too, very early showed signs of developing a sense of corporate identity coupled with a spirit of independence. It is more than a little surprising, furthermore, to discover that the House of Peers also liked to think of itself as representing public opinion, not just the opinion of the nobles and similar dignitaries. Thus, Tani Kanjō and his supporters in the matter of a speedy restoration of tariff autonomy often had phrases like 'the forty million compatriots' on their lips.

Perhaps the government expected that it would be subjected to this sort of demagoguery by Tani, for he had been on bad terms with his old colleagues in the ministry for a number of years. What must have been really galling for the cabinet ministers of the time, however, was the fact that so many of the ordinary run of Members of the House of Peers sided with Tani. These were the people, hereditary peers and nominated Members alike, whom the authorities over the years loaded with honours, status and responsibilities. Many of them formed part of the administration's *corps d'élite*. Yet one after another they got to their feet in the new parliamentary bastion which their own patrons and the nation's rulers had presented to them, and roundly condemned the government for failing to implement a more decisive foreign policy. Clearly, men of prefectural governor rank or its equivalent were a tiny and privileged minority, but they could be an extremely influential group when they chose to exercise to the full the very real prerogatives enjoyed by Members of the Imperial Diet, and at the same time claimed to be speaking or acting in response to 'public opinion' or on behalf of the 'national interest'. By and large, in these first years of the constitutional system, the Peers represented informed, metropolitan and politically 'neutral' opinion, as opposed to the partisan, provincial and often somewhat uninformed opinion that abounded in the House of Representatives.

The contrasting tones of debate in the two Houses reflect this last distinction. Oratory in the Lower House tended to be heated and patently against the government. What it lacked in sustained argument or verified fact, it made up for in emotional outburst and moral indignation. Peers' speeches, on the other hand, were altogether more solid and better researched, and usually delivered in a quieter and more moderate style of address. There was an appropriate air of senatorial gravity about the Upper House from the first. Yet, precisely because of its ponderous qualities, a good and polite but undeniably anti-government speech in the House of Peers could be more telling in its criticism than the customary pyrotechnic display in the House of Representatives.

One wonders whether Itō Hirobumi, who had been in a sense relegated from high political office to the Presidency of the House of Peers, ever exerted himself to bring about a degree of informal reconciliation between the attitudes of the government and the views of its opponents in that House. Mutsu Munemitsu, who was Minister for Communications in the first Yamagata cabinet, as well as a newly elected Member for Wakayama Prefecture, was favourably placed to play a similar role as mediator *vis-à-vis* the House of Representatives. Nor was Mutsu alone in this; the Lower House contained many people who managed to maintain reasonably good links with the cabinet on the one hand, and the political parties on the other. Moreover, cabinets – even those outwardly upholding the doctrine of 'transcendence' – invariably had some members who were more ready than the others to treat with the opposition. Nothing has been said on this subject of informal contact and dialogue in this chapter, because it has been based on the formal Diet Record. Even the latter, though, seems to indicate that by the time of the second session of the first Diet, there was tacit agreement to disagree on foreign policy between governments and the various groups opposing them.

Such a truce, if indeed it can be said to have ever existed, did not last. With the rise of the 'strict enforcement' campaign from the end of 1892, any theory of consensus politics, so popular with scholars as a standard explanation of Japanese political processes, is clearly inapplicable; and one may shed a tear in passing for the ministers who were forced to pick their way to their chosen goal of orderly revision of the treaties through so many mine fields, domestic and foreign. Yet, if matters cannot be packed away in a box marked 'consensus', what view of the constitutional process will help to illuminate those first disturbed years of its operation? Perhaps the constitutional and parliamentary forms of government from 1890 to 1900 are best thought of as some kind of ritualized warfare. At the very least, the Diet gave a new and a more civilized structure and potential to a continuous political conflict.

NOTES

1 The treaty ports tended to vary in number and importance. The principal ones were Hakodate, Niigata, Yokohama, Kanagawa, Ōsaka, Kōbe, Hyōgo and Nagasaki.

2 Ozaki may in fact have heard Aoki's words on this occasion, as he was a member of the House of Representatives from its inaugural session in 1890 until 1953 (Mason and Caiger 1972: 274).

3 A rescript dated 12 October 1881 had announced the convening of a national Diet in 1890 (Mason 1969: 215–16).

4 DNTGS: 533; it was under the aegis of Itō, nevertheless, in his second term as Prime Minister that Japanese diplomats finally managed to negotiate equal treaties.

5 Notably Jones (1970: 124), where he writes: 'It is impossible not to feel that Ōkuma deserved to succeed.'

6 This article read: 'Deliberative assemblies shall be widely established and all matters decided by public discussion.'

7 DNTGS here refers twice to Rule No. 171, but as this deals with the need to wear formal attire in the House of Representatives chamber, it hardly seems relevant, and presumably either the speaker or the transcript writer was in error. Rule 141, on the other hand was designed to facilitate the

recall of recalcitrant ministers to the House for further questioning, in keeping with Article 50 of the Law of the Houses.

8 This article stated that various categories of 'already fixed expenditures' could not be arbitrarily interfered with by the Diet.

9 Rule 142 stated that a motion could be tabled concerning the failure of a government spokesman to reply to questions, providing such a motion had at least thirty sponsors.

10 The actual date of the ratification of the treaty with the US had been 1879.

11 The 'few officials' included himself; he had resigned from the post of Minister of Agriculture and Commerce 1887, in protest against the terms for treaty revision agreed to by Inoue Kaoru.

12 Behind the remark that scholars would turn into 'dried vegetables' seems to be the general idea that unless there took place an extensive modernization of the Japanese economy, which was the vital basis of society, modernization of elements of its superstructure like public buildings or universities would prove to be ineffective, sterile, somehow 'dried-up'.

13 Tomita's history was sound.

14 Article 10 runs (in part) as follows: 'The present Convention shall take effect when Japan shall have concluded such conventions or revisions of treaties with all the other treaty Powers holding relations with Japan as shall be similar in effect to the present Convention, and such new conventions or revisions shall also go into effect.'

15 A further check of the relevant pages in the Diet Record shows that a proposal on treaty revision was sponsored in the House of Representatives by Maeda Kagashi (1828–1904). This was first set down in the order paper for 14 December 1891 and marked as requiring a secret sitting; however, it was never debated. In addition and also in the House of Representatives, Suzuki Shōji tabled on 15 December 1891 a series of general questions to the government on its handling of the revision problem. The purpose of these was to enquire whether the cabinet had actively taken up the task of re-negotiation once more and, if so, by what steps it intended to retrieve full judicial and fiscal sovereignty (DNTGS: 1387, 1402, 1415).

16 Figures from *Meiji Taishō kokusei soran*, pp. 445–6, show a deficit of ¥25 million on the trade account for 1890, and a loss of ¥12 million in specie.

17 For a diametrically opposite, but clearly self-centred, view on this, see the brilliant article by M. B. Jansen (1970: 329–30).

6 The Japanese Commercial Code of 1890, and its reception in the first two sessions of the Imperial Diet, 1890–1

Philip Mitchell

THE BIRTH OF THE CODE AND ITS BACKGROUND

A special supplement to the Official Gazette (*Kampō*) of the Japanese government on Saturday 26 April 1890 bore the following proclamation:

> We hereby sanction and promulgate the Commercial Code. We decree that this law shall take effect from the first day of January, 1891.
> PRIVY SEAL
>
> Twenty-seventh day of March, 1890[1]

Japan's Commercial Code had taken more than nine years to produce. Despite this and the seeming authority and simplicity with which this proclamation decreed that the Code would take effect within eight months, a further nine years elapsed before Japan had a Commercial Code with the force of law. For the Code was to ignite a vehement controversy, the consequences of which have influenced Japanese law to this day.

Law and the last years of the Tokugawa government

The law of Japan as it developed during the Tokugawa period can be described as fragmentary in two senses. The first arose from the *baku-han* system whereby local lords owed allegiance to a central government but enjoyed a large measure of regional autonomy. The social and economic relations which complemented this regionalism meant that not only did administrative pronouncements on legal matters often differ according to locality, but that the same was true even in circumstances where law was founded purely upon custom.[2] Secondly, legislation during the Tokugawa period consisted mainly of small-scale edicts. These, intended as they were to be a pragmatic way of dealing with specific needs, rather than a more sophisticated approach to a grandiose legal system, were necessarily piecemeal.

The earliest Japanese efforts to understand Occidental law were made by scholars of the government's *Bansho Shirabesho* (Office for Research of Barbarian Writings). The *Bansho Shirabesho* had been established in 1857 following the commencement of direct official relations with Western Powers, to meet a need for knowledge about those Powers. Its main subjects of study were science, geography, philosophy and art[3], but in 1862 two of its scholars, Nishi Amane and Tsuda Mamichi, were sent to Leiden University, where they attended the law lectures of Simon Vissering. After their return to Japan in 1866 they both lectured on Western law at the *Bansho Shirabesho*, which was by then officially called *Kaiseijo* (Institute of Development). Nishi prepared a translation from his notes of Vissering's lectures on *volkenregt* (international law), which was completed in 1867 and published under the title *Bankoku kōhō* in 1868; Tsuda did the same for Vissering's lectures on *staatsregt* (constitutional law), and this was published under the title *Taisei kokuhō ron*, also in 1868. As a subject of study, then, Occidental legal ideas entered Japan shortly before the Meiji Restoration of 1868, though as a constituent of the actual law of Japan they did not.

One should, however, hesitate to judge simply from the fragmentary nature of Tokugawa law and the fact that it remained uninfluenced by Occidental thought, that the Tokugawa legal system fits the sometimes popular image of Tokugawa Japan as 'backward'. It is true that Tokugawa methods of interrogation and punishment of criminals rank with the most physically severe in world history[4], and that even words as fundamental as *kenri* (*right*) and *gimu* (obligation) did not exist until coined for the purpose of writing about the law of foreign countries.[5] A legal system which is said to have no word for 'rights' might seem primitive to a nineteenth- or twentieth-century Western observer; but one should remember that 'rights' in the sense referred to in the American Declaration of Independence or the French Declaration of the Rights of Mankind are a relatively modern development in Western jurisprudence. Also, ideals of duty, akin to *gimu*, pervaded Tokugawa society, even though that word itself was apparently not known. John Wigmore, who pioneered academic study of Tokugawa law within Japan and whose efforts have scarcely been added to by non-Japanese scholars in the ensuing ninety years, argued persuasively that Tokugawa judicial officials displayed an intellectual level equal to that of English judges of the same period. Furthermore, as will be mentioned later, the customary law relating to commerce bore some astounding resemblances to its counterpart in Europe.

The need for 'Western-style' codes of law

The leaders who gained power in 1868 as a result of that concatenation of portentous changes called the Meiji Restoration faced important questions of policy, not the least of which concerned Japan's legal system. Eventually, the decision made was to enact codes of law fashioned after those of Western countries. The motivation most frequently cited for this is the new Meiji government's desire to rid Japan of treaties which derogated from Japanese sovereignty. The foreign Powers required, as a prior condition for treaty revision, the modernization of Japanese law so that it would pay respect to Occidental principles of justice.

There can be little doubt this was an important motivation; but it should be remembered that internal factors, too, demanded great changes in law, and explanations purely in terms of diplomatic pressure are far too simplistic. In the sphere of criminal law, the new government used codes[6] as an auxiliary to the centralization of administrative power; whilst in the sphere of private law, that is, the Civil and Commercial Codes, there was the further point that by the time they were promulgated they were needed to reflect massive social and economic changes since the Restoration. On this view, the law of the Meiji period illustrates the dual truths that law may help to effect change in a nation and must also reflect change in a nation.

The early Meiji period and Occidental law

On 26 May 1868,[7] Soejima Taneomi on behalf of the *Dajōkan* (Great Council of State) ordered Mitsukuri Rinshō to translate the five French codes into Japanese. This, it is said, was with a view to wholesale adoption of these codes as the law of Japan, though one must question whether the idea of wholesale adoption was ever taken seriously. Further, it is not altogether clear why French law, rather than any other system, was chosen. The Napoleonic Codes appeared self-contained whereas the Common Law seemed nebulous and tied to English culture, and they had already been used to modernise the legal systems of several other countries.[8] Considerations like these presumably carried weight.

The enormous difficulty of Mitsukuri's task can be appreciated when it is borne in mind he was not a legal specialist, did not have the advice of any French lawyer, at least until the arrival of Georges Bousquet in 1872, and had no useful French–Japanese dictionary. However, owing partly to Mitsukuri's talent and partly to the enthusiasm of Etō Shimpei, head of the government's Office of Laws and future Minister for Justice, who is reputed to have commanded Mitsukuri, 'Don't bother too much about mistranslations, just translate it quickly!' – the translation was completed by 1874. As to the drafting of Japan's codes, Mitsukuri's work was of great influence; drafting committees later drew extensively on his translations and also relied directly upon him as an interpreter.

Further, Mitsukuri's efforts meant that French law was accessible to Japanese students. Indeed, French law had been taught since November 1871 in the *Meihōryō*, a law school established through Etō's efforts and placed under the government's *Sain* (Left Chamber).[9] English law, too, was taught from 1874 at *Tōkyō Kaisei Gakkō* which in 1877 became part of Tokyo University. Also, a number of private law schools were established in the late 1870s and early 1880s. Thus, there was in early Meiji Japan a current of keen investigation into Occidental law. As already mentioned, this current had its origins before the Meiji period itself, with scholars of the *Bansho Shirabesho*.

Compilation of a Civil Code

The history of Japan's Civil Code has attracted detailed attention elsewhere, and it is not intended here to add to those researches. However, the Civil Code bears a special relationship to the Commercial Code due to Article 1 of the Commercial Code, which in the 1890 version[10] said:

> In commercial matters, so far as in this Code not provided for, the usages of trade and the provisions of the Civil Code apply.

Even if one discounts the theory that Mitsukuri's translation was to be adopted as Japanese law, attempts to compile a Civil Code certainly date to as early as September 1870, when a drafting committee was established in the government's Office of Laws with Etō Shimpei as its chairman. There is no indication of what became of this attempt after the Office of Laws combined with the Left Chamber in September 1871. At least five other attempts to draft a Civil Code were made before 1880, but each seems to have met with opposition from within the government due to the compilers' reliance on the French code and alleged disregard for Japanese customs. None the less, a noteworthy event associated with one such attempt took place in 1873. It was the despatch of a committee throughout Japan to gather data on civil customs. This demonstrates that even during the early 1870s, a period sometimes regarded as characterized by a blind rage for knowledge of foreign law, some attention was given to customary indigenous law.

From 1880, the name of Gustave-Emile Boissonade de Fontarabie (1825–1910) figures prominently. He had been a professor at the Faculty of Law in Paris, and he had come to Japan as an adviser to the Japanese government in November 1873. In 1877 he had finished drafting what became the Criminal Code and Code of Criminal Procedure and his skills were in 1880 turned to drafting a Civil Code. Boissonade wrote of his methodology: 'Doubtless what Japan adopts should not be French law purely and simply. I want your government to adopt our laws only to the extent that they have been proved good by the experience of three-quarters of a century.'

His code consisted of five books, on Property, Acquisition of Property, Securities, Persons and Evidence;[11] it was promulgated in two parts in 1890 and due to go into effect on 1 January 1893. True to Boissonade's comments, the code was not simply a copy of the French one. Native Japanese custom was the basis of certain provisions, in particular those dealing with family and inheritance. Overall, though, the influence of the French code was strong.

In the legal history of the Meiji period, there is a strong thematic identity between the Civil and the Commercial Codes. No doubt this arose partly from the technical link forged in Article 1 of the Commercial Code, which has already been mentioned. Moreover, as will be shown below, the two Codes met a common fate in the postponement debate in the Diet. Last but not least, they were alike in being derived from French law, albeit with modifications.

Commercial legislation in the early Meiji period

Despite what has just been said, it would be wrong to view the law of Meiji Japan purely in terms of new French-style codes and the difficulties encountered therewith. As already mentioned, the Commercial Code did not finally take effect until 1899, more than thirty years after the Restoration. Returning to the government's legislative policy during the earlier years of the Meiji period it was, at least in the commercial field as opposed to criminal legislation, a policy of particularism rather than the universalism implicit in a code. An instance of this early legislation is the National Bank Regulations of 1872; other prominent examples are the Stock Exchange Regulations (1874) and the Rules for Companies Trading in Grain (1875). These, as their titles suggest, were specific responses to the rapid commercial growth which took place during the early Meiji period. As such, they represent a continuation of the Tokugawa legislative policy of *ad hoc* responses to particular needs.

Commercial growth during the 1870s involved the formation of a large number of companies and other business associations. By 1880 a detailed law entitled Company and Partnership Regulations had been drafted,[12] and from September of that year its provisions were discussed and revised in the *Genrōin* (Senate). Deliberations were completed by 14 April 1881. A new detailed scheme of laws prepared within the Ministry of the Navy to govern commerce at sea, including provisions for special Maritime Courts, was also in an advanced stage of preparation by April 1881.

However, at this time a change of government policy apparently took place; it was decided to compile a Commercial Code and not to enforce these company and maritime laws. Precisely who made the decision, how it was made, and the reasons therefor, are worthy topics for future research, as in one sense the decision was a linchpin of transition from the Tokugawa approach of specific legislation to the modern approach of a general Commercial Code.

Hermann Roesler

Hermann Carl Friedrich Roesler was the man chosen to draft the proposed Commercial Code. He was born in Lauf, near Nürnberg, in 1834, and died in Bozen (Tyrol) in 1894. Before coming to Japan, he had been a scholar of economics and law in Germany, rising to the position of professor at the University of Rostock in 1862. He became deeply dissatisfied with the political trends in Germany under Prussian hegemony. In particular, he condemned Prussia's 'rigid legal formalism', arguing that it stifled the free development of society. When in 1877 he was invited by the Japanese minister at Berlin, Aoki Shūzō, to become legal adviser to the Foreign Ministry in Tokyo, he seized the opportunity, and in the autumn of 1878 he departed with his family for Japan.

He began with treaty revision and relations with Korea. By 1881 he had advanced to the post of first legal adviser to the government and regularly lectured at Tokyo University. He enjoyed to a remarkable degree the confidence of government leaders: Siemes writes, 'there seems to have been hardly any important affair of state in which his advice was not requested'. Roesler remained in Japan until April 1893, during which time his most visible contribution was in legislative drafting. Several English-language studies have publicized his role in drafting the Meiji Constitution, but his work on economic legislation, including the Commercial Code, remains largely unexplored in either Japanese or English.

Searches in Tokyo[13] did not reveal a document commissioning Roesler to draft the Commercial Code, but it appears he started on this particular task in April 1881. Although a member of the Legislative Division of the *Dajōkan*, he worked mainly by himself. Thus, little is known of his methods and the actual course of his work, apart from the fact that he initially undertook a worldwide study of commercial laws.

By 29 January 1884 he submitted to the *Dajōkan* a draft entitled *Entwurf eines Handelsgesetzbuches für Japan*. This was published[14] in three volumes later that year. An official Japanese version was also prepared and published.[15] The draft consisted of 1133 articles divided into four books concerning Commerce in General, Maritime Commerce, Bankruptcy and Commercial Litigation.

A Japanese compilation committee established in March 1882 and headed by Tsuruda Hiroshi, had undertaken a survey of the commercial practices of each district of Japan. However, either the committee's findings were not available to Roesler[16] or he chose not to use them, for in an explanatory essay presented to the government with his draft he wrote:

> Japanese commercial customs are not incorporated in this draft. . . .
> They are, though, given effect by Article 1, which applies commercial customs where they do not conflict with the Commercial Code. The provisions of the draft may be altered to accord with commercial customs peculiar to Japan, but in this great care must be taken. If it is desired that Japan's Commercial Code conform to present-day commercial activities, it must be made harmonious with the commercial laws of foreign countries, and this is particularly so if Japanese sovereignty is to be extended to foreigners. . . . The law of each nation has characteristics which must develop in accord with experience, but in that commerce is an international as well as a local matter, harmony with the practices of other nations must be achieved.

Despite echoes of the jurist Friedrich Carl von Savigny's view[17] that law, like language, is peculiar to each nation, Roesler here stressed the special need for Japanese commercial law to conform to the usage of other nations.

From Roesler draft to Commercial Code

Even after the decision to compile a code, the earlier particularist legislative policy was by no means extinguished. Roesler's full draft was not complete until 1884, but already in 1882 the need for provisions on Bills of Exchange was so pressing that a law based heavily upon a part of the draft concerning them was prepared. This was discussed in the *Genrōin* from October to November 1882 and then enforced as Decree No. 57 on 11 December 1882. In the later 'postponement controversy', the existence of this law provided ammunition for those opposed to the Code, for it meant the Code's provisions on Bills of Exchange were not urgently needed.

From 1884 to 1887, attempts at similar specific legislation on companies and on bankruptcy postponed deliberations on the Roesler draft. In a submission to the *Dajōkan*, Itō Hirobumi wrote on 20 May 1884: 'Even though we now have a draft Commercial Code admirably prepared by Mr Roesler . . . the need for provisions regarding companies is most urgent and I respectfully submit that the same should be compiled without delay.' However, these efforts did not come to fruition. On 17 March 1886, after considerable delay, the committee set up to prepare company provisions took the view that such laws would be of insufficient effect without the supporting provisions of the remainder of the Code.

Yet another obstacle to deliberations on the Roesler draft was the sudden transfer of responsibility for the various codes from the Justice Ministry to the Foreign Ministry in August 1886, and back to the Justice Ministry in October 1887.[18]

From 4 November 1887, deliberations and amendments were finally carried out by a Committee for Investigating Laws headed by the Justice Minister, Yamada Akiyoshi. The draft was then sent[19] to the cabinet[20] which sought the comments of various organs of government[21] and incorporated further amendments before submitting the final draft to the *Genrōin* for approval on 7 June 1889. The proclamation of 26 April 1890, which finally promulgated the Code, is reproduced above.

As well as supporting the conclusion that the legislative particularism of the Tokugawa period did not die easily, the imbroglio of delays and discussions concerning the Commercial Code demonstrates that the pre-constitutional process of government in Japan by no means allowed an impetuous move regarding codification. Putting the matter another way, the procedure and discussion to which the Code was subjected manifest a gradualist approach as well as a commitment to due process, which were typical of Meiji period leadership and can be seen in Japanese law and administration to this day. This approach allows more than one, or even a few, at the very top of the hierarchy to influence a decision.

What changes had been made to the Roesler draft by the time it was promulgated? The deletion of the entire fourth book on Commercial Litigation and of another 36 articles is sufficient to raise the issue whether it is a misnomer to call the 1890 Code the Roesler code. Yet on the other hand, a recent study by Hirose Hisakazu of the development of *receptum* liability[22] in Japan from the Roesler draft to the present day indicates that many of the changes are likely to have been alterations of style and wording, not substance. Furthermore, the writer's own comparison of Roesler's first three articles with those of the 1890 Code revealed only syntactic changes which would scarcely be discernible if translated into English. Questions such as to what extent this is true of the entire code, and in particular the important issue of just how much and in what manner the draft was altered to accommodate Japanese customs, must be left to a study investigating each provision at each stage of amendment.

WHAT THE CODE SAID

An English translation

As well as consulting the Japanese text of the Code published in the Official Gazette, the writer has been able to read an English translation found in the National Diet Library in Tokyo. The identity of the translator is not known, but the work had official sanction, having been published by order of the Justice Ministry. This suggests it might have been translated by an officer or officers of the government.

Code translations had been promised by the government during negotiations on treaty revision as early as June 1887, but the 1887 negotiations were 'wrecked by a typhoon of hostile public opinion' which opposed any concessions to foreign Powers. The priority of translations seems afterwards to have been relegated; for when the Japanese text of the Commercial Code was promulgated, it was more than two years before a translation appeared. None the less, when the translation did appear it featured near-perfect expression, faithful to the original Japanese, and it seems to have been well received by resident English speakers.

The provisions of the Code

The Code's 1064 articles were divided into a portion entitled General Provisions and three Books entitled Commerce in General, Maritime Commerce and Bankruptcy.

The General Provisions consisted of only the first two articles, which dealt with the relationship between the Code and other laws. Article 1, quoted above, applied the Civil Code and the usages of trade to 'commercial matters' not provided for in the Commercial Code.

Article 2 preserved the validity of existing or future laws promulgated with reference to particular classes of commercial matters or traders. The Commercial Code, then, established a branch of law which, to the extent it was inconsistent with the Civil Code and the usages of trade, was a special exception, but which was in turn subject to the special exceptions of more particular laws. A technical problem would very likely have arisen where the Commercial Code was silent and trade usage (*shōshūkan*, which might equally have been translated 'commercial custom') and the Civil Code conflicted, for Article 1 did not make clear which of the two, trade usage or the Civil Code, should apply in such cases. In the wording of present-day Article 1, this has been resolved in favour of trade usage.

Book I: Commerce in General (Articles 3–823)

This Book began by defining the Code's two most essential terms. 'Commercial Matters' was the generic term for the subject matter touched by the Code. They included 'commercial transactions' (a very wide range of transactions, from the sale of produce to insurance transactions to the publication of newspapers) if performed with the object of making a profit, plus *all* transactions performed by a 'trader' in the course of business. A trader was defined as a person whose *normal business* it is to engage in 'commercial transactions'; and a commercial transaction was such even if only one party to it was a trader. For example, if A, an ordinary citizen, dealt with B, a trader, in the course of B's business, the dealing was thereby 'commercial' and would thus attract the application of the Code.

The Code, then, defined its subject matter basically in terms of acts of a certain character, though that character was partly determined in turn by the class of persons performing it. It is beyond the scope of this chapter to compare comprehensively the Japanese Commercial Code with other Commercial Codes; but as to its method of demarcating subject matter mainly with reference to the nature of acts not the status of persons, it can be said the Japanese Code followed the egalitarian approach of the French Commercial Code of 1807.

Among the provisions in Book I was the establishment of a system of local registers open to public inspection in which were to be recorded such matters as trading names, details of companies, and permission from guardians for minors to engage in trade.

Every trader was also required to keep books, giving a daily account of obligations entered into, merchandise received and delivered, and payments made and received.

The Code provided for the formation, maintenance and dissolution of partnerships and companies. It is noteworthy that a *kabushiki kaisha* (a public limited liability company) could not be formed without permission from the government. This gave the authorities the ability to veto risky or unscrupulous ventures and also to control activity in particular industries.

Other subjects covered by Book I include agency, sale according to sample, sale by auction, insurance, bills of exchange, promissory notes and cheques.

Book II: Maritime Commerce (Articles 824–977)

The law of maritime commerce, due to its special subject matter, developed in Europe as a body distinct from that concerning commerce on land. Further, owing to the international character of shipping, it developed with a high degree of international uniformity from an early date. The French Commercial Code dealt with maritime commerce separately from commerce on land, partly because of the need for conformity with international usage and partly because that Code's drafters recognized the two were discrete due to their discrete origins. The same division was later followed by other codifications such as the German Commercial Code of 1861 and the Japanese Code at present under discussion.

The Japanese Code provided that vessels were entitled to fly the Japanese flag only if they belonged wholly to Japanese subjects or to companies, partnerships or other entities subject to Japanese jurisdiction.

Provisions applicable to commerce involving Japanese ships dealt with matters such as the rights and duties of master and crew (for example, the master had the right to select and engage members of the crew, and the crew were entitled to a proportionate addition to their contracted wages where a voyage was extended), apportionment of loss in case of damage to cargo, and rights of creditors.

In relation to creditors, the Code's separate treatment of commerce by sea as opposed to commerce by land is illustrated by the period of prescription (that is, extinction of rights of claim a certain time after they accrue). In Book I for commerce by land this was set at six years; but in Book II for rights of ships' creditors it was set at one year.

Book III: Bankruptcy (Articles 978–1064)

This third and shortest book of the Code, containing only 87 articles, restricted its application to those engaging in the business of a 'trader', but included partnerships and companies so engaged. In this restriction it followed the model of the French Commercial Code. By contrast, the German Bankruptcy Law, which was enacted as a law separate from the Commercial Code in 1877, extended to merchant and non-merchant alike.

The term bankruptcy (*hasan*) was not specifically defined in the Code. A trader became bankrupt when he (or 'it' in the case of a company) was adjudged so by 'the Court'. This the Court could do of its own motion, or on the application of one or more creditors, and was required to do when a trader 'suspended payment' of debts and notified the Court within five days of the suspension.

An individual trader, or member of a partnership, or director of a company adjudged bankrupt was disqualified from trading in any of those capacities until he had been 'rehabilitated' (i.e. it had been proved that all debts had been fully paid).

The Code as a whole

The Japanese Code established a broad framework of commercial law, but it still required much interpretation, particularly as to the precise meaning of some terms and as to the relationship between some of its provisions. In this, it reflected the formula expressed in 1802 by Jean Etienne Portalis and the other drafters of the French Civil Code, a formula in which lies much of the secret of the French Code's success during the past one hundred and ninety years: 'The role of legislation is to fix, by taking a broad perspective, the general maxims of the law; to establish principles which will be richly productive, not to delve in detail into every question which may arise.'

As to its relationship to the two archetypal Commercial Codes – the French (1807) and the German (1861) – the generalization has been made that it reflected the French in structure but the German in content. However, some exceptions to this have been seen, for example, the Code's treatment of bankruptcy. On the other hand, it is certainly true that the Japanese Code followed neither the French nor the German Code blindly. Bearing these points in mind, a more acceptable statement of the Japanese Code's relationship to other contemporary codes might be that it bore considerable evidence of Roesler's methodology, which involved drafting in the light of comparative study rather than adherence to any single precedent.

THE CODE AND THE DIET

A controversy looms: the *Hōgakushikai* resolution and its antecedents

Law schools established during the 1870s and 1880s amidst the growing current of keen study of Occidental law tended to specialize in either French or English law, as has already been mentioned. French law at the time was strongly influenced by 'natural law' thinking, which basically holds proper law to be the embodiment of universal human reason, or, even further, to have been divinely instilled. This natural law emphasis was accentuated in Japan by Gustave Boissonade, who was an outstanding exponent of natural law thinking (Takayanagi 1957: 28). However, Henry Terry and John Wigmore, *doyens* of English Common Law teaching in Japan, took an analytical-historical view of law, and disapproved greatly of natural law. Terry wrote of natural law as 'a species of pseudo-law' which had given rise to 'obscurity' and 'wild and foolish theorizing', and was 'the very tap root of communism' (Takayanagi 1957: 29) The national qualifying examinations for judges and barristers could be taken in either French law or English law, so that no one was required to have a knowledge of both (Nakamura 1962: 76). Against this background it is not surprising that two groups strongly opposed in their theoretical views of law developed.

During the late 1880s, an amount of what has been called chauvinist or 'super-patriotic' (Ishii 1958: 584) feeling had been expressed by such figures as Nishimura Shigeki, Miyake Setsurei and Tani Kanjō.[23] The essence of this feeling was that to rely on foreigners and their ideas would be to destroy Japanese morality and culture. Thus, the re-modelling of Japan's laws along Western lines was, according to this view, to be deplored.

The *Hōgakushikai*, composed of law graduates of what had by then become Tokyo Imperial University (at the time a stronghold of English law teaching), as early as its general meeting in May 1889 stated its objection to the government's efforts at codification (Hoshino 1944: 26–9). The objection was on three grounds: (1) that if the Commercial Code is drafted under German influence (Roesler) whereas the Civil Code is drafted under French influence (Boissonade) then the law of Japan will not be based on any consistent principle;[24] (2) implicitly taking up the views of Tani *et al.*, that importation of European law would not be in accord with existing Japanese legal usages and would do harm to Japanese culture; and (3) that drafts should be published so that members of the public could criticize them and offer amendments. It is highly likely that the members of the *Hōgakushikai* were interested not only in the good of the nation but in the welfare of their own careers: if European continental law were allowed to gain a stronghold in Japan, their own training in English law would be of less value. The 'natural law' thinking implicit in European jurisprudence must anyway have been to some extent repugnant on intellectual grounds to the members of the *Hōgakushikai* because of their Common Law training. However, the bold suggestion that Japan should have a Common Law system rather than continental-style codes seems not to have been made, at least at this stage of the debate.

Initial reactions to the Code

The promulgation of the Commercial Code and most of the Civil Code in April 1890 afforded matters for concrete comment. In this, attention was centred upon the Commercial Code because of the mere eight-month interval before its due date of enforcement. Immediate expressions of surprise and regret at this short interval are to be found in the press (*Japan Weekly Mail*, 3 May 1890). Expressions of discontent were not, however, confined to the press. On 28 June 1890, the *Genrōin* passed a resolution arguing that the interval was too short for the nation to become familiar with a new code and that it was inconsistent to sever the Commercial Code from the Civil Code by a disparity of two years in their enforcement dates (Kumagai 1967: 116). It should be noted that the *Genrōin* did not object to the Code itself, which it had approved barely a year earlier on 7 June 1889. It merely urged, on what it saw as practical grounds, postponement of the Commercial Code until the enforcement date for the Civil Code, i.e. 1 January 1893. The cabinet, however, stood firm. Its answer, which Kumagai suggests (Kumagai 1967:117) was prepared by Justice Minister Yamada, stressed the immediate need for proper control of companies and pointed out that the period for assimilation of the Code was not as short as had been alleged, for under the Commercial Code Enforcement Regulations (Law No. 59 of 1890) existing companies would have six months' grace from the date of enforcement before having to comply with the Code.

Business circles, notably the Tokyo Association of Commerce and Industry (*Tōkyō Shōkōkai*), called for postponement. They echoed both the *Hōgakushikai*'s philosophical objections to the Code itself and the *Genrōin*'s pragmatic objections to the date of enforcement. The Tokyo Association obtained agreement from many kindred provincial

Associations (Kumagai 1967: 117), which is some evidence that the Code had produced genuine and widespread alarm in the business community. The Tokyo Association was, however, vigorously opposed by the Ōsaka Chamber of Commerce. On 27 October, a resolution of the latter called for enforcement of the Code. It claimed that the Code would: (1) inspire general confidence within Japan's commercial community; and (2) provide a legal footing upon which foreigners would be encouraged to transact business with Japanese merchants, thus contributing to Japan's economic development (Kumagai 1967: 117).

The *Genrōin* had tried and failed to secure postponement. In November 1890, that institution was disbanded to make way for Japan's first Diet. As has been explained, some sectors of influential opinion, both legal experts and commercial experts, were clearly opposed to the Code, but the government had remained steadfast. Rumours and theories now circulated as to how the new Diet might express hostility toward the government. These were founded on the fact that as a result of the general election held on 1 July 1890 the government could in general count on the support of 129 of the 300 Members of the House of Representatives whereas the generally anti-bureaucratic Liberal Party and Progressive Party together would command 171 seats (Ōtsu 1927: 542).[25]

The first session of the Diet: a bill for postponement

On Tuesday 25 November 1890, as Akita writes, the tall iron gates fronting the Diet were opened, and Japan began its days as a constitutional state (Akita 1962: 33). The Diet was at the same time an experiment and a cause for pride. It may be regarded as the world's first legislature and national assembly apart from those of Europe and countries colonized by Europe. During the first week of December 1890, even before the legislative sittings had begun, the Tokyo Association of Commerce and Industry speedily made use of the right to petition the Diet granted to all subjects by Article 50 of the Constitution. It submitted to both Houses a petition which reiterated the Association's earlier arguments for postponement (Kumagai 1967: 118). There followed a bill proposed in the House of Representatives by Nagai Matsuemon, a prominent businessman and a member of the House of Representatives political grouping known as the *Taiseikai*. As with most bills considered by the Diet in its first session, Nagai's bill was short and to the point. Entitled *A Bill Concerning the Time of Enforcement for the Commercial Code and Commercial Code Enforcement Regulations*, it provided:

The Commercial Code (Law No. 23 of April 1890) and the Commercial Code Enforcement Regulations (Law No. 59 of August the same year) shall take effect from 1 January 1893.

(DNTGS: 501)

The bill ultimately passed both Houses, but not before a lively debate that occupied almost the whole sitting time for two days in each House, a total of some sixteen hours of talking. Before turning to consider the course of proceedings and the issues in debate, three preliminary points should be made.

Firstly, it would be rash to conclude a simple relationship of cause and effect between the Tokyo Association's petition and the subsequent introduction and passing of the bill. These events are to some extent an indication of the influence a group of respected merchants could exert upon the Diet, but it should be remembered that the Tokyo Association was by no means the only group calling for postponement and that many Members of the Diet[26] had previously urged postponement as members of the *Genrōin* and could be expected to maintain their earlier position.

Secondly, Nagai's affiliation with the *Taiseikai* is noteworthy. The *Taiseikai* has been described as 'an association of those Members who had a general sympathy for the aims and methods of the Government' (Mason 1969: 195).

The cabinet was formally committed to the doctrine of non-responsibility to (or independence from) the Diet, so that it was bad politics from its point of view to have an openly pro-government party in the House of Representatives. However, certain Members of the House who were elected as ostensible Independent (i.e. non-party) candidates but whose 'general sympathy' lay with the government, had formed an intra-mural association with the outwardly non-partisan name of *Taiseikai* (Accomplishment Society) (Mason 1969: 194). In that he introduced a bill which attempted to thwart the government's insistence on enforcement of the Commercial Code from January 1891, should Nagai, then, be thought of as a maverick member of the *Taiseikai*? A glance at the table on page 216 below will reveal the answer to be 'no', for it appears that of all those who spoke in debate on Nagai's bill, not a single *Taiseikai* Member supported the government's wish for enforcement from January 1891. The general characterization of the *Taiseikai* as pro-government is therefore clearly not applicable in the specific context of debate on the Commercial Code. This opposition from the *Taiseikai* shows that the first Diet in its attitude to the Code was quite capable of developing its own doctrine of independence, i.e. Diet independence from the cabinet.

Thirdly, from the foregoing it can be seen that the question 'when and why did the government decide to submit the Code to the Diet?' is based on a false premise. Rather, the bill was a bid from the Diet to secure last-minute postponement of a law which had been promulgated before the Diet existed and had not been submitted to it. Was it, then, simply a mistake on the part of the government not to have enforced the Code two months earlier and thereby caused it to take effect before the Diet sat? Bearing in mind the acumen of the then Prime Minister Yamagata Aritomo and other oligarchs, this may not have been just a mistake. One possibility is that it was realized the Diet might oppose the Code, and thus it was thought better to allow time for possible postponement than to suffer the greater humiliation of having the Code actually repealed by the new Diet. A less extreme, and therefore more easily acceptable, form of this view is that although the ministers did not actively submit the Code to the Diet, they recognized that it was a document of great public importance and decided to allow time for the legislature to consider it on its own initiative before it took effect.

The postponement bill in the House of Representatives

The sole business on the House of Representatives order paper for Monday 15 December 1890 was Nagai Matsuemon's bill. After a short announcement by the Speaker of the House, Nakajima Nobuyuki, that various ministers would appear in the House the following day to answer questions which had been presented by Arai Shōgo, Nagai moved to the centre of the chamber and ascended the rostrum. He stated just two grounds for presenting the bill. Firstly:

> Article 1 of the Commercial Code makes it clear that the Commercial Code is complementary to the Civil Code. For this reason the Commercial Code should be enforced at the same time as the Civil Code, that is 1 January 1893, the date provided for in the present bill.

Secondly:

> The Commercial Code contains many unsuitable provisions and abounds in institutions which are unknown in Japan. Its operation could not fail to produce great inconvenience in the practical transaction of business. . . . My original idea was to submit a bill for amending these defects but as the date of the Code's operation is imminent, there is no choice but to propose postponement.
> (DNTGS: 501)

He did not, however, specify the defects or unfamiliar institutions.

Toyoda Bunzaburō, a Liberal and public spirited entrepreneur elected from Ōsaka, was first to speak in opposition to the bill. He admitted the Code was not free from defects but argued that no law could be perfect from the outset, and that the Code must be gradually amended in accordance with practical experience. As to the reason why speedy enforcement was necessary, he argued that during the past few years the country's economic condition had been harmed by speculative and untrustworthy companies (DNTGS: 502). The only remedy, he said, was to enforce the Code. It was true the provisions on companies and bankruptcy were considered by some people to be too strict, he said, but these were people who realized that the operation of the Code would put an end to their cunning and deceitful business schemes (DNTGS: 502).

As the foregoing glimpse suggests, the debate was determined but earnest in nature. The content of the speeches was mostly confined to points relevant to the Code, and no Member lowered himself to the arguments *ad hominem* which characterize parliamentary debates in many countries today. Few Members were interrupted during their speeches. The earnest character of the debate can be taken as a measure of the seriousness with which the Code was regarded (Kudō 1901: 76); for at some other times during the first session of the Diet, the House of Representatives reached a state of uproar. What, then, were the issues covered in the debate?

The first point raised by Nagai, that the relationship between the two Codes meant they ought to be enforced from the same date, was answered by Suematsu Saburō (Independent from Yamaguchi Prefecture) with the argument that the word *mimpō* in the Article 1 of the Commercial Code referred not to the Civil Code but to the general civil law already in existence and that therefore there was no need to have the two Codes operate from precisely the same date (DNTGS: 504). This argument, though ingenious and appealing in the abstract, carried with it the problem that it could scarcely be said that a general civil law existed. Judicial decisions were at the time guided by a *Dajōkan* edict (entitled *Rules Concerning Judicial Administration*) published in 1875, Article 3 of which provided: 'Civil cases shall be judged in conformity with custom in the absence of statutory provisions and by means of reason [*jōri*] in the absence of custom' (Nakamura 1962: 71). Judges, who were apparently often at a loss to find a suitable custom, varied widely in their exercise of 'reason'. For example, some saw fit to base their exercise of 'reason' upon the unenforced Civil Code, while others did not (Takayanagi 1963: 31). The argument that a general civil law did not exist, however, had the inherent difficulty that it drew attention to such inadequacies and inconsistencies. As has been seen, these latter were a prime reason for the government to introduce codes, and were therefore not likely to be stressed by those advocating postponement, though Okayama Kenkichi did mention them.

The second point raised by Nagai, that unfamiliar matters in the Code would disrupt Japanese commerce, may be regarded as a more moderate form of the xenophobic reaction which was one element in the 1889 *Hōgakushikai* resolution. This second point was countered partly by the argument (from Suematsu Saburō) that rapidly increasing foreign commerce created a need for conformity with Occidental methods, even if they were unfamiliar at present, and partly by the argument (Suematsu and Miyagi Kōzō) that the Code did take account of Japanese customs. Apart from one instance, that of the method for keeping trade books[27], advocates of postponement did not discuss the specific 'unfamiliar elements' in the Code. Neither did advocates of enforcement deign to demonstrate specific ways in which the Code took account of Japanese customs. In this connection, though, the striking resemblance between certain traditional concepts in pre-Meiji Japanese commercial law and its counterpart in Europe is noteworthy. This affinity of basic commercial legal concepts was pointed out in an article[28] in the *Japan Weekly Mail*. There Wigmore argued that, for example, the concept of the bill of exchange seems to have been developed by the Japanese at about the same time it was developed by the Lombards in Europe, i.e. in the thirteenth century (*Japan Weekly Mail*, 10 December 1892). Similarly, in 1850 the idea of a business as a legal entity distinct from the individuals who make it up was as comprehensible in Japan as in England or America. This remains far from proving that no concept in the Commercial Code was new to Japanese merchants; but it does suggest that no matter how little those responsible for drafting it had actually altered it in the light of Japanese usages, the Code had more conformity with Japanese usages than the advocates of postponement would have liked to believe.

Another ground emphasized by supporters of the postponement bill was the point earlier made in the *Genrōin*, and by some others, that eight months was not sufficient time to become familiar with the Code before it took effect. Opponents of the bill[29] sought to refute this by saying that even after the two extra years required by the bill there would still be many people who had not studied the Code, whereas less than eight months had already been sufficient for crooked merchants to come to grips with the fact they would have to mend their ways under the Code.

Finally on the postponement side, the statement by Okayama Kenkichi, one of the two Progressive Members who spoke on the bill, that 'Commercial law is a private law and should not be too much interfered with by the legislature', is noteworthy. Okayama, who had graduated from the Law Faculty of Tokyo University in 1882 and was therefore imbued with English Common Law conceptions, was hinting at the view that customary law would be better than legislation, or, put in another way, that common law would be better than codes.[30] However, this Pandora's box of jurisprudential argument was opened no further by the advocates of postponement. Neither was it tampered with by the advocates of enforcement.

As well as making the points already mentioned, advocates of enforcement (i.e. speakers against the bill) reminded the House that Japan's hopes for treaty revision would be weakened by non-introduction of the Code (Suematsu Saburō, DNTGS: 502); that although the Code might contain defects, these could be remedied in the light of experience with the practical operation of the Code (Toyoda, DNTGS: 502); and that the merchants who objected to the Code were a minority concentrated in Tokyo, whereas those in Ōsaka, the acknowledged centre of commerce, favoured enforcement (Kikuchi Kanji, DNTGS: 508). This last point appears not to have been refuted by supporters of the bill, though the reply could have been made that the Tokyo Association of Commerce and Industry had been supported by some regional chambers of commerce in its call for postponement. The point that the Code should first be put into operation and then revised was condemned by one supporter of the bill as a 'cruel and deceitful idea' to use the Japanese people as a subject for experiments in law (Motoda Hajime, DNTGS: 503). To hasten enforcement for the purpose of treaty revision was also, on this view, undesirable, for it subordinated the interests of forty million Japanese to the demands of foreigners.

The expression of a view in favour of revision of the Code before it was implemented shows that some speakers for the bill went beyond the earlier position of the *Genrōin*. The *Genrōin* had called for the delay in enforcement so that the nation could become familiar with the Code. Nagai and others called for a delay in enforcement so that the provisions of the Code could be altered.[31]

Such were the issues raised in debate on Nagai's bill in the Lower House. However, in studying Diet history, indeed in studying any history, it should be kept in mind that debate can never take place without persons to take part in debate. It is legitimate to divorce the issues raised from the persons raising them in order to reduce the issues to a manageable topic; but even here understanding will be enriched if it is remembered that the nature of what is said in debate is determined by the convictions, beliefs and backgrounds of the persons involved.

Table 6.1 lists basic information for each Member who made a substantive speech (i.e. declared support or opposition to the bill and did not just raise a point of procedure) in the House of Representatives.

Table 6.1 Members speaking on the postponement bill in the House of Representatives

	YC	*GS*	I	*T*	P	E	
Nagai Matsuemon				x	x		Aichi
Toyoda Bunzaburō	x					x	Ōsaka
Motoda Hajime				x	x		Ōita
Suematsu Saburō			x			x	Yamaguchi
Okayama Kenkichi		x			x		Shizuoka
Kikuchi Kanji	x				x		Ōsaka
Konishi Jinnosuke	x				x		Kagawa
Inoue Kakugorō	x					x	Hiroshima
Ōyagi Biichirō				x	x		Tokyo
Miyagi Kōzō			x			x	Yamagata
Tanaka Gentarō				x	x		Kyōto
Ienaga Yoshihiko	x					x	Nagasaki
Suematsu Kenchō				x	x		Fukuoka
Takanashi Tetsushirō			x			x	Tokyo
Seki Naohiko		x			x		Tokyo
Inoue Seiichi			x			x	Yamaguchi

Key:
YC = Yayoi Club (Liberal)   *T = Taiseikai*
GS = Giin Shūkaijō (Progressive)   P = favoured postponement
I = Independent   E = favoured enforcement

One of the few patterns that emerges from this table is that already mentioned. *Taiseikai* members all spoke for the bill (i.e. against enforcement). What explanation, then, can be given for the various speakers' sympathies? One key seems to be that four of the nine 'postponement' speakers, namely Motoda, Okayama, Ōyagi and Seki, were law graduates from Tokyo University in the late 1870s and early 1880s. They were thus part of the 'English law faction'. Suematsu Kenchō very likely also belonged to this faction, for he was a graduate of Cambridge University. Among the 'enforcement' speakers, on the other hand, Miyagi, Takanashi and Inoue Seiichi had studied French law. In this light, the division of sympathies seems to have been at least partly connected with the division between rival schools of juris-prudence. The uniform *Taiseikai* support for the bill may well show that members of that group such as Motoda, Ōyagi and Suematsu Kenchō, who belonged to the 'English law faction' were able to persuade their colleagues to support the bill.

Just as noteworthy as the apparent defection of *Taiseikai* members who are supposed to have had a general sympathy for the government, is the seeming waywardness of Liberal speakers in the debate. No doubt some Liberals (and possibly the two Progressives) were actuated by a desire to fulfil party aims to oppose and embarrass the cabinet. None the less, it should be borne in mind that three of the five Liberals who spoke, including Toyoda, in fact supported the government's enforcement date. Thus, Nakamura's criticism[32] of the Liberals for opposing the government in a partisan fashion on the issue of the Code seems to be misplaced.

Finally, another element in the division of sympathies was the split between Tokyo entrepreneurs, represented by Nagai, and Ōsaka entrepreneurs, represented by Toyoda. It can, then, be seen that general political sympathies or intra-mural party loyalties in at least some cases bowed in this debate on the Commercial Code to longer established extra-mural loyalties formed by speakers' academic and professional or business backgrounds. Future detailed study may well confirm or deny these suggested reasons for individual Members taking the attitude they did, possibly discovering new ones in the process. This task could prove daunting, as is illustrated by the matter of rivalry between the 'English law faction' and the 'French law faction': speakers in the Diet largely steered clear of the grandiose issue of the applicability of a Code system as against a Common Law system. Yet, when one discovers the backgrounds of the speakers, rivalry between French and English jurisprudence clearly had an important bearing upon the debate. Partakers in debate may honestly state reasons for what they say, yet the underlying reasons are often more complex and have an air of the inscrutable.

Towards the end of the afternoon of 16 December, the bill's second day in the House of Representatives, Horiuchi Chūji (a Liberal Member elected from Nara Prefecture) moved that debate be closed (DNTGS: 525). This motion was put and carried on the number of Members standing. A vote was then taken on the bill itself, by collecting the *meishi* (name cards) of Members voting for and against it. The result was 189 votes for to 67 against. This result is notable for two matters. Firstly, more than fifty Members of the three-hundred-strong House did not vote. Secondly, the vigorous and apparently evenly matched nature of the debate belies the fact that opponents of the bill were outnumbered by almost three to one, a reminder that in politics then, as in politics now, logic and vigorous argument are not all that count.

Suematsu Kenchō then moved that the second reading of the bill take place the same day (DNTGS: 527). This was carried on the number of

Members standing, after which the Speaker announced there would be a short recess. The House rose at 5.28 p.m. and resumed at 6.30 p.m. By 6.43 p.m. the bill had passed the second reading, again on a vote determined by Members standing,[33] and the House had voted to dispense with a third reading.

The postponement bill in the House of Peers

Having been passed by the House of Representatives, the postponement bill was then considered by the House of Peers on 20 and 22 December 1890.

Possibly because the House of Representatives itself provides such a complex and intriguing topic of study, the activities of a second equally complex and intriguing component of the Japanese Imperial Diet, namely the House of Peers, tends to be overlooked. On the object of having a House of Peers, Itō Hirobumi, whose role was decisive in preparing the Meiji constitution, wrote:

> The object of having a House of Peers is not merely admittance of the higher classes to some share in the deliberations upon legislative matters, but also representation of the prudence, experience and perseverance of the people, by assembling together men who have rendered signal service to the State, men of erudition and men of great wealth.
>
> (Itō 1906: 66)

Since the Constitution gave almost identical powers to the two Houses and provided that no bill could become law without the assent of both Houses, a study of proceedings concerning the Commercial Code postponement bill would clearly be incomplete without some treatment of its fortunes in the House of Peers.

When debate did begin in the House of Peers on the morning of 20 December, Watanabe Jinkichi moved that because such a short interval remained before the date originally fixed for the operation of the Code, the House should dispense with the second and third readings of the bill. He also moved that the President of the House should appoint a special committee to consider the bill, this committee being required to report to the House by 2 p.m. the same day (DNTGS: 43). The idea of appointing a committee required to report in such a short time was criticized by the *Japan Weekly Mail* (27 December 1890) on the ground that the Code could not possibly be considered on its merits in the space of a few hours; but it seems that if the postponement bill was to attain the desired effect, it was imperative that the Peers avoid a drawn-out or adjourned discussion. As the *Japan Weekly Mail* itself pointed out on the same page, there remained only six days until the government departments were to close for the New Year holiday. During these six days the bill would have to be passed by the House of Peers, sanctioned by the Emperor, and published as a law allowing sufficient time for outlying areas to be notified that the operation of the Commercial Code was to be postponed.

The President of the House, Itō Hirobumi, first put the motion regarding the special committee. The motion was passed on the number of Members standing. After a brief adjournment the President announced the Members he had appointed to the committee: namely, Kuroda Kiyotsuna, Murata Tamotsu, Watanabe Jinkichi, Okauchi Shigetoshi, Obata Umashine, Watanabe Kiyoshi, Miura Gorō, Maeda Masana and Obata Tokujirō (DNTGS: 44).

A majority also stood in favour of the motion to dispense with the second and third readings. However, because a two-thirds majority was required by the Law of the Houses for such a motion, the President ordered that there be a roll-call. The outcome was 174 votes for the motion to 104 against the motion, tantalizingly short of the required majority (DNTGS: 46).

Even though a committee had been appointed, the President allowed the House to begin debating the bill. Many of the substantive issues raised in the Peers had already been raised in the Lower House. For example, several Members[34] opposed the bill on the ground that the proper interpretation of Article 1 of the Commercial Code was that the word *mimpō* referred to civil customary law, not the Civil Code, and that therefore there was no need to wait until the enforcement date for the Civil Code before enforcing the Commercial Code.

However, the debate in the House of Peers was by no means a mere repetition of that in the House of Representatives. Differences in procedure[35] are obvious, but also, as might be expected from the different composition of the House of Peers, a number of fresh issues were raised. For example, Watari Masamoto argued that the bill was unconstitutional. He said:

> Article 6 of the constitution provides that the Emperor gives sanction to laws and orders them to be promulgated and executed, and although Article 38 empowers the Diet to initiate projects of law, it does not confer any competence to fix the date for putting a law into operation.
>
> (DNTGS: 47)

A popular image of the Meiji Constitution has been that it was totally undemocratic and allowed only authoritarian rule by a handful of oligarchs. The fact that Watari's view did not prevail (i.e., the Diet did overcome the government's wish for enforcement of the Commercial Code from 1 January 1890) is one of many instances counter to this popular image.

It has been argued that the motions moved by Watanabe Jinkichi to dispense with the second and third readings, and to appoint a special committee to consider the bill rapidly, were justifiable on grounds of urgency. Later, reporting as a member of the committee, he made a suggestion which, it may be felt, was not justifiable. He said that because the House of Representatives was more representative of merchants and manufacturers than was the House of Peers and for the sake of preserving good relations between the Houses, the House of Peers should follow the House of Representatives in supporting the bill. Hirata Tōsuke in reply predictably protested that to advance such a theory was to deprecate the bicameral system, the very *raison d'être* of the House of Peers (DNTGS: 48–50).

Katō Hiroyuki, who earlier in the Meiji period as a founding member of the *Meirokusha* had been influential in spreading Western knowledge throughout Japan, was in favour of postponement. Katō argued (DNTGS: 51–2) that the rapid advances made by Japan in the past twenty years still needed to be complemented by sufficient education of society before it would be appropriate to introduce a Commercial Code. He therefore suggested the government should display the same caution as that shown toward introducing codes in Germany. Katō was thus drawing a parallel between the argument regarding codification in Japan and the earlier controversy between Friedrich Carl von Savigny and Anton Friedrich Justus Thibaut in Germany.[36]

The basic similarity between the two controversies is that each concerned the appropriateness of codification at a particular time in a particular country. The German controversy, however, involved the question whether it would be appropriate to compile a code, whereas the Japanese controversy arose once compilation had taken place. Fear of foreign elements played a part in both controversies. In Japan, this actuated those who opposed codification. In Germany, there were no doubt some who viewed the very idea of codification as foreign (in particular, as French), but the perception of Thibaut and his followers was that codification was needed to unite and strengthen Germany against foreign elements. In Germany, in other words, fear of foreign elements actuated those who supported codification. Moreover, the German controversy was essentially a learned disagreement between two professors of law, whereas the Japanese controversy was a complex and vehement public debate. On a broad conceptual level, there was the common factor that the anti-codification arguments involved a degree of aversion to 'natural law' thought. Also, in the speeches of some Diet Members, of which that of Katō is a good example, it is possible to identify undertones of Savigny's theory that law must be a product of the people's spirit. However, it should be noted that Katō's argument put simply was: 'do not codify: the people's spirit is not yet ready'; whereas Savigny's argument was 'do not codify: the lawyers do not yet understand the people's spirit'. In short, the relationship between the two controversies is one of broad similarity but underlying differences.

Returning to the House of Peers, debate on the postponement bill continued through the afternoon of 20 December. By 5.50 p.m., although the members of the special committee had reported to the House, there still remained a number of other Members who wished to speak and the President thus determined to adjourn proceedings. The following day being Sunday, proceedings were adjourned until Monday 22 December. The fact that a motion to close debate on 20 December was not forthcoming suggests that supporters of the bill may have believed voting would be close. However, when voting took place[37] on the morning of 22 December, 104 Members voted for the bill and only 62 against it (DNTGS: 86).

As with the House of Representatives, the exact motives for voting of individual Members must be a matter of further research. Of those mentioned above, Kuroda Kiyotsuna, Murata Tamotsu, Watanabe Jinkichi, Okauchi Shigetoshi, Obata Umashine, Maeda Masana and Katō Hiroyuki had previously been members of the *Genrōin*. In this light, the earlier opposition to the Code by the *Genrōin* would seem to have been a powerful influence in the House of Peers, possibly more so than in the House of Representatives.

Approval by the Diet of the postponement bill was no doubt a crushing blow to Justice Minister Yamada Akiyoshi. Since 1887 he had diligently supervised what he had hoped were the government's final efforts to produce a Commercial Code. At 10 p.m. on the evening of 22 December 1890, the day on which the House of Peers passed the bill, Yamada submitted his resignation to the Emperor. This was officially on grounds of ill health, but from the timing there can be little doubt Yamada's decision was strongly influenced by the success of the postponement bill.

The bill received Imperial Sanction on 23 December 1890 and was published as law number 108 of 1890 in the Official Gazette on 26 December 1890.

The Code and the second session of the Diet

The issue of the Commercial Code in the Diet did not end in the first session. The advocates of enforcement did not accept the passage of the postponement bill as a final defeat. On 10 December 1891, early in the second session of the Diet, a bill in the following terms was introduced to the House of Representatives by Watanabe Matasaburō:

> *A Bill Relating to the Enforcement of a Portion of the Commercial Code and the Commercial Code Enforcement Regulations.*
>
> Chapter 6 of Book 1 and Book 3 of the Commercial Code (Law No. 32 of March Meiji 23 [1890]), together with the provisions relating to Commercial Companies and Bankruptcy from the Commercial Code Enforcement Regulations (Law No. 59 of August the same year) shall take force from the first day of March Meiji 25 [1892], provided that the enforcement of Book 3 of the Commercial Code shall be restricted to cases of bankruptcy of Commercial Companies.

The bill was debated by the House of Representatives on 10 and 17 December 1891. Three key speeches were those of Watanabe Matasaburō (the proposer of the Bill), Nagai Matsuemon (who maintained his opposition to the Code), and Tanaka Fujimaro (the new Justice Minister), who addressed the House not as a Member but as the government representative.[38]

Watanabe Matasaburō, an independent Member elected from Hiroshima Prefecture, was an influential lawyer. He was vice-president of the Hiroshima Law Society and had been a member and vice-chairman of the Hiroshima local assembly. His experience in law and in addressing assemblies are evident in his speech to the House.

As soon as the bill was read to the House, he ascended the rostrum and spoke as follows:

> Before proceeding to mention the substance of this bill, I should make a correction. I trust you are aware that 'April Meiji 24' in the bill is a mistake for 'March Meiji 23'.
>
> As to a summary of our reasons for proposing this bill, we have already said something in the written explanation accompanying the bill, and I believe you gentlemen are aware of the main points therein. I cannot here state how much of a panic the mismanagement of commercial companies in recent years has caused among our nation's economic community. This is something about which the general public has been clamouring for a long time, and the matter of producing an elaborate and strict law as a means of dealing with the

situation is one of the current issues taken up unanimously by men of learning in society.

The portion of law we seek to enforce is Chapter 6 of Book 1 plus Book 3 of the Commercial Code. Calculated in terms of articles, this is from Article 66 to Article 273 and from Article 978 to the last Article, namely 1064; 295 articles in all, which amounts to less than a third of the whole text of the Commercial Code. Besides this, there are the rules relating to commercial companies and bankruptcy in the Commercial Code Enforcement Regulations. Something I must mention here is the problem of whether or not one can enforce a part of the promulgated Code without the difficulties of inconsistency. Examples of enacting and promulgating a particularly expedient law are not at all rare in countries with uncodified law. As you gentlemen know, England in 1849 promulgated insolvency laws, in 1862 made an enactment relating to commercial companies, and later after many developments, in 1883 revised and augmented them. Also, the United States first produced a Bankruptcy Act in 1800 and after frequent changes finally made a revised enactment of it in 1878. Thus there are so many different examples that in fact I am not at leisure to mention them all. Also, in the case of countries with codified law, France has produced separate laws relating to commercial companies. France in 1807 promulgated the law of bankruptcy as part of its Commercial Code, and in 1835 revised this law of bankruptcy. Then Spain, in 1830, promulgated bankruptcy laws, and Holland in 1838, Prussia in 1855, Austria in 1868, Italy in 1865, Germany in 1877, each respectively did so. There are many examples of this. Thus, both those who oppose the enforcement of the entire Code, and those who oppose the enforcement of part of the Code, which is made necessary by present circumstances, would, I think, say that, after all, as to the enforcement of a portion of a law, there are frequent examples in foreign countries.

The next issue with which we must concern ourselves regarding the enforcement of a portion of the Commercial Code is the relationship between the Commercial Code and other major laws. The first matter we must examine is the relationship with the Civil Code. As the drafters of the Commercial Code explain in the preface, as the Commercial Code and Civil Code both cover property law and contract law, the general ambit includes both Codes. Also as the Commercial Code makes clear in Article 1, that which is not provided for in the Commercial Code is left to the Civil Code as well as commercial custom. Consequently there may be a feeling that when one lays aside the Civil Code and enforces one part of the Commercial

Code, it is like making a bird unable to fly by taking away one of its wings, or making a cart unable to move by taking off one of its wheels.

However, the Civil Code, though now compiled, is not ready to go into force, and something as important as a Civil Code essentially needs to be enacted as a separate piece of legislation and as something based on reason and custom. On the other hand, I think that not enforcing a part of the Commercial Code would be tantamount to saying there should be no regulation of commercial companies. Thus, I think it is not worth being at all distressed that enforcement of the Civil Code does not accompany enforcement of this part of the Commercial Code.

The next point is the relationship between the Commercial Code and other specific laws. I think this is a very important matter especially with regard to the Commercial Code Enforcement Regulations. These Regulations are absolutely indispensable to the enforcement of the Commercial Code, and in the present case of trying to apply them to the enforcement of a part of the Commercial Code it is in fact easy to distinguish the articles relating to commercial companies and bankruptcy, so I do not think there is a need to feel at all uneasy.

Next, in regard to bankruptcy, the fact that Article 32, that is, a part of the non-enforced portion, is referred to in Article 1051 looks rather as though it may present problems, but if one simply ignores this portion it presents no difficulty whatsoever. Regarding the penal provisions for culpable bankruptcy in Articles 1050 and 1052 etc., there is certainly a need to enforce Law No. 101 of 1890.[39] Also, Law No. 66 of the same year relating to stamp duty in non-contentious commercial matters, is really necessary; and I believe that if this bill passes both Houses and receives the Emperor's sanction, the government will not neglect that fact for a moment. I think again there is no obstacle here.

Next is the matter of relationship between different parts of the Commercial Code, in other words, discord between the part which will be enforced and the part which will not be enforced. As I explained before, if one totally ignores everything except that which relates to commercial companies and bankruptcy of commercial companies, again I believe that will present no problems.

There is still one point I must say something about. What must be called one major excuse from the advocates of postponement of the Commercial Code is to urge a partial revision. When I examine the portion it is now proposed to enforce, I can find no point that requires major recasting. If for argument's sake we concede there may be defects, and look at the matters the supporters of postponement point to, there are, as the members of the Tokyo Association of Commerce and Industry's investigation committee made public in their Opinion on Revision of the Commercial Code, fourteen places in the 208 articles of Chapter 6. In particular, there are five involving revision of the wording, eight involving substantial alteration, and one involving the addition of an article. As to those involving substantive alteration, there are only such matters as altering the interest rate of 7 per cent in Article 95 to 10 per cent; making 'three people' in Article 191 'one person' or 'several people'; or making 'any person' and so on in Article 222, 'creditors' and so on. I do not think these are very major modifications. Coming to the other matters of suggested revision, if we do not revise the Code in the ways proposed, I cannot see there will be any great evil or huge problems in putting it into operation. Not only am I unable to see anything to this effect in documents advocating amendment; the same also applies in the case of people who wish to reject the Code completely. I think this is clear from the resolution of the Ōsaka Chamber of Commerce and from the arguments of lawyers and businessmen. In the 87 articles of Book 3 on Bankruptcy there are only two points nominated for revision. One involves alteration of wording, and one involves substantive change, but I do not think they are very well-grounded. Bearing all this in mind, revision is not needed. Even if the Code is enforced today there really will be no difficulty. To sum up, even businessmen and experts cannot easily see the legal appropriateness of partial revision. For these reasons I do not think we should be at all slow to put this Code into force.

To conclude I should like to mention a point concerning enforcement of bankruptcy law together with company law. Fundamentally, this thing called bankruptcy applies not only to companies in our Commercial Code, but to commercial persons in general, but here we are only enforcing the law of commercial companies, and considering the possible results, we have decided to apply it only to cases of bankruptcy of commercial companies. In recent years in various countries, the law of bankruptcy has developed considerably and reached a state of perfection. Despite this, our own regulations regarding bankruptcy are far from perfect. I think that if the law of commercial companies is enforced, but the law of bankruptcy is not enforced, then it will be a waste. Therefore we intend to enforce only those provisions that deal with bankruptcy of commercial companies. As experts in commercial law say, generally speaking, the way we deal with bankruptcy of merchants must be more rigorous than that for ordinary persons. This is particularly so with commercial companies, and commerce being a special case, special provisions are most urgent. The reasons we need to establish a law concerning bankruptcy are partly to maintain confidence in traders and partly also to afford proper protection. I believe that, when explained, the need for bankruptcy law is clear. As I said when I outlined my chief aim in proposing this bill in my opening paragraph, at the same time as hoping to rid ourselves of nefarious companies by means of a rigorous and just law, and dispelling panic in our nation's economic community, we hope for the establishment of fine companies which will inspire confidence.

There may be an argument that because we expect our Commercial Code to be enforced in its entirety from January 1893, which is only a short period of ten months from 1 March 1892, it would be better to wait until January 1893 and not to trouble ourselves with the present bill. But I think there are a number of points which require revision in the whole text of the Commercial Code and also in the Civil Code. It may possibly be that the Commercial Code cannot be enforced from January 1893. It is certainly hard to guarantee that it will be enforced from January 1893. Thus, since it is easy to see that every day company law and the corresponding law of bankruptcy is delayed is a day lost, and every day hastened is a day gained, I now present this bill. I sincerely hope it will have the support of as many Members as possible and that it will pass this House swiftly.

Nagai Matsuemon, who together with Motoda Hajime and Okayama Kenkichi was one of the three main speakers against the enforcement bill, spoke as follows:

I oppose this bill. I should like to have your attention while I outline some opinions in opposition to the bill. My reasons for opposing this bill are not only that it seems you gentlemen are being called upon to go back on your decision made last year.

According to the proposer of the bill, we hear that we must prevent panic amongst companies by means of strict and detailed rules; but on the contrary, I think that if we hasten enforcement we will bring on panic amongst the economic community. Consequently I am opposed to such a thing.

As for postponement of the Commercial Code, prior to the opening of the Imperial Diet last year, there were various opinions regarding the merits and demerits of enforcement, from the academic and business communities. Then, in the first session of the Imperial Diet, in this very chamber, the question arose, and, while these merits and demerits were being debated, they were also debated outside the Diet in newspapers, speeches and so on. Also from every region many petitions came to this House and the House of Peers. Among these petitions there were those which approved of enforcement, but the majority in fact approved of postponement. Thus, this Diet, accepting legitimate public opinion, by a large majority postponed enforcement until 1 January 1893. Without me reiterating the reasons for that postponement, I think you gentlemen will remember them from that material, but, to quote the main views therein which led to postponement: the Commercial Code is a law complementary to the Civil Code and thus it would be inconvenient to enforce it while the Commercial Code is not in force; and therefore it is appropriate first of all to postpone it until 1 January 1893, the same as the enforcement date for the Civil Code. This was one reason. However, I do not think this was the most important reason. If we look at the main reason it is that the drafting is faulty: the process of drafting has not been carried out well, and there are inappropriate provisions among its contents. And not only are there inappropriate provisions, there are many points that do not correspond to the condition of the people and thus are undesirable. There are also many points which do not accord with custom.

Since, if we were to enforce this Code, we would straight away cause disruption among the commercial community, we should rather carry out a proper revision so that it accords with the condition of the people – I think that was one main reason. Another was that, with respect to enforcing a Code like this, the period from the day of promulgation until enforcement was short, only six months, and for all those involved in commerce to become familiar with and comply with a huge Code within this period would be very difficult. Thus we must postpone enforcement to allow for proper preparation. I believe it was for reasons like these that this House as well as the House of Peers approved of postponement until 1 January 1893.

I thus fear that if we were now to enforce a portion, namely the law of commercial companies and bankruptcy, from March next year, we may cause another panic amongst the commercial community. If we look at commercial companies at present, all these companies are carrying on business on the basis that the Code will be enforced from 1 January 1893, and dubious companies are reorganizing themselves into companies that befit this Code. I believe it would be very disloyal to the people to disregard the fact that they have already been given this grace and suddenly to shorten the time to March next year.

None the less, in my opinion, if one asks what provisions are the necessary ones in the Commercial Code, they are those regarding company law, bankruptcy law and the like. If one takes away company law and bankruptcy law from the many provisions, one may as well say the remaining provisions are useless.

There are many provisions which are not yet needed in Japan. I am not greatly opposed to enforcing these, but I think that to shorten the time until enforcement and make it March next year is utterly inappropriate. I strongly believe that the way to maintain economic order is to enforce the Code from 1 January 1893, as was decided last year.

The proposer has just said there is a great need for enforcement, but I do not believe there is a very great need. The reason there is not a need is that, at the moment, when we look at the economic community in general, it has fallen into panic, and having fallen into panic, the panic is now being eased. (Someone calls out 'We can't hear'.) In other words, the various companies are mainly remedying this situation. Even if this bill did not now exist, they would mainly be remedying the situation. By the time it is proposed to enforce this bill, January [sic] next year, one can expect the situation to be remedied. So not only is there no need to enforce the law and use it to coerce companies to remedy the situation, it may instead be that the companies now reorganizing would be ruined by such a move. Or again, it may be thought there is a need regarding newly established companies, but if you consider the present commercial community, last March and April there were virtually no companies newly formed. Thus I believe there is nothing compelling us hastily to enforce this law for the sake of newly established companies.

For such reasons I think there is no need to hasten the enforcement date for this Commercial Code, and so I hope that, in accordance with the present position, it will be enforced from 1 January 1893. I thus speak against the bill.

In that there had been no general election between the first and second sessions of the Diet, the composition of the House of Representatives was almost the same in both sessions. Indeed, all Members who spoke on both Nagai's bill in the first session and Watanabe's bill in the second session maintained their views in favour of postponement or enforcement as the case may be. The notable change was in the position of the government, as is shown by the short speech of Justice Minister Tanaka Fujimaro. He said:

Regarding the bill at present being debated by you gentlemen, I should like briefly to outline my views. Earlier, in March 1890, the government promulgated the Commercial Code, and decided upon enforcing it from January 1891. This was, of course, due to it being a matter of urgency. After this, the first Imperial Diet decided on postponement for two years. The government was not unwilling to accept this public opinion, and soon it expressed the same view. It has been decided that the Commercial Code will go through the remaining due procedure and be enforced from 1 January 1893. That is to say, I think it eminently suitable that the Code as it already stands should be enforced at the time which already stands. Now, to bring that time closer and enforce a portion of the Code will surely begin to bring disorder and complications to that which has already been decided upon. This is the point I find regrettable about the bill.

What, then, was the reason for the government's change of position? It is suggested that, as Tanaka openly claimed, this was a case of the government bowing to what it perceived as public opinion. The influence of public opinion upon decision-making in Japan is a complex theme which would reward considerable study. Such study could beneficially test the hypothesis that governments in the Meiji period were seldom willing to antagonize public opinion for more than a short period. In the present instance, the fact that the composition of the government itself had changed in May 1891 (the first Yamagata cabinet being replaced by the first Matsukata cabinet) no doubt facilitated a change in government position concerning enforcement of the Code.

Proceedings on the enforcement bill occupied most of the afternoon on 10 December 1891. Towards 5 p.m., Katō Rokuzō, a *Taiseikai* Member, moved that debate be closed. The closure motion was passed on the number of Members standing, as was the first reading vote. Amano Saburō, a Liberal elected from Saitama, moved that the second reading be proceeded with. This was opposed by Orita Kanetaka, also a Liberal but from Kagoshima Prefecture, on the ostensible ground that the order paper provided only for the first reading that day, and that the House should observe the order paper to ensure proceedings were carried out in an orderly manner. Amano's motion was then lost on the number of Members standing.

The second and third readings took place on the afternoon of 17 December, exactly a week later. On a motion by Itō Daihachi to carry the bill to a third reading forthwith, which was possibly merely a time-saving device (i.e. a means of combining the second and third readings into one vote at the end of a day of sitting), the voting appeared to be close when Members were asked to stand. Inoue Kakugorō thus asked for a roll-call. The result was sixty-four votes each way, and the deputy-Speaker, none other than the ex-*Genrōin* member and longtime scholar of Occidental law Tsuda Mamichi, exercising a casting vote in accordance with Article 47 of the constitution, voted in the negative. The enforcement bill had been defeated.

In the light of the large majority who favoured postponement in the first session, and of the fact that the enforcement bill did not have the support of the government, it would seem more surprising that the vote was so close than that the bill was defeated. In fact, only 129 of three hundred Members of the House voted. The remainder were presumably either abstaining or absent, but it is not clear in what proportion. The close vote in a sense foreshadowed that the debate in the first and second sessions of the Diet was to be but one chapter in an extended controversy.

An outline of later developments

As Watanabe Matasaburō had anticipated in December 1891, the postponement bill had a sequel. In late May and early June 1892 the Diet in its third session resolved to postpone enforcement of both the Civil and the Commercial Code until 1 December 1896.[40] Those opposed to enforcement of the Codes called for a committee to undertake a complete revision of them. Eventually, in March 1893, a Codes Investigation Committee was set up for this purpose by the government. The three members with special responsibility for the Commercial Code were Ume Kenjirō, Ōkano Keijirō and Tabe Hō.

Meanwhile, however, the enforcement bill also had a sequel when in December 1892 legislation to enforce the portions of the original Commercial Code concerning companies, bankruptcy and bills of exchange was proposed in the House of Peers. Interestingly, the bill was this time proposed by the government. After several minor amendments to the provisions to be enforced, it was passed by both Houses and received Imperial sanction as Law No. 9 of 1893. It provided that the specified provisions of the Commercial Code would take effect from 1 July 1893. The urgent need of these provisions for the orderly conduct of commerce had finally overcome the Diet's resolute opposition to enforcement of the Commercial Code.

Neither of the re-compiled Codes was completed by 1896, though the first portion of the Civil Code had been promulgated, so in December 1896 the Diet was obliged to postpone the enforcement date yet again to 30 June 1898. The Civil Code, which has continued to operate down to the present, was promulgated in two parts, and, after approval by the

Diet, took effect from 1 July 1898. The re-compiled text of the Commercial Code was submitted to the Diet for approval in May 1898. However, owing to an untimely dissolution of the House of Representatives, a period of further postponement of the 1890 version had never been approved by the Diet. The effect was that, to the apparent consternation of supporters and opponents of the government alike, the 1890 version became law. Diet approval of the new version was finally obtained in March 1899, becoming Law No. 48 of that year. It took effect from 16 June 1899 and with some amendments[41] remains in force today.

To what extent, then, did the new version differ from the 1890 Commercial Code? A complete answer to that is not possible, but in brief, regarding its source, the 1899 version seems to have been subject to more German influence than was the 1890 version: the Codes Investigation Committee had at its disposal drafts of a new German Commercial Code[42] of which it made prudent use. On the other hand, even though the 1890 version was originally drafted by Roesler, the latter's willing departure from his native Germany in 1878 is symbolic of the fact that he did not wish to be blinkered by a purely German approach. Regarding structure, some difference is obvious, for the 1899 version is divided into five Books[43] whereas the 1890 version was divided into only three Books. Yet close similarities may be observed between some provisions of the two Codes, for example those concerning Trade Books, or, as the 1899 version calls them, Books of Account. To draw an analogy, the 1899 Code is like an edifice built to a new design but utilizing many bricks from its predecessor on the same site.

CONCLUSION

As Frederic William Maitland rightly observed, 'such is the unity of all history that any one who endeavours to tell a piece of it must feel that his first sentence tears a seamless web'.

Throughout this chapter many questions have necessarily been left unanswered; for the writer takes the view that in the interpretation of history, as in the interpretation of law, a new question is born of the answer to any given question. For this reason, it is hoped that future work will test and build upon what is herein presented, and gradually repair the seamless web which is torn by what is not herein presented.

The significance of the 1890 Commercial Code and its reception in the first and second sessions of the Imperial Diet is manifold. In the context of legal development from the Tokugawa to the Meiji period, the Code represents transition from particularism to universalism. Difficulties encountered in drafting and enforcing it, and the fact that eventually early sessions of the Diet approved only of enforcing a particular portion, indicate that the legal particularism of the Tokugawa period did not end in 1868. In the context of the study of foreign law in Japan, postponement can be seen as a triumph of the 'English law faction' over the 'French law faction', and indicates that Japan did not receive the foreign idea of a Commercial Code as willingly and rapidly as it is sometimes supposed Japan accepts foreign ideas. In the context of constitutional politics, postponement was an early triumph of the Diet over the Cabinet. Political power was not so concentrated in the hands of an elite few as to allow an impetuous move regarding codification. Finally, in the broad context of the development of Japanese law, it was reactions to promulgation of the 1890 Commercial Code that ignited the vehement controversy concerning the Civil and Commercial Codes. The resolution of this controversy, in turn, was crucial in shaping the legal system of modern Japan.

NOTES

1 Accompanying this proclamation was the full text of the Code, which thus became Law No. 32 of 1890.
2 One illustration is the law regarding avulsion: in Izu domain land torn from one bank of a river to the other remained the property of the owners of the bank from whence it came, whereas in Echigo domain the former owners of the detached land had to bear the loss: 'New Codes and Old Customs', *Japan Weekly Mail*, 26 November 1892, p. 658.
3 It functioned as the official translation bureau as well as a research unit, and was also known as *Bansho Torishirabesho* or *Bansho Shirabedokoro*.
4 See the illustrations and descriptions of tortures such as 'The Lobster' in Hall (1913: 804ff.).
5 George Sansom wrote that 'a Japanese scholar who had been sent to the University of Leiden to study law . . . invented the compound word Kenri' (1950: 471–2). However, this word seems in fact to have been borrowed from William Martin's Chinese translation of Wheaton's *Elements of International Law*, which was published in Beijing in 1864 (Havens 1970: 52).
6 Basically Chinese-style criminal laws embodying some Western ideas, until 1882 when a Criminal Code and Code of Criminal Instruction, showing mainly French influence, came into operation.
7 Robert Epp (1967: 19) gives this date but does not quote its source.
8 These ranged from countries conquered by Napoleon e.g. Belgium (1811), to Turkey (1850) and Egypt (1875): Ōsumi Kenichirō (1957: 8–12). Whilst it might not be accurate to say that French law was 'used to modernise' the law of Germany, it is certainly true that, for example, the French Commercial Code influenced the German Commercial Code of 1861, which brought about a unified system of commercial law for the whole of Germany.

9 Legislation was one of the chief responsibilities of the *Sain*, which was founded on 29 July 1871 and abolished on 14 April 1875, to make way for the *Genrōin*.

10 I.e. the Code which is the topic of this work. In the Code at present in force (Law No. 48, 1899), the provision remains the same except that the wording has been altered to make it clear that the usages of trade prevail over the Civil Code.

11 In more detail, these dealt with such matters as succession and sale; mortgages; matters of personal legal status including domicile, marriage and divorce; and methods of proof in court.

12 Enquiries by the writer at the National Diet Library in Tokyo indicated that the draft has not survived. Neither was it possible to discover by whom the drafting was done.

13 At the National Diet Library, Tokyo University Law Library, and the National Archives at Takebashi.

14 Presumably by the government. It simply bears the words 'Tokio. 1884', no publisher's name being given.

15 This was entitled *Shōhō Sōan*. It bears the characters for *Shihōshō* (Justice Ministry) but no date.

16 Bearing in mind the confidence he enjoyed it seems unlikely that the findings were actually kept from him, but they might not have been produced until after his work was complete, for they were not published until 1884.

17 This view is stated forcefully in Friedrich Carl von Savigny, *Vom Beruf Unsrer Zeit für Gesetzgebung und Rechtswissenschaft*, translated by Abraham Hayward as *Of the Vocation of our Age for Legislation and Jurisprudence*.

18 A likely suggestion, for which the writer is indebted to R. H. P. Mason, is that the transfer to the Foreign Ministry was part of the novel *Rokumeikan* diplomatic strategy and that the return to the Justice Ministry was a result of the collapse of this strategy and the resignation of Inoue Kaoru from the position of Foreign Minister in October 1887.

19 In two parts, 2 May and 24 December 1888 (Itō Sumiko 1976: 218).

20 This had replaced the *Dajōkan* on 22 December 1885.

21 E.g. the Shipping Bureau of the Communications Ministry and the Banking Bureau of the Treasury (Itō 1976: 212).

22 This doctrine, derived from Roman Law, places upon those whose business involves receiving guests (e.g. hoteliers, bath-house proprietors) strict liability for loss or damage to property which a guest has brought on to their premises.

23 None of these three should, however, be condemned as totally blind fanatics. For example, Nishimura had been a member of the Meiji Six Society (*Meirokusha*), which was influential in diffusing Western knowledge throughout Japan.

24 Contrary to the belief of some laymen, German and French law were not greatly similar during the nineteenth Century. The 1804 *Code Civil* and the 1807 *Code du Commerce* were imposed by Napoleon upon parts of Germany but were quickly discarded by most German states after his fall.

25 Another ground for fears that the Diet might oppose the Code was that many former members of the *Genrōin* would have seats in the Diet.

26 Including Tsuda Mamichi, deputy Speaker in the House of Representatives, and Nishi Amane in the House of Peers.
27 Cited by Suematsu Kenchō (DNTGS: 520). The comment may be made that the Code's provisions on trade books presumed a high degree of literacy and numeracy among Japanese merchants.
28 Entitled 'New Codes and Old Customs' published in instalments from October to December 1892. John Wigmore later claimed to be the author of this (Wigmore 1928: 529)
29 Notably Toyoda Bunzaburō (DNTGS: 502), and Suematsu Saburō (DNTGS: 505).
30 As the *Japan Weekly Mail*, 20 December 1890, reports, he made the additional complaint that the Code provided for practices not yet current in Japan and if this approach were taken one might as well provide for other future contingencies such as commerce with inhabitants of the moon. In contrast, customary law (by definition) dealt with current practices. The full Japanese transcript of his speech is to be found in DNTGS: 506–7.
31 Some six weeks after the Diet had passed Nagai's bill, this question (as to whether the bill had been passed to allow familiarization or actual revision) arose in the House of Peers in discussion of a motion proposed by Obata Umashine. The motion urged the government to revise the Commercial Code and Civil Code, and, in that the motion was carried, the question was resolved in favour of the 'revision' view. See DNTGS: 412 (13 February 1891).
32 Based on his view of the Civil and Commercial Codes as 'progressive measures' which the Liberals on the basis of their manifesto should have supported (Nakamura 1962: 88).
33 On the motion of Aoki Eiji, a *Taiseikai* Member elected from Aichi Prefecture (DNTGS: 529).
34 Including Okauchi Shigetoshi, who reported as a member of the committee (DNTGS: 52).
35 Many of these, such as appointment of the special committee in the House of Peers, would seem to be a result of the urgency with which the bill had to be considered.
36 The Thibaut–Savigny controversy has not been fully studied in English. The most comprehensive work in English is Small 1924, Chapter 2, 'The Thibaut–Savigny Controversy'. For those who cannot read German, study of the controversy is difficult because the essay of Thibaut is yet to be fully translated into English, and although a translation of Savigny's reply does exist, it is a collector's item on account of its rarity. Bibliographical details of the primary sources and some useful secondary sources may be found in Small. The Thibaut–Savigny controversy, which took place in 1814, involved an essay published by Thibaut, calling for the compilation of a unified code of law for Germany. Thibaut's call was made amidst a current of francophobic German nationalism which had been promoted by the Napoleonic wars. Napoleon had imposed on the parts of Germany he conquered the adoption of a German version of the French Civil Code. With the defeat of Napoleon at the Battle of Leipzig in 1813, the conqueror was repelled and most of the numerous German states took the opportunity to rid themselves of this code which was seen as part of the conqueror's chains. Yet value was seen by Thibaut and others in the concept of a code. There

existed what may be called a philosophy of 'natural law optimism': that an ideal and universally applicable scheme of law could be discovered by the exercise of reason and then embodied in a code. Thibaut saw a unified code of law compiled by Germans to suit German conditions as a step toward political unification of the German people. Savigny's reply was directed against the idea that one could simply decide to draft a code and successfully present it to a people as that people's law. Rather, he argued, law is determined by the whole past of a people and is tied to the people's character. He developed this argument by means of the concept of *Volksgeist* ('folk spirit' or 'people's spirit'), claiming that the proper role of the legislator is first through the study of history to understand the *Volksgeist* of the particular people for whom he is legislating, and then in legislation to give accurate expression to that *Volksgeist*. Savigny thus strongly disapproved of the 'natural law' premise that proper law is the embodiment of universal human reason. With regard to Germany and Thibaut's call for a unified code, he argued it would not be possible to compile a suitable code until German jurists had given up 'natural law' notions and attained an historical understanding of the German *Volksgeist*. Savigny's views became influential to the extent that a unified German Commercial Code was not enacted until 1861 and a unified German Civil Code was not enacted until 1900.

37 On the motion of Watanabe Kiyoshi, who had opposed the bill during debate, the first reading vote was taken by secret ballot. The second and third readings followed almost immediately and were simply determined by the number of members standing.

38 Under Article 54 of the Constitution, cabinet ministers had the right to address the Diet at any time. This was an eminently useful provision in a Constitution which allowed for non-Diet and non-party cabinets.

39 This was a law specifying penalties, which were not specified in the Code itself.

40 The requisite bill was initially proposed in the House of Peers by Murata Tamotsu, and has received some scholarly attention in Japanese (Hoshino 1943 and 1969).

41 One of the most consequential of these took place in 1932 and 1933 when the provisions of the Code relating to the bills of exchange and cheques were deleted and replaced by separate laws on these subjects (Law No. 57 of 1933 and Law No. 20 of 1932 respectively), because Japan entered the Geneva Convention on Uniform Law for Bills of Exchange and Cheques. Other reasons for a number of amendments have been (1) United States influence since 1945, and (2) the natural development of commerce during more than ninety years.

42 The *Handelsgesetzbuch* (HGB), eventually enforced in 1900.

43 I.e., General Provisions, Companies, Commercial Transactions, Maritime Commerce, and Bills of Exchange.

Conclusions

History, regardless of whether it is being made or written, is anything but one-dimensional. A study of the first decade and a half of the Japanese Diet ineluctably reminds us of this well-honed truth. So much of the testimony does much more than merely call back political matters avidly discussed in days gone by. It also deepens our knowledge of the standing and development of the parliament as an institution; and at the same time it re-kindles our awareness of the past as a record of the aspirations, activities, disappointments and achievements of individual men, in this case thousands of them. Accordingly, issues, institutional elements and personal careers, along with reference as need be to individual chapters and their findings, will form the cardinal points of the following conclusions.

ISSUES

The particular matters for parliamentary debate covered in this book are as diverse as they are momentous: land tax; poor relief; public order and emergency police powers; foreign affairs, foreign trade, and the national economy; the drafting of Japan's Commercial Code and initial attempts to have it enacted. In addition, there were a number of issues, such as education or the independence of the Judiciary, which were raised from time to time in the House of Peers as described in Chapter 1. Even the full list of issues raised in the foregoing chapters remains, of course, a very small sample of the policies and measures laid before the Diet during its first fifteen years of existence. Nevertheless, in its diversity the list is representative, and a good indication of parliament's role as a national clearing house of legislative and political concerns from all sides of public life and all regions of the country. Here such concerns could be aired, tabled, formally and informally debated, and perhaps acted on.

There can be no doubt either about the intrinsic importance of the issues described in this book. They all went to the heart of national life; and debate on them was serious and sustained, even if for the time being it seemed negative or inconclusive. This was because any one issue had a much longer currency than any one session of parliament. Thus, the really poor were always with the Meiji period Japanese; as was the difficult question of land tax. Treaty revision had its origins in events well before the Restoration of 1868, and was not completed until the end of the first decade of the twentieth century. Likewise, a Commercial Code began to take shape in the 1870s and 1880s, but did not become the settled law of the land until 1899. From this point of view, it can be argued that the Diet acted as a sounding board as well as a clearing house, with particular debates giving government leaders, in addition to politicians and lobbyists, a good idea of the actual standing of a political issue at the time in question. On the desirability or otherwise of retaining the Peace Preservation Ordinance, for instance, opinion in the House of Representatives seems to have been about evenly divided in 1891, and the government must have felt accordingly hardened in its resolve to keep this legislation on the statute book. On the other hand, it correctly read the storm signals in the Diet's obstructive attitude toward the draft Commercial Code, with the criticisms raised by its friends in the House of Peers coming as a specially cruel blow, and soon decided on a policy of tactical retreat and regrouping. In all these manoeuvrings, opinion in the Diet was reflected and extended in that other great organ of popular expression and debate, the press. As a result, the concerns treated in this book were not just matters for debate between government and Diet or among Diet Members themselves; they also involved a wider public and its opinions, however hard these other elements may be to estimate.[1]

Any discussion of the broad historical meaning of the various programmes and measures rehearsed in the Diet and examined in the preceeding chapters must take account of their apparent lack of specific and fruitful outcome. There is an air of inconclusiveness, or at best negativism, which is typified by the failure of the Peers' protests on the unfair dismissal of Lieutenant-General Ozawa Takeo and the even more disgraceful treatment of Chief Justice Takano Takenori. To continue talking in concrete terms: land tax revision was actually achieved, with the second Yamagata cabinet getting much of its way after having thoroughly prepared the ground. However, the first Yamagata cabinet's 1890 bill on poor relief was comprehensively rejected by the House of Representatives. In contrast, the government's ordinance on peace preservation remained in force until 1898, despite Diet objections.

Similarly, in foreign affairs, the authorities followed their own moderate and forbearing counsels with regard to treaty revision and relations with Korea, regardless of insistent pleadings and urgings from both Houses of the Diet, until the mid-1890s. By that time they had succeeded in settling the former issue in accordance with their own lights and to the satisfaction of public opinion, and were at war with China over the destinies of the adjacent peninsula. Decisive diplomatic gains were at length achieved; but by a government acting as it thought best and in spite of, rather than because of, the Diet's attitudes. With the draft Commercial Code, on the other hand, inconclusiveness stemmed not from official ignoring of the Diet but from a directly contrary source: namely, opposition in the early Diets to the Sat–Chō leaders' well worked proposals, and their enforced revision. In these respects the fate of the Commercial Code was absolutely linked with that of the Civil Code.

Given the 'sounding board' character of the Diet, the problem of inconclusiveness, where it exists, does not in fact loom so large. Opinion on important issues was thoroughly aired, tested, and where necessary reserved for future action. But there is more to it than this. Seeming trivia – dead-end or deadlocked debate, procedural wrangles, point scoring, displays of egoism, bad temper or hard feelings and general jockeying for position – are hallmarks of parliamentary systems the world over. Moreover, it is only with the advantage of (sometimes considerable) hindsight that we latter-day *epigoni* are able to say that such and such an initiative or point of view was 'relatively unimportant' or 'futile' or 'lacked result' and so on. Thus, the House of Representatives (and even more so the ministerial Upper House) might well have accepted the government's bill on poor relief, especially in the form it took after being amended by the House's own committee; or, to take a contrary example, it is not too hard to imagine the government adopting the advice of Tani Kanjō and his friends in the House of Peers, and chosing to concentrate on the regaining of tariff autonomy as a first priority in treaty revision. In the same general fashion, it can be argued that initial Diet obtuseness with regard to the new legal Codes led to better ones in the end, so the early debates were not simply abortive or a waste of time. In other words, pondering the alleged ineffectiveness of so much of Diet politics makes us realize the 'openness' of the system, both in its inward and contemporary relation to its own activities at any one time and in its forward relation to future possibilities, i.e. history. Further, this quality of 'openness' was especially evident in the early years of the Diet, when it was more a gathering of individuals and less a conglomerate of organized factions and parties.

Does all this amount to a chaos theory of history? Not quite. In the first place, the Diet increased its efficiency as a legislative machine as time went by, owing in no small part to the very growth of more cohesive groupings within its walls. Secondly, some longer-term trends can be discerned, and so a certain amount of legitimate interpretative analysis made, with respect to the institution's first few years. Thirdly, regardless of future development, the Diet always had a day-to-day significance in terms of its personnel and in its role as in many ways the highest organ of national life and opinion.

INSTITUTIONAL STATUS AND INSTITUTIONAL DEVELOPMENT

The Diet could not have achieved what it did achieve without its high status. To a considerable degree, it possessed this from the outset; but its own activities and personnel combined with the general flow of events to transform and in many practical ways to enhance its standing during the first years of its existence. This is really the pith of the matter, but elaboration is called for.

The 'given' status of the Diet, that which it had from its inception, derived from a number of factors. One of these, clearly, was the official pomp and general circumstance of popular rejoicing that marked its ceremonial opening in November 1890, and the high expectations held of it. A related, and usually unremarked, influence was the important place accorded the new parliament in the 1889 Constitution. In the main text of that document, the provisions relating to the legislature occupy a substantial third chapter, coming after a Chapter I on the Emperor and a Chapter II on the rights and duties of subjects. In short, the 1889 Constitution put the Diet at the illustrious forefront of national life, as well as endowing it with a by no means meagre political potency; and this aura of attention and acclaim was heightened by three of the other great foundation documents of the mid-Meiji political settlement dealing specifically with the new national assembly: the Law of the Houses; the Imperial Ordinance concerning the (formation of) the House of Peers; and the Law of Election for the first House of Representatives.[2]

Furthermore, in the section of the Constitution dealing with the Emperor, the Diet receives more than honourable notice, the monarch's role in relation to it being put ahead of his position *vis-à-vis* the army and navy for instance; while the preamble to the document is full of such parliamentary concerns as the rule of law and the protection of civil rights, and goes on to make specific mention of the Diet alone among the major organs of state, and in particular that body's role in any process of constitutional amendment. By way of contrast, the articles directly concerning the Executive are restricted to two in all, on the Privy Council and the ministers of state (i.e., cabinet), and form a very truncated Chapter IV. The fact that the esteem and authority allotted to the Diet under the Constitution were subject to bureaucratic constraint and sniping, and had frequently to be fought for and enlarged, even in order to be maintained, should not blind us to their existence in the document from the start, or their initial significance as a status-endowment.

The Diet must have also derived much of its 'given' status from the attention, by no means all of it adulatory, it received in the press and other organs of contemporary publicity such as books and wood-block prints; and, as always, the exceptionally high calibre of the early memberships made a significant contribution in this respect too. Finally, credence must also be given to the notion that the Diet had status from the time it opened because it functioned immediately and fully in the manner it or any other parliament was supposed to do. Certainly, it became the butt of all kinds of aspersions and more measured criticism from both within and without; and it was often bedevilled by procedural wrangles, threats of violence, sordid 'money politics' (something which has lasted to this day) and fierce disputes with the government of the time especially over financial policies. Nevertheless, too much should not be made of these negative factors; the chapters of this book show that from the start the Diet was perfectly capable of conducting its affairs with the good sense and seriousness of purpose required of it by the Constitution. Critics, whether native or foreign, who miss this truth and belittle the Diet – or, indeed, the reality of *Japanese* modernization in general – do themselves no credit and are a positive danger to their publics.

This brings us to consideration of the institutional development of the Diet during the 1890s and early 1900s. Although the Diet was created *ab initio* in 1889–90, it did have useful and respectable antecedents in such earlier institutions as the Conference of Prefectural Governors (1874–1880), the Senate or *Genrōin* (from 1875), and the prefectural assemblies (from 1878 and 1880). The prior existence of these bodies – with their diverse memberships, elected in the case of the prefectural assemblies, comprising experienced men of affairs and substance; with their secretariats of presiding officers, secretaries and clerks; with their agendas, rules and procedures – did much to make possible the ready working of the Diet. In terms of this book, this side of things, which admittedly qualifies in some ways as 'given' status rather than institutional development, is never far from the surface. Apart from the generally orderly running of Diet affairs, and in a more directly political context, it can be discerned in the confidence some of the government's critics in the House of Peers on such matters as the Commercial Code or foreign affairs drew from their own earlier membership of the *Genrōin*. Likewise, the fact that so many Representatives had already served before the inauguration of the Diet as chairmen, deputy-chairmen, committee heads or just plain members of the prefectural assemblies gave them a store of proto-parliamentary and political skills which they could put to good use after 1890. Nor, when considering the immediate antecedents and subsequent development of the Lower House, should the politicizing and emancipating effects of the pre-constitutional agitation for liberty and popular rights be forgotten. In the early 1880s, this movement had spread far and wide, and had come to consist of a multiplicity of political associations and politically minded papers at both the national and local levels.[3]

What happened after 1890 was a, by no means easy, scaling down of expectations on all sides. The government found that it could not automatically get its way in the Diet; equally, the popular party opposition discovered that it could not browbeat the government. Both Houses had to adjust their relations to each other; and each of them had to allow for intra-mural differences of opinion, and accept, if not indeed preside over, the steady rise of party and factional influence within their membership even when theoretically unwelcome, as shown in Chapter 1. All of this produced a certain amount of disillusion with the system, especially among informed members of the public; and it led too to a lowering of political standards, as evidenced by the career of Hoshi Tōru, the notoriously corrupt and domineering Liberal Party leader who ended by being assassinated in 1901. But what was really taking place was a much more important re-routinization of national politics, following the obsolescence and breakdown of the old *baku-han* system, into new patterns that took account of the creation of the Diet as their main arena and symbolic centre. Without such a re-adjustment – many of the essentials of which had been achieved by the end of the nineteenth century – it is hard to see how the Diet system could have survived; and it is worth noting some of the evidence for this all important process of re-routinization to be found in the various chapters of this book.

To begin with, none of the parties to a particular debate were willing to go outside the system to avert or avenge a rebuff.[4] Thus, the authorities accepted their defeat on poor relief without demur; but on peace preservation the battle honours, if anything, went the government's way, with its opponents in the House of Representatives divided among themselves and a majority of them ultimately resigned to the existing situation. In foreign affairs and commercial law, even the most ardent advocates of this or that point of view in the early 1890s were prepared to admit defeat and plan to fight another day, still within mutually accepted bounds. Thus, Inoue Kakugorō declared himself satisfied with the Foreign Minister's replies when ending their exchange in the first session of the House of Representatives; and the actual point of *impasse* (and so disengagement) between government and opposition in the early discussions on the Commercial Code was the seemingly technical matter of the date from which it was to be enforced. This neatly deferred substantive, and possibly very damaging, debate about both the Commercial and the Civil Code to a conveniently later date. It is in the land tax debate of 1898, however, coming appropriately enough towards the end of the decade, that one can most clearly see the process of routinization and the 'politics of compromise' at work.

The relationship between the two Houses of the Imperial Diet does not really figure as a separate topic in its own right in this book. In some ways, this is unfortunate, because here was an important aspect of the new constitutional order which was completely untried, there being no precedent for a fully bicameral system in the unicameral prefectural assemblies or the older national consultative bodies such as the Conference of Prefectural Governors and the *Genrōin*. Moreover, the working-out of the relationship between the Peers and the Representatives during the 1890s did have its moments of tension and drama, as when the Representatives objected strongly to the Peers restoring cuts the Lower House had made in the naval estimates contained in the first Matsukaka cabinet's budget for 1892. The resulting dispute between the two Houses over their respective rights in the matter had to be ultimately settled by a ruling from the Privy Council.

As opposed to these excitements, the chapters of this book depict a more mundane reality of relations between the Houses being conducted more or less as envisaged by the Constitution. Thus, at the pragmatic level of actually getting bills through the legislature, the proposed changes to the land tax in 1898 had to be discussed in, and approved by, both Houses before they could become law; and the House of Representatives could fulminate against the Peace Preservation Ordinance from one year's end to the next, but, until the House of Peers accepted a Lower House bill to that effect, there was no way of having the Ordinance abolished. The same stamp of legally necessary bicameralism can be seen in the Diet's handling of the draft Commercial Code where the bills for postponement of the date of enforcement acquired all the greater authority for having been discussed and passed in both Houses.

The debates on foreign affairs, and in some ways the discussions on the Commercial Code, raise questions of a more amorphous nature concerning the combined influence and activities of the two Houses. In the first place, the abundant outpouring and general strength of criticism of the government's diplomacy or its plans for legal codification, voiced by both Peers and the Representatives, vindicated the Diet's claim to act as a unified body of public opinion at the highest level, as well as the state's supreme legislative organ. This claim was of course advanced in each House separately, but is best testified to by the numerous joint conferences (*kyōgikai*) between the two Houses, which totalled as many as twenty by 1900. There had even been a case by then of an inter-House committee to consider legislation. Secondly, the same general considerations lead us to ask whether individual Members of the two Houses opposed to this or that government policy engaged in behind-the-scenes and informal liaison when mounting attacks on the cabinet. It is evident that the public record of what was said in one House was taken into account by the other. For instance, Aoki Shūzō was questioned by Tani Kanjō in the House of Peers about his earlier description in the House of Representatives of the 1878 Japanese treaty with the United States as 'ineffective'. On the question of possible sustained, *private* co-operation between Peers and Representatives, on the other hand, this book does not provide conclusive answers one way or the other. Nevertheless, in the case of the debates on the Commercial Code in particular, it is hard to believe that this did not take place.[5]

Obviously, the Diet could not function, even in the most basic legislative and interpellative manner, without informal groupings *within* each House, since any bill, motion or questions to a minister had to have the prescribed quota of sponsors before it could be tabled. Informal groups were often contained and nourished inside larger and more formal structures: the nascent parties, factions, associations and clubs that proliferated in the Diet from the first. Such intra-mural atomism, and the wider societal pluralism that it reflects, are striking features of Japanese politics in any age. Chapter 1 shows how, in the case of the House of Peers, the tendency during the first decade or so of the Diet's existence was for Independents and individuals to give way to more tightly organized groups under recognized and capable leaders; and, further, for these entities to take an increasingly conservative stance in politics, sometimes even more conservative than the Sat–Chō national leaders wanted. Hence Itō Hirobumi's threat to embark on a wholesale reform of the Peers. Despite the emptiness of this particular threat, one way or another brave, independent souls – to say nothing of wild men – appear to have been tamed, though perhaps not completely eliminated, in the House of Peers. This was partly a result of the routinization of politics; partly the result of eventual government success, in achieving such important objectives as treaty revision and implementation of new legal codes.

In the House of Representatives, matters stood rather differently. Organized groupings along party or quasi-party lines were a far more conspicuous feature of the political landscape from the outset. In fact, the three hundred Members of the first House of Representatives, elected in July 1890, divided quite schematically and easily, on paper at any rate, into four major components. These were Liberals (130), Progressives (forty), *Taiseikai* (eighty) and Independents (forty-five). The first two of these on the whole combined to produce a popular party (*mintō*) majority in this and subsequent Lower Houses. But serious complications arose, firstly, from the failure to maintain a semblance of Liberal and Progressive unity on all occasions, and, secondly, from the fact that, although the Progressives remained reasonably united among themselves, the Liberals were fissiparous and apt to split and re-group throughout the 1890s. Even at the time of the election to the first Diet, they had stood as the three separate entities of *Aikokutō*, *Daidōha* and *Jiyūtō*, only coming together after the results of the polls were known to form the intra-mural *Yayoi Club* (Mason 1969: 193). This restored unity of the Liberals was extremely shaky, however; as can be readily seen in their subsequent and bitter divisions of opinion over the government's budget for 1891, the ramifications of these divisions in the forms of 'hard' and 'soft' factions, *sōshi* violence, and changes of heart on the Peace Preservation Ordinance.

Despite continuing ructions and recriminations, the Liberals managed to hold together; and in June 1898 they merged with the Progressives to form the *Kenseitō* (Constitutional Government Party). This new organization actually succeeded in forming the government of Japan for a brief and rather inglorious six months in 1898 (Ōkuma–Itagaki cabinet), before being split by internecine rivalry. The two former partners now once more went their separate ways as the *Kenseitō* (Liberals) and *Kenseihontō* (Progressives). Nevertheless by 1898, the position had considerably stabilized, at any rate so far as the Liberals were concerned, and in some ways they could be thought of as the 'natural' party of government. They had always been the largest single grouping in the House of Representatives; and their leaders, notably Itagaki Taisuke, had remained on good terms with Itō Hirobumi and other senior bureaucrats. Moreover, the inbuilt tendency of constitutional politics was to lead them to some form of accommodation with the Sat–Chō chiefs; and they themselves seem to have enjoyed a new access of unity and confidence after the disasters of the coalition cabinet. Thus, it is not altogether surprising that the basis of the largely successful second Yamagata cabinet of 1898–1900 was an informal agreement with the Liberals, by which that astute veteran of national politics bought their parliamentary support in return for some major concessions.[6] This was the prime political reality that underlay the enactment of the 1898 tax reforms, as detailed in Chapter 2.

What had been more or less covert at the time of the second Yamagata cabinet, and even at the time of the third Itō cabinet a little earlier, was to be quite overt two years later in 1900 when Itō Hirobumi once more became Prime Minister by entering into open alliance with the *Jiyūtō/ Kenseitō* group. The latter now reformed itself into the *Seiyūkai*, with Itō as its first President. Thus, Itō's fourth cabinet can be equally thought of as the first *Seiyūkai* cabinet; and the new party was to prove far stronger, more durable, and generally more effective than any of its predecessors in the previous decade.

One of the major institutional trends of the 1890s then, in Diet politics, was the uneven growth of the Liberals in cohesiveness and unity under generally accepted leaders. Linked with this was their ability to maintain, if not to improve, their standing in the House of Representatives relative to the other groupings. These two advances in turn allowed them by the end of the decade to 'assist' the second Yamagata cabinet and to 'form' the fourth Itō cabinet. In this way, the first stages of the politics of compromise (which meant in about equal proportions the bureaucratization of politics and the politicization of the bureaucracy) were played out. It all made for a more easily manipulated Diet, as trends in the House of Representatives paralleled those in the House of Peers. Moreover, the crucial domestic political events of the ten or twelve years after 1900 seem to have been prefigured in the differing strands of opposition posed by the Liberals to the government in the early sessions of the Diet. One must always remember that those early Liberal Representatives were a pretty mixed bag, and individual members of the party could be found standing on either side of any particular issue. Nevertheless, in general it can be said that dogged antagonism on matters like poor relief, or on the obligation of ministers to reply to questions, or on the fiscal proposals for 1891 was mitigated by a readiness to see the government's point of view (foreign affairs), or to give it the benefit of the doubt at any rate for the time being (peace preservation), or to compromise (budget, Commercial Code).[7]

The Progressives (*Kaishintō/Kenseihontō*), meanwhile, tended through all this to be little brothers at first, and then mirror image, of the Liberals. Generally speaking, though always somewhat less radical than the Liberals, they joined the latter in a popular party stance of opposition to the Sat–Chō leaders, based on common aspirations for party cabinets and enlargement of civil rights. This was until the discomforting episode of party merger and the short-lived 1898 *Kenseitō* cabinet. Immediately before that misadventure, the Progressives had provided tacit and vital parliamentary support for the second Matsukata cabinet of 1896–8. In this, they adopted a role very similar to that subsequently played by the Liberals during the second Yamagata cabinet, and in fact had shown the latter how to go about the all-important business of working one's passage into the cabinet room. Despite this auspicious start, the Progressives were to fall on relatively evil days after 1898, until revived from 1911, first under Katsura Tarō and then under their veteran founder, Ōkuma Shigenobu.

The other two major groups in the Representatives, namely the so-called pro-government party (*Taiseikai*, later *Teikokutō*) and the Independents, underwent rather varying changes of fortune during the years from 1890 to 1905. The government supporters seem to have definitely lost ground dropping from eighty in the first Diet to a mere eighteen in 1903. The Independents are more difficult to track, and at different times the bulk of them are listed as affiliated with the popular parties or with the pro-government minority of Members; but on the whole, their numbers seem to have held up at around forty (out of three hundred Representatives), to seventy (out of 376). However, this was not sufficient really to halt the trend to popular party, and especially *Seiyukai*, domination of the Lower House; and the fundamental picture is best revealed in the following figures for the state of the parties *circa* 1900: *Seiyūkai*, 156; *Kenseihontō*, 103; *Teikokutō*, 14; *Independent*, 27 (total 300) (Uyehara 1972: 245).

As genuine Independents in both Houses tended to dwindle, and the ranks of avowedly pro-government Representatives reduced to virtual insignificance, the need for an understanding in principle between bureaucrats ensconced in cabinet and the leaders of the popular parties in the Diet took on all the colour and urgency of a political imperative. This, of course, is what did happen, and the process culminated in the relatively long and fruitful years of the Katsura–Saionji partnership at the beginning of this century. However, it is as well to realize that this development in constitutional politics was in some ways a defiance of the Constitution or, at any rate, a defiance of certain possible major assumptions about how that document should operate in practice.

Notably, cabinet–party compromise in its very self involved two entities studiously ignored by the Constitution's drafters. The Meiji Constitution, just like its European counterparts, quickly came to depend in all its particulars on the existence and operation of a 'modern' cabinet system and representative political parties, though neither of these things is mentioned in its text.[8] Going further, it would appear that the continued rise of popular parties was predicated on the simultaneous evolution of a cabinet which came to be the key structural and policy co-ordinating element in the system as a whole, and especially between the Executive and Legislative branches. This role it could fulfil only by acting as a quasi-party or party institution, and bound by principles of collective responsibility and secrecy of discussion. So an effective system of government based on cabinet–Lower-House co-operation emerged in Japan in the late 1890s and early 1900s; but this belied earlier ideas of ministers serving the Emperor in a strictly individual capacity, rather like the Duke of Wellington saw his position in relation to British monarchs in the 1820s and 1830s, and of Members of both Houses of the Diet, and not just the House of Peers, acting as free thinking, loyal retainers, almost in the traditional Confucian mould. It is obvious that of all the recently established institutions it was the House of Peers that suffered most from the developing cabinet–popular-party nexus. This cannot by any means have been the only reason for its increasing marginalization, but it was doubtless an important one.[9]

THE DIET AND INDIVIDUALS

Increasing coalescence of the Liberals and Progressives into two large, distinct parties, coupled with a corresponding decline of the *Taiseikai* and Independents in the House of Representatives; similar trends in the House of Peers – all these were doubtless necessary complements of parliamentary and political growth. But as has been noted, they came at the cost of a reining-in of individualism and personality. Looking back, the first ten or so years of the Diet were a feast – if not indeed at times a near riot – of personality. Independents in both Houses were entitled to be just that; but in the debate on poor relief in the first House of Representatives, Liberal spoke against Liberal, Progressive against Progressive. The same was true of the discussions on peace preservation. Foreign affairs was anybody's game; while Chapter Six disposes of the contention that the *Taiseikai* was normally pro-government, at any rate so far as the proposed new Commercial Code was concerned.

In many ways this strong individualism must have been part of the legacy of the Diet from the twenty or thirty years preceding its opening.

Both its Upper and Lower Houses were upper-class and upper-middle-class institutions, but within that parameter they had mostly capable memberships. Despite its name, the House of Peers was by no means a collection of effete and antiquated aristocrats. As Chapter 1 demonstrates, about half the total membership lacked titles, being appointed on personal merit or elected as wealthy commoners. Even in the case of titled Members, the majority owed their seats in the House to the votes of their order at special elections arranged for that purpose. Furthermore, all those who were in the House as a result of mutual election or Imperial appointment, whether titled or not, would, in those positive years, have tended to represent the brightest and best of their generation. Having come to the fore in the stirring and revolutionary circumstances of the Meiji Restoration, they were well versed in politics, administration, warfare, industry and education. Apart from this quality of personal distinction, Chapter 1, and to a lesser extent the Introduction, give some indication of the varied social and political backgrounds of individual Peers. This too can only have enhanced the standing of their House, while making for animated and informed political debate.

Within the House of Representatives, broad historical forces roughly similar to those operating on the House of Peers had come together to produce a varied and individualistic body of Representatives, within the predetermined 'gentry' categories of wealth and social position. Even for farmers and businessmen, the samurai–Confucian ethos, based on ideas of personal honour, endeavour and accountability, was by no means a thing of the past. Nor was the traditional Confucian regard for education and learning. Bakumatsu and post-Restoration political tensions had shaped the mentality of many Members, as had the hopes and traumas of the Liberty and Popular Rights Movement. Finally, the Members of the early House of Representatives – together with their families, associates and constituents – would have all been influenced to a greater or lesser extent by the grand example of Western economic and political individualism.

Much of this has changed, as indeed it had to, since the first decades of Diet politics. Again, the blame, if that is the right word, lies in the routinization of politics and the development of party machines. Yet one can hardly suppose that the early qualities of personal distinction and individualism have disappeared entirely from the halls, corridors and tea rooms of the present Diet building; if only because it would be next to impossible to imagine the proper functioning of any parliament without these elements somewhere in its make-up. It has been well said that Japan's greatest resource is its people. The history of the Diet affords plenty of splendid – and not so splendid – insight into this truth, both in its collective and its individualistic aspects. But it is the individualism that needs to be stressed here.

NOTES

1 One source of difficulty was that although leading newspapers all professed a generalized allegiance to one political camp or another, they also, rather like the Diet men themselves, reserved the right to take an independent stand on any particular issue. Thus, in the case of the government's bill on poor relief, the *Chōya shimbun* published an editorial which obliquely criticized the popular parties for their rejection of the measure, and was at the same time a scathing attack on the political morals of the Representatives as a whole; whereas the similarly 'oppositionist' *Kokumin shimbun*, in its editorial on the subject, considered that the Lower House had been right to reject the government's bill, but should now move to introduce a new social insurance law in its place (*Chōya shimbun*, 16 December 90; *Kokumin shimbun*, 6 December 90).

2 The six great foundation laws of the settlement were the Constitution itself; the Imperial House Law; the Imperial Ordinance on the House of Peers; the Law of the Houses; the House of Representatives Election Law; and the Law of Finance. All of them were by definition and substance 'constitutional'.

3 Many of the points made in this paragraph are amplified in the biographical Appendix.

4 This was most clearly seen in the 'dust-up' following the 1892 general election, when gross government interference was bitterly criticized in the Diet, and eventually resolved, by the resignation of the cabinet responsible as a result of these parliamentary attacks. Here was one occasion when remonstrances by the House of Peers, which took the lead in the matter, did take effect.

5 Apart from famous incidents like the 1891 budget *imbroglio* or the 1892 election interference scandal, which one imagines must have given rise to considerable informal inter-house liaison, Andrew Fraser has given a detailed account of how Representatives and Members of the House of Peers from Tokushima Prefecture worked together, with their Tokushima fellows in the bureaucracy, to promote the interests of their native district (Fraser 1970, 1971). A further point on inter-House relations: it is obvious from the following Appendix that, as time went by, many Representatives were 'promoted' to the House of Peers. Such people must have come trailing clouds of experience and friendships (or enmities).

6 There were: (1) a public announcement by the government of its willingness to co-operate with the Liberals; (2) an adherence by the government to Liberal policies, such as railway nationalization and widening of the suffrage; (3) government acceptance of the permanence of the arrangements newly entered into (Hackett 1971: 192–3).

7 In debates to amend the existing Newspaper Regulations and Publications Regulations, held in the first and second sessions of the Diet, it is notable how frequently Liberal and Progressive Members preferred a bureaucratic

and authoritarian stance to a more liberal one when discussing particular sections of the proposed legislation (Mason: forthcoming article).

8 The cabinet (*naikaku*) was in fact established in a major administrative reform in 1885, in preparation for constitutional government. 'Modern' here means a cabinet which, while nominally responsible to the Sovereign, is in fact an independent holder and wielder of Executive power.

9 The hereditary Peers rather quickly grew out of touch with the rest of society, and for this reason and because they were so privileged, they tended to become very conservative in politics after about 1910. However, there were exceptions to this trend, notably their support for universal manhood suffrage after the First World War; and, on analogy with the British House of Lords, a conservative, if not reactionary, temper was only to be expected from a mainly hereditary Upper House.

Appendix: Brief biographies

Amakazu Fumie (1847–1927) Liberal; Mie fifth constituency; born Mie Prefecture. Member of prefectural assembly, Imperial Agricultural Society; also active in Kansai Local Government Mutual Progress Association; president of Mie Prefecture Agricultural Bank. Returned four times to House of Representatives; afterwards elected to House of Peers as a High Taxpayer.

Amano Jakuen (1851–1909) *Taiseikai*; Gifu first constituency. Jōdō Shinshū Buddhist priest and educator. Also taught in state primary schools and in prisons. Elected three times.

Andō Kyūka (1825–1904) *Taiseikai*; Ōita first constituency; born Ōita Prefecture. Educated in Chinese studies and literature. Local official in Fukuoka Prefecture; head of Nishi–Kunisaki District in Ōita Prefecture. Elected three times.

Andō Sokumei (1828–1909) Imperial Nominee to House of Peers; born Kagoshima Prefecture. After 1868, worked as a police officer in Tokyo; as a public prosecutor in the Ministry of Justice; and as a Chief Superintendent of Police. Senator (*Genrōin*).

Aoki Shūzō (1844–1914) diplomat and government minister; born Yamaguchi Prefecture, Chōshū domain samurai. Initially studied medicine, but in 1868 sent at domain expense to Germany where he studied politics and law. In 1873 became a diplomat, subsequently ambassador to Germany and conjointly to Austria, Holland and Denmark. In 1886, having returned to Japan, he was appointed deputy-Foreign Minister and worked hard with Inoue Kaoru on treaty revision. Negotiations failed. In 1889 Foreign Minister in first Yamagata and Matsukata cabinets; worked again for treaty revision but resigned in 1891 over Ōtsu attack on visiting crown prince of Russia. In 1892 ambassador to Germany for third time; 1894 ambassador to Britain where, acting in close liaison with the incumbent Japanese Foreign Minister, Mutsu Munemitsu, he signed the first equal treaty (Aoki–Kimberly Agreement of 1894). In 1898 Foreign Minister in the second Yamagata cabinet, during the Boxer Rebellion in China; 1906–7 ambassador to the United States. His wife was a German noblewoman.

Arai Shōgo (1856–1906) Liberal; Tochigi second constituency; born Tochigi Prefecture. Studied Chinese and English. Chairman of prefectural assembly. In 1885 imprisoned for plotting 'Liberal' revolt in Korea; 1889 amnestied. Published newspapers. Founded the Uji River Hydro-electric Company. Later worked for a period with the Ministry of Colonial Affairs. Diet Member 1890–1902, 1904–6.

Bandō Kangorō (1861–1918) Independent born Tokushima Prefecture. Farmer. In 1878 graduated from Tokushima Middle School; 1880s member, deputy-chairman of prefectural assembly; 1890s president of Tokushima Railway Company. In 1894–1917 House of Representatives. Elected ten times.

Enomoto Takeaki (1836–1908) Tokugawa retainer and Meiji government minister; born in Tokyo, son of Tokugawa councillor. Studied Western learning at Nagasaki, concentrating on naval studies. In 1861–6 sent to Holland by *bakufu* to study military science, law and mechanics. Became a *bakufu* naval commander, and his surrender in May 1869 to Meiji government forces in Hokkaido marked end of War of Restoration. Jailed for three years. Later served in the Hokkaidō Development Board, the new navy, and as ambassador to Russia where he signed an important treaty regarding the allocation of sovereignty over Sakhalien (to Russia) and the Kurile Islands (to Japan). At this time he was also involved in treaty revision. In 1880 Navy Minister; 1882 ambassador to China where he helped Itō Hirobumi conclude the Treaty of Tientsin. Subsequently Communications, Education, Foreign, and Agriculture and Commerce Minister in various Sat–Chō cabinets. In 1890 Privy Councillor and Viscount.

Haseba Sumitaka (1854–1914) Liberal; Kagoshima third constituency; born Kagoshima. Educated at domain college. Tokyo metropolitan and Kagoshima prefectural police officer. Served in the Satsuma campaign. Member of prefectural assembly, and a District head. Later, head of the Home Office secretariat; Speaker of the House of Representatives; Minister of Education. Elected eleven times.

Hashimoto Kyūtarō (1855–1926) Progressive; Tokushima fourth constituency; born Tokushima Prefecture. Educated at *Kyōkan Gijuku* and

Keiō University. Member of Tokushima prefectural assembly, and local hygiene and conscription committees. Member of the prefectural association for encouragement of industry; also interested in education. Later mayor of Kōjimachi ward in Tokyo. Elected ten times.

Hashiyama Chūzaemon (1845–1915) *Taiseikai*; Aichi seventh constituency; born Aichi Prefecture. Local official; member and later chairman of Aichi prefectural assembly; interested in forests and fisheries; managing director of the Chita Spinning Co.

Hirata Tōsuke (1849–1925) Imperial Nominee to House of Peers; bureaucrat-politician; count. Second son of a Yonezawa domain (Yamagata Prefecture) retainer; adopted by official domain physician. Educated first at domain college; later studied and worked at various colleges in Tokyo and Osaka. In 1872 accompanied Iwakura mission, staying in Europe to study politics and law at the Universities of Heidelberg and Leipzig; 1876 returned to Japan. Posts in Home Office and Treasury, also on secretariat of Council of State; worked on regulations for management of government property and fire insurance. In 1882 accompanied Itō Hirobumi on his tour of Europe to study constitutions. Subsequently occupied a succession of high administrative and political posts such as head of legislative bureau in Home Office, chief secretary of the privy council, head of the cabinet Pension Bureau, Home Minister, and Minister for Agriculture and Commerce.

Horikoshi Kansuke (1860–1916) Liberal; Saitama fourth constituency; born Saitama Prefecture. In 1889 graduated from Waseda University (Japanese language, politics). Farmer, village head, member of prefectural assembly and local government association. Chairman of warehouse and life insurance companies; auditor for the Tōbu Railway Co. Chairman of *Jiyū shimbun* (Liberty Newspaper) and published a law journal. Elected four times.

Ienaga Yoshihiko (1849–1913) Liberal; Nagasaki first constituency; born Nagasaki Prefecture. Studied Chinese and German. Warden of Saga Middle School dormitory. Later, practised law; president Nagasaki Lawyers Club. Chairman of Nagasaki city assembly; member of Nagasaki prefectural assembly. Elected three times.

Inoue Kakugorō (1859–1938) Liberal; Hiroshima ninth constituency; born Hiroshima. Graduated from Keiō University 1882. Was employed as counsellor and chief secretary in a Korean government office for foreign relations and trade. Wrote articles for Liberal newspaper. Later, deputy-president of the Tokyo chamber of commerce; manager of the

Hokkaidō Colliery and Steamship Co.; president of the Yahagi Water Power Co.; and a manager of the *Seiyūkai*. Elected fourteen times.

Inoue Seiichi (1850–1936) Independent; Yamaguchi second constituency; born Yamaguchi Prefecture. Graduate of *Daigaku Nankō*. Ministry of Justice trainee; sent to France for study; LL.D. Judge; member of higher civil service examinations board; lectured in law at Tokyo University.

Inukai Tsuyoshi (Ki) (1855–1932) Liberal; Okayama second constituency; born Okayama Prefecture. Graduate of Keiō University. Journalist; member of Tokyo prefectural assembly. Later, cabinet minister and Prime Minister; president of *Seiyūkai*. Elected nineteen times.

Ishida Kannosuke (1849–1935) Liberal; Hyōgo fourth constituency; born Hyōgo Prefecture. Member and later chairman of Hyōgo prefectural assembly. Governor of Toyama Prefecture; newspaper publisher. Elected six times.

Ishizaka Sennosuke (1849–1915) Liberal; Toyama first constituency; born Toyama. Studied at the Daigaku Nankō. Professor at Keiō University and at Dōjinsha Academy (Tokyo). Worked for Ministry of Education, and later in local administration as a District head. Chairman of Toyama prefectural assembly.

Itakura Chū (1856–1938) Liberal; Chiba fifth constituency; born Chiba. Lawyer and scholar of French law. Chairman of prefectural assembly. Published *Tōkai shimbun*. Elected eight times.

Itō Hirobumi (1841–1909) bureaucrat, cabinet minister and statesman. Born Yamaguchi Prefecture (Chōshū domain) son of a farmer, later adopted by low-ranking samurai. Educated privately and by Yoshida Shōin. Ardently anti-foreign and anti-*bakufu*; associate of Kido Kōin and Takasugi Shinsaku. Insurgent and terrorist. Sent by domain to Nagasaki to study drill, and later to England. After 1868 employed in Treasury. In 1870 travelled to United States to study banking; on his return introduced modern banking system in to Japan. In 1871–3 member of Iwakura mission; 1875 negotiated Ōsaka compromise between still incumbent ministers and disaffected colleagues, notably Kido Kōin and Itagaki Taisuke. Thereafter increasingly involved with high-level political disputation and change. In 1878 Home Minister; 1882–3 sent to Europe to study constitutions; 1885–8 first modern Prime Minister; concurrently Imperial Household Minister and chairman of constitutional preparation commission. In 1890 first President of House of Peers. Prime Minister 1892–6, 1898, 1900–1. In 1900 founded *Seiyūkai*; 1906–9 resident-general in Korea; 1909 president of Privy Council, but assassinated in this year at Harbin by a Korean nationalist when about to hold talks with the Russian Finance Minister. Though best remembered for his achievements as a civil politician in the domestic fields, especially the framing of the 1889 Constitution, Itō was heavily involved at times with foreign affairs, especially relations with Korea, China and Russia. He has been called the 'pre-eminent statesman of modern Japan'. Well read, affable, resourceful and many-sided, he rose to the occasion time and again, supplying the politics of inspiration not simply as a matter of tactical possibilities but in conscious response to deep-seated historical trends. (Cf. Akita 1967.)

Kamata Katsutarō (1862–1942) Independent; born Kagawa Prefecture, farmer. 1880s member, chairman of prefectural assembly. Head of Kagawa Education Society; president of banks and commercial companies; 1894 House of Representatives (elected twice); 1897–1925 High Taxpayer, House of Peers (elected four times).

Kaneko Kentarō (1853–1942) born Fukuoka Prefecture, samurai. In 1871–8 studied at Harvard University, honorary degree in Law. In 1878–90 secretary in *Genrōin*, Council of State, and Privy Council; 1890 chief secretary, House of Peers; 1895 deputy-Minister of Agriculture and Commerce; 1898 Minister of Agriculture and Commerce; 1900 Minister of Justice. In 1890–1906 Imperial Nominee to House of Peers. Then created Baron, Privy Councillor.

Kanno Ryō (1851–1919) Progressive; Ishikawa third constituency; born Ishikawa Prefecture. Local official; chairman of Ishikawa prefectural assembly; director of local railway company; later lived in China as a trader.

Katō Heishirō (1854–1935) Liberal; Okayama seventh constituency; born Okayama Prefecture. Governor of Shizuoka and Yamanashi Prefectures; mayor of Kōfu city. Member of organizing committee of fourth national industrial exposition. Elected four times.

Katō Hiroyuki (1836–1916) Imperial Nominee to House of Peers; legal scholar and political philosopher. As a *bakufu* retainer had taught at the Kaiseijo; later took up German studies. After Restoration, held posts in Tokyo University and Ministries of Education and Foreign Affairs. Later senator; imperial tutor; president of Tokyo University; palace adviser; Privy Councillor; president of the Imperial Academy. At first advocated Liberalism, but afterwards adopted a more conservative stance.

Katsuki Yukitsune (1842–1894) *Taiseikai*; Fukuoka second constituency, born Fukuoka Prefecture. Studied Chinese classics and attended Akizuki domain college. Employed as a local rural teacher and administrator. Later, principal of Amaki Middle School in Fukuoka Prefecture. Founder and editor of local newspaper. Elected twice.

Kikuchi Kanji (1850–1932) Liberal; Ōsaka fifth constituency; born Ōsaka Prefecture. Lawyer; member of Osaka city, prefectural assemblies. Principal of Ōsaka Commercial College; governor of Ōsaka Prefecture; principal of Hagoromo Girls' High School. Newspaper publisher. Elected three times.

Konishi Jinnosuke (1855–1928) Liberal; Kagawa second constituency; born Kagawa Prefecture. Member of local conscription board and primary school textbooks committee. Elected three times.

Koretsune Makaji (1851–1892) *Taiseikai*; Ōita sixth constituency; born Ōita Prefecture. Studied Chinese classics; member of Ōita prefectural assembly. District head and tax official. Elected twice.

Kudō Yukimoto (1842–1904) Liberal; Aomori first constituency; born Aomori Prefecture. Studied at the Hirosaki domain school (*Keikokan*) and later pursued military science. Served as a civil engineer in the Ministry of Popular Affairs (*Minbushō*) also as a senior official and police inspector in Mie Prefecture. Subsequently appointed head of various Districts and then Principal of Goshogahara Normal School, all in Aomori Prefecture. Elected nine times.

Matsudaira Nobumasa (1852–1909) House of Peers; Viscount; former *daimyō* of Kameyama (Kameoka) *han*, near Kyōto. Served the Meiji government in various offices of an administrative and advisory nature.

Matsukata Masayoshi (1835–1924) bureaucrat, cabinet minister and statesman. Born Kagoshima city, son of a samurai involved in Satsuma–Ryūkyū trade. Studied Chinese classics and military arts at domain college. From 1862 was an increasingly important figure in Satsuma politics. In 1866 sent by domain to Nagaskai to study naval matters. After Restoration, employed by new government as governor of a district in north Kyūshū and distinguished himself in that post. In 1871 entered Ministry of Finance. In 1878 studied in Paris under incumbent French Minister of Finance. In 1881–1901 Minister of Finance for all but two of these twenty years. Greatly distinguished himself. From about 1889 was virtually the sole leader of the Satsuma party in Sat–Chō governments. In 1891–2, 1896–8 Prime Minister. *Genrō*; 1903–12 president International Red Cross in Japan; 1883 Count; 1905 Marquis; 1922 Prince.

Matsuoka Kōki (1846–1923) born Tokushima Prefecture; country samurai. Studied classics, swordsmanship. In 1871–90 secretarial official in Justice Ministry; chief judge of Tokyo and local courts; 1890 head of Tokyo Appeals Centre; 1891 chief prosecutor; 1894, 1898 deputy-Home Minister. In 1903 president Nihon University; 1906 Minister of Agriculture and Commerce; 1917 Baron; 1920 Privy Councillor; 1891–1919 Imperial Nominee to House of Peers.

Misaki Kamenosuke (1858–1906) Liberal; Kagawa fourth constituency; born Kagawa Prefecture. Had been secretary of the Japanese legation in America, and later a senior Home Office official. Newspaperman and president of the Kyoto *Chūgai shimbun*. Became manager and deputy-president of the Yokohama Specie Bank. Later, Member of House of Peers. Elected four times.

Miura Yasushi (1829–1910) Home Office bureaucrat and Imperial appointee to House of Peers. At one stage in his career he was governor of Tokyo Prefecture and later a Court adviser.

Miyagi Kōzō (1852–1893) Independent; Yamagata first constituency; born Yamagata Prefecture. In 1876 Ministry of Justice trainee; sent to France for study at Paris and Lyons Universities. Procurator; judge; member of Codes Investigation Committee. President of Tokyo Lawyers Club and founded Constitutional Association. Worked hard to disseminate legal theory, and helped found Meiji Law College (later Meiji University) where he was principal and lectured on criminal law. Elected twice.

Motoda Hajime (1858–1938) *Taiseikai*, later *Seiyūkai*; Ōita second constituency; born Ōita Prefecture. In 1880 graduated Tokyo University; lawyer; 1890 elected to House of Representatives where he sat almost continuously until the early 1930s. After 1900, Speaker of the House of Representatives; Minister for Communications; Minister for Railways; Privy Councillor. Elected sixteen times.

Nagai Matsuemon (1853–1913) *Taiseikai*; Aichi Prefecture second constituency; born Aichi Prefecture. Studied at domain college. Worked hard in connection with founding of Aichi hospital. Published *Aichi Illustrated Newspaper*; prominent banker. Elected twice.

Naitō Rihachi (1856–1921) Progressive; Hyōgo seventh constituency; born Hyōgo Prefecture. Deputy-chairman of prefectural assembly.

Chairman of Bandan Railway Co. and Himeji Hydro-Electricity Co.; manager of Himeji Commercial Bank. Elected five times.

Nakajima Nobuyuki (1846–1899) Liberal; Kanagawa fourth constituency; born Kōchi Prefecture. Formerly senior government official, and governor of Kanagawa Prefecture. Resigned posts in 1880 to campaign actively for the Liberty and Popular Rights Movement. Deputy-president of Liberal party. Later, ambassador to Italy; became a Baron and sat in House of Peers.

Nakamura Eisuke (1849–1938) *Taiseikai*; Kyōto second constituency; born Kyōto. Active in local government and at one time chairman of Kyōto prefectural assembly. Deputy-president of Kyōto chamber of commerce and industry. Interests in banking, railways, spinning, warehousing and Kyōto cereals exchange. Later, member of the *Seiyūkai* and a director of the *Dōshisha*. Elected twice.

Nishi Amane (1829–1897) Imperial Nominee to House of Peers; bureaucrat, educator and philosopher. Son of a Tsuwano domain (Shimane Prefecture) official doctor. Studied first at domain college (Confucianism) later at Ōsaka, and Okayama, and Tokyo where he took up Western learning including English. In 1862–5 sent by *bakufu* to study law and philosophy at Leiden University. In 1868 principal of Numazu Military College, afterwards served in Army, Education and Imperial Household Ministries. Chief concern was education, helped draft Imperial Rescript to Soldiers and Sailors. Member of Imperial Academy; Senator; Baron. (Cf. Havens 1970.)

Nishimura Shigeki (1828–1902) Imperial Nominee to House of Peers; Confucian-minded philosopher and educator who was never far from the centre of political affairs. (Cf. Shively 1965.)

Okauchi Shigetoshi (1842–1915) Imperial Nominee to House of Peers; higher court judge; later, Baron.

Okayama Kenkichi (1854–1894) Progressive; Shizuoka third constituency; born Shizuoka Prefecture. In 1882 graduated Tokyo University. Lawyer; consultant for Mitsui Bank and Japan Mailship Company (NYK). Lectured at Tokyo University and other metropolitan tertiary institutions.

Orita Kanetaka (1858–1923) Liberal; Kagoshima second constituency; born Kagoshima. Pursued Japanese, Chinese and English studies. Chairman of prefectural assembly. Member of prefectural school board, conscription board, and hygiene and education committees. Manager of the Kagoshima Agricultural and Industrial Bank. Elected four times.

Ōtsu Junichirō (1856–1932) Progressive; Ibaraki second constituency; born Ibaraki Prefecture. Founded a local newspaper, and took part in the Liberty and Popular Rights Movement. Member of the Ibaraki prefectural assembly. Elected fourteen times to House of Representatives. In 1927 entered House of Peers as an Imperial Nominee. Parliamentary and political party elder. Wrote *Dai Nihon Kensei Shi* (*Constitutional History of Japan*) in ten large volumes.

Ōyagi Biichirō (1858–?) *Taiseikai*; Tokyo seventh constituency; born Tokyo Prefecture. In 1882 graduated Tokyo University, Lawyer; president Tokyo Lawyers Association; lecturer at Law College.

Ozaki Saburō (1842–1918) Imperial Nominee to House of Peers; bureaucrat. At one time he had been a secretary to the Council of State (*Dajōkan*).

Saga Kintō (1863–1941) House of Peers; Marquis; lower first court rank. Domiciled in Tokyo.

Seki Naohiko (1857–1934) Independent; Wakayama third constituency, later represented Tokyo constituency; second son of a Wakayama domain retainer. In 1883 Tokyo University law graduate, but became a journalist with close connections to the Sat–Chō leaders. After Diet opened, close political associate of Inukai Tsuyoshi. Elected to House of Representatives ten times. In 1927 Imperial Nominee to House of Peers.

Shimoiisaka Gonzaburō (1852–1923) Liberal; Iwate fourth constituency; born Iwate Prefecture. Member of prefectural assembly and board of education. Studied Chinese; raised cattle. Elected four times.

Shioda Okuzō (1849–1927) Liberal; Tochigi fourth constituency; born Tochigi Prefecture. Local official; member and deputy-chairman of Tochigi prefectural assembly. Director of the Tokyo rice exchange; worked for Keihin Bank, and later managed its branch office in Hawaii. Manager of Tamagawa Electric Railway Co.; president of the Hawaii Japanese Association. Elected three times.

Shirane Senichi (1849–1898) son of Chōshū (Yamaguchi Prefecture) samurai. Educated at domain college and at Keiō University. Ministry of Justice and later Home Office official. Governor of Ehime and Aichi Prefectures. In 1890 promoted to deputy-Home Minister. Guilty of grave interference in 1892 general election, resigned position in Home Ministry. Given post in Imperial household; 1895 Minister of Communications in second Itō cabinet; 1897 Baron.

Sone Arasuke (1849–1910) Independent; Yamaguchi fourth constituency; born in Hagi (Yamaguchi Prefecture) third son of a Chōshū retainer; adopted into Sone family. Studied at domain college and participated in War of Restoration. In 1870 attended Osaka Military College where he learnt French; 1872–7 studied in France. On return to Japan, served in the Army and later as a junior secretary to the Council of State. Editor of *Kampō* (Official Gazette) involved in preparations for opening of Diet. In 1890 first Clerk of the House of Representatives; 1892 elected to the House of Representatives; deputy-Speaker; 1896 ambassador to France where he worked on treaty revision; 1898 Minister of Justice in third Itō cabinet. Subsequently Minister of Agriculture and Commerce (second Yamagata cabinet); Treasurer and at times Minister of Foreign Affairs and of Communications in first Katsura cabinet. In 1900 Imperial Nominee to House of Peers; 1906 Privy Councillor; 1906 deputy-resident general in Korea; 1909 resident-general. Baron, later Viscount.

Suehiro Shigeyasu (1849–1896) Independent; Aichi sixth constituency, born Aichi Prefecture. Studied Chinese at domain college. Treasury official; later, influential journalist and publicist. Elected twice.

Suematsu Kenchō (1855–1920) *Taiseikai*; Fukuoka eighth constituency; born Fukuoka Prefecture, fourth son of a village headman. Educated at home and later in private school of Murakami Butsuzan (Chinese studies); 1871–3 attended various private schools in Tokyo; 1873–5 staff writer for *Tōkyō nichi nichi shimbun*. Befriended by Itō Hirobumi who had him appointed to secretariat of Council of State; also as an assistant on an important diplomatic mission to Korea. In 1876 posts in Industry and Legislative Bureaus; also junior secretary to the Council of State. 1897 served under Yamagata Aritomo in campaign against Satsuma rebels. In 1878–86 in England, where for four years he studied law, classics and modern languages at Cambridge University; graduated LL.B. and B.A. In 1886 senior Home Ministry official: head of Prefectural Government Bureau, later Legislative and Pensions Bureaus. In 1889 married Itō's daughter. In 1895 financial adviser to Korean government; Baron; 1896 Imperial Nominee to House of Peers; 1898 Minister of Communications in third Itō cabinet; first president of the Japan Society of Arts. In 1900 Home Minister in fourth Itō cabinet, held post in Imperial Household Ministry; 1904–6 special envoy to England in connection with Russo-Japanese War; 1906 Privy Councillor; 1907 member of Imperial Academy; tutor to crown prince of Korea; Viscount. Japan Red Cross committee member. Advocate of theatre reform; published many important original works and translations, including *Bōchō kaiten shi* and translations of Emperor Justinian's *Codex*. Elected three times. (Cf. Mason 1979.)

Suematsu Saburō (?–?) Independent; Yamaguchi first constituency; born Yamaguchi Prefecture, third son of a high-ranking Buddhist priest (Suō Kōmyōji). Made no attempt to enter priesthood, and by 1890 he was a senior official in the Ministry of Communications. Earlier, travelled to France where he had studied law and worked as a clerk in the Japanese embassy. Returned to Japan and found employment as a public prosecutor attached to the Supreme Court. Given to eccentric opinions; leading member of Gotō Shōjirō's *Daidō Danketsu*.

Suzuki Manjirō (1860–1930) Liberal; Fukushima second constituency; born Fukushima Prefecture. Studied medicine and foreign languages in native area, and later medicine in Tokyo. Doctor; founded Kanda hospital in Tokyo. President Aikoku Life Insurance Company; other business interests included hotels and brewing. Chairman of the Kita Toshima District ward (Tokyo) doctors' association. Elected six times.

Suzuki Shōji (1841–95) Liberal; Niigata eighth constituency; born Niigata Prefecture. Member and later chairman of Niigata prefectural assembly. Elected four times.

Taguchi Ukichi (1855–1905) Financial Reform born Tokyo, samurai. Studied Chinese classics, English, medicine, economics. LL.D.; 1874 clerical official in Finance Ministry; 1878 journalist; 1879 proprietor and chief editor of *Tōkyō keizai zasshi*. Director of railway, banking and commercial companies; member of Tokyo stock exchange. Elected six times.

Takagi Seinen (1856–1934) Progressive; Tokyo fifth constituency; born Tokyo Prefecture. Studied Japanese and Chinese, later politics. Member of Shinagawa ward education committee and Tokyo Prefectural assembly. Elected thirteen times.

Takanashi Tetsushirō (1856–?) Independent; Tokyo sixth constituency; born Tokyo Prefecture. Lawyer. Colonial official in Taiwan; chairman Yokohama stock exchange. Elected seven times.

Taketomi Tokitoshi (1855–1938) Liberal; saga second constituency; born Saga Prefecture, samurai. In 1880s member, deputy-chairman, chairman of prefectural assembly; 1890s bureau head in Agriculture and Commerce Ministry; councillor in Finance Ministry; 1898 chief secretary in first Ōkuma cabinet; 1913 Minister of Communications, Finance. General secretary of *Rikken Dōshikai* and *Kenseikai*; 1890–1920 House of Representatives (elected thirteen times). In 1924–38 Imperial Nominee to House of Peers.

Tamura Koremasa (1857–1926) Progressive; Toyama fourth constituency; born Toyama Prefecture. Deputy-chairman Toyama prefectural assembly; member prefectural committee for the encouragement of industry; managing director of the *Toyama Nippō* newspaper. Elected four times.

Tanaka Fujimaro (1849–1909) bureaucrat, diplomat and cabinet minister. Son of Owari domain retainer. Before 1868 he was active supporter of Imperial Restoration in Kyōto, and had a place in the new government from its inception working in areas of legislation and education; 1871–3 member of Iwakura mission; 1873 Minister of Education; 1880 Minister of Justice. In 1884 ambassador to Italy; 1887 ambassador to France, also Belgium, Switzerland and Spain; 1890 Privy Councillor, 1891 Minister of Justice in first Matsukata cabinet; 1892 re-appointed to Privy Council. In 1896 deputy-chairman of committee for implementation of (equal) treaties; 1904 head of Senior Prize Court.

Tanaka Gentarō (1853–1922) *Taiseikai*; Kyōto fifth constituency; born Kyōto. Pioneer interests in South Manchurian Railway Co., the Oriental Colonization Co., and the Japan Industrial Bank. Also president of Kyōto companies interested in electrification and railways, and in the development of a jute industry in Hokkaidō. Later, Member of House of Peers. Elected four times.

Tanaka Shōzō (1841–1913) Progressive; Tochigi third constituency; born Tochigi Prefecture. Landowner and village headman; chairman of prefectural assembly; published *Tochigi Shimbun*. Active in the campaign for counter-measures against metal poisoning caused by Ashio copper mine. Elected six times. (Cf. Strong 1977.)

Tani Kanjō (1837–1911) House of Peers; Viscount; army general and cabinet minister. Born Kōchi Prefecture (Tosa domain) son of lecturer at domain college. Studied Chinese and military arts, at first under his father and others in Kōchi, later in Edo. Sent by domain to observe conditions in Nagasaki and Shanghai. At the time of the Restoration, he was in Kyōto; commanded Tosa troops in Kantō and Tōhoku during the War of the Restoration. He entered the new government, but soon recalled to Tosa to help with domain reforms; 1871 re-entered national government on its military side and soon appointed major-general; 1873 commander of Kumamoto garrison. In that post he took action against *shizoku* (former samurai) uprisings in Saga and Fukuoka; and in 1877 his stout defence of Kumamoto castle was a turning point in the government's campaign against the Satsuma rebels. In 1878 lieutenant-general and commander of Eastern Region garrison; principal of Army Officer Cadet College. In 1881 left these posts and joined Torio Koyata in founding a conservative political party (*Chūseitō*) to oppose Liberals. Principal of Peers' School and Peeresses' School; 1885 Minister of Agriculture and Commerce in first Itō cabinet, and travelled to Europe in that capacity; 1887 resigned from cabinet in protest against its Westernizing policies in connection with treaty revision. Thereafter worked with kindred spirits and through the *Nihon* newspaper to advocate policies of 'considered' nationalism. Sat in House of Peers from 1890 as a formidable critic of successive Sat–Chō governments. (Cf. Mason 1969: 112–26.)

Tateiri Kiichi (1844–1929) Progressive; Mie sixth constituency; born Mie Prefecture. Studied at domain school. Worked on land tax reform in the 1870s as a government official; also as a prefectural official. Member of prefectural assembly. Elected twice.

Tateishi Kanji (1827–1894) Liberal; Nagasaki fourth constituency; born Nagasaki. Studied fencing, gunnery and military sciences. Before 1868 had been commissioner in charge of domain cannon foundries, and a senior page to the *daimyō*. Deputy-chairman of prefectural assembly. Member of prefectural conscription board and hygiene and education committees. Elected twice.

Tomita Tetsunosuke (1835–1916) Imperial Nominee to House of Peers; bureaucrat with varied experience in diplomacy, banking and Tokyo local government.

Torio Koyata (1847–1901) House of Peers; viscount; born Yamaguchi Prefecture, son of Chōshū retainer. Took part in domain anti-*bakufu* insurrection as member of *Kiheitai* (irregular militia). Disowned by parents. Participated in War of Restoration; later served in Army Ministry. In 1875 member of Council of State; 1876 Chief of Staff; 1879 commander of Imperial Guards. In 1886 travelled in Europe; senator. 1888–90 Privy Councillor; 1895 resigned from House of Peers on re-appointment to Privy Council. (Cf. Mason 1969: 112–26.)

Toyama Masakazu (1848–1900) Imperial Nominee to House of Peers; noted scholar, specializing in philosophy, psychology and sociology. He held chairs at Tokyo Imperial University, and was Minister of Education in 1898.

Toyoda Bunzaburō (1853–96) Liberal; Ōsaka second constituency; born Ōsaka Prefecture. Member of Ōsaka prefectural assembly. Founder and managing director of Ōsaka Electric Light Co.; also interested in education (including pre-schools) and hygiene. Elected twice.

Tsuda Masamichi (Mamichi) (1839–1903) *Taiseikai Kaiseijo*; Tokyo ninth constituency; born Tokyo, son of a Tsuyama domain retainer. Before 1868 had studied Western law, economics and military sciences both in Japan and Holland; taught in Kaiseijo. Published a number of influential writings on the elements of his academic specialisms. Senior central government official, and an associate judge on the higher courts. Senator; member of the Tokyo Academy. Later, Baron and Member of the House of Peers. Elected twice.

Ueki Emori (1857–1892) Liberal; Kōchi third constituency; born Kōchi Prefecture. Educated at domain main college (Chinese studies) and teachers' college, and also at Kainan private school. Involved in Liberty and Popular Rights Movement from its earliest days. Journalist, writer, and ideologue. (Cf. Ike 1950: 130–5.)

Uozumi Itsuji (1857–1899) Progressive; Hyōgo fifth constituency; born Hyōgo Prefecture. Studied Chinese. Local government official. Deputy-chairman of prefectural assembly. Concerned himself with schemes for control and use of rivers. Elected three times.

Utsunomiya Heiichi (1858–1896) Liberal; Kagoshima fourth constituency; born Kagoshima. Studied at domain college and at private schools. Served in the Satsuma campaign. Later a teacher at colleges in Shanghai and in the Tokyo area. Elected twice.

Wakao Ippei (1820–1913) House of Peers; industrialist with interests in sericulture, banking and railways. A native of Yamanashi Prefecture, he had been mayor of Kōfu. He was elected to the House of Peers by the fifteen most wealthy taxpayers of Yamanashi in 1890.

Watanabe Jinkichi (1856–1925) High Taxpayer, House of Peers, 1890–1897; 1902 elected to House of Representatives for one term. Born Gifu Prefecture. Banker and director of Hokkaidō coal and railway companies. Before 1890, he was a member of the Public Works Association and the Currency Investigation Committee; also mayor of Gifu city and chairman of Gifu Chamber of Commerce.

Watanabe Kiyoshi (1835–1905) Imperial Nominee to House of Peers; Home Office bureaucrat; rose to be governor of Fukuoka and Fukushima Prefectures.

Watanabe Matasaburō (1850–1910) Independent; Hiroshima first constituency; born Hiroshima Prefecture. Officer in pro-Restoration militia

(Aki *han Jūtai*). Lawyer; vice-president Hiroshima Lawyers Club; president Shikoku Lawyers Association. Deputy-chairman Hiroshima prefectural assembly; chairman Hiroshima city assembly; mayor of Hiroshima. Published *Chūgoku shimbun* newspaper. Elected three times.

Watari Masamoto (1829–1924) Imperial Nominee to House of Peers; domiciled in Tokyo. In 1869 studied in France. Later worked in Foreign Affairs Ministry, Mines Department, Army Ministry. Appointed to secretariat of Council of State; senator. Travelled in Europe.

Yamada Akiyoshi (1844–1892) count; member of House of Peers, Privy Councillor and cabinet minister. Born Yamaguchi Prefecture; samurai. Very active in anti-*bakufu* campaigning in Chōshū before 1868, and participated in War of Restoration. Later employed in Army Department. In 1871–3 member of Iwakura mission to United States and Europe; 1874 served against Saga rebels; 1877 served against Satsuma rebels; lieutenant-general; 1883–91 Minister of Justice and in this role oversaw the inauguration of Japan's modern judicial system.

Yamada Tōji (1858–1899) Liberal; Kanagawa third constituency; born Kanagawa Prefecture. Graduated from the Tokyo Law School 1885; published law journals; governor of the Japanese–French Law School. Elected three times.

Yamagata Aritomo (1838–1922) bureaucrat, cabinet minister and statesman. Born Yamaguchi Prefecture, son of a very low-ranking samurai. Studied briefly under Yoshida Shōin. Ardently anti-*bakufu* and noted leader of *Kiheitai* militia before 1868. Senior commander on government side during War of Restoration. In 1869–70 travelled in Europe and America, studying military organizations; 1870 entered Ministry of War, and during the ensuing twelve years laid the foundations of the modern Japanese army with the introduction of universal conscription, an independent general staff, and the Imperial rescript to soldiers and sailors. In 1874 Army Minister, personally lead troops against Saga rebels; 1877 commanded government forces sent against Satsuma rebels; 1878 first chief of general staff; 1883 head of Legislative Board of Council of State; 1883 Home Minister, responsible for prison reform and inaugurator of Japan's modern system of local government; 1889–91 Prime Minister. In 1892 Minister of Justice in second Itō cabinet; 1893 president of Privy Council; 1894 field commander in Sino-Japanese War, later Army Minister; 1898–1900 Prime Minister. In 1904–5 chief of general staff during Russo-Japanese War; Influential *genrō*; 1903–22 president of Privy Council; 1872 lieutenant-general; 1890 general; 1898 field-marshal. In 1884 Count; 1895 Marquis; 1907 Prince. Yamagata was a notable poet and garden designer, as well as being a master of politics both domestic and foreign. (Cf. Hackett 1971.)

Yamaguchi Naoyoshi (1839–1894) Imperial Nominee to House of Peers; Home Office bureaucrat.

Yasuda Isao (1853–1917) Progressive; Chiba eighth constituency; born Chiba Prefecture. Graduate of Keiō University. Lawyer; teacher at Chiba Middle School and Normal School; local government official. member of prefectural assembly. Raised cattle. Elected six times.

Yasuda Yuitsu (1853–1904) Liberal; Miyazaki second constituency; born Miyazaki Prefecture. Studied surveying. Worked as a teacher; and as an official in the Departments of War and Foreign Affairs. Miyazaki local government official. In 1889 toured the whole of Japan when acting as interpreter for a visiting Austrian prince. Farmer. Elected twice.

Yokobori Sanshi (1852–1914) Liberal; Tochigi first constituency; born Tochigi. Studied Chinese. Local government official (District head) and chairman of prefectural assembly. Farmer. Elected four times.

Yuasa Jirō (1850–1932) Liberal; Gumma fifth constituency; born Gumma Prefecture. Studied Chinese and arithmetic. School board member and local government official. Member and chairman of prefectural assembly. Manufactured *miso* and soy sauce. Established reading-room in Annaka-machi. Also founded and managed a silk worm raising business, a silk thread factory, and a Christian book publishing firm: all to give employment to former samurai who were Christians. president of Usui Bank; director of Japan Railway Co.; member of founding committee of *Kokumin Shimbun* newspaper. Committee member of the evangelical association of the Congregational Church of Japan and Dōshisha University trustee. Elected twice.

Bibliography

REFERENCES

Note: Mss. referred to in Chapters 1 and 2 are listed under Kenseishiryōshitsu.

Akita G. (1962) 'The Meiji Constitution in Practice: The First Diet', *Journal of Asian Studies* vol. 22.

Akita, G. (1967) *Foundations of Constitutional Government in Modern Japan, 1868–1900*, Harvard University Press, Cambridge, Mass.

Allen G. (1938) *Japan: The Hungry Guest*, Allen and Unwin, London.

Araki Moriaki (1964) 'Daiichi gikai ni okeru jinushi giin no dōkō', *Shakai Kagaku Kenkyū* vol. 16, no. 1.

Ario Yoshishige (1914) *Hompō chiso no enkaku*, Tokyo.

Azuma Tōsaku (1936) *Meiji zenki nōseishi no shomondai*, Tokyo.

Banno Junji (1971) *Meiji kempō taisei no kakuritsu*, Tokyo.

Banno Junji (1973) 'The Transformation of the Political Party Movement before and after the Sino-Japanese War, 1890–1900', *Papers on Far Eastern History* no. 7.

Beasley W. (1955) *Select Documents on Japanese Foreign Policy 1853–1868*, Oxford University Press, London.

Berger G. (1977) *Parties out of Power in Japan 1931–1941*, Princeton University Press, Princeton.

Bosanquet H. (1909) *The Poor-Law Report of 1909*, Macmillan, London.

Conroy H. (1960) *The Japanese Seizure of Korea, 1868–1910*, University of Pennsylvania Press, Philadelphia.

Crawcour E. (1963) 'The Japanese Economy on the Eve of Modernization', *Journal of the Oriental Society of Australia* vol. ii, no. 1.

Dai Nihon Teikoku Gikai Shi (*DNTGS*, the Diet Record) (1926) Dai Nihon Teikoku Gikai Shi Kankōkai, Tokyo.

Duus P. (1968) *Party Rivalry and Political Change in Taishō Japan*, Harvard University Press, Cambridge, Mass.

Epp R. (1967) 'The Challenge from Tradition: Attempts to Compile a Civil Code in Japan, 1866–78', *Monumenta Nipponica* vol. 22.

Fraser A. (1971) *A Political Profile of Tokushima Prefecture in the Early and Middle Meiji Period 1868–1902*, Occasional Paper no. 11, Faculty of Asian Studies, Australian National University, Canberra.

Fraser A. (1972) *National Election Politics in Tokushima Prefecture, 1890–1902*

Occasional Paper no. 14, Faculty of Asian Studies, Australian National University, Canberra.

Fraser A. (1986) 'Local Administration: The Example of Awa-Tokushima' in M. Jansen and G. Rozman (ed.), *Japan In Transition: From Tokugawa to Meiji*, Princeton University Press, Princeton.

Fukushima Masao (1962) *Chiso kaisei no kenkyū*, Tokyo.

Fukushima Masao (1971) *Chiso kaisei*, Tokyo.

Gikai seido nana(shichi)jūnen shi, (1960–3) 12 vols (vol. 1: House of Peers biographies; vol. 11: House of Representatives biographies), Okurashō Insatsu Kyoku, Tokyo.

Hackett R. (1971) *Yamagata Aritomo in the Rise of Modern Japan*, Harvard University Press, Cambridge, Mass.

Hall J.C. (1913) 'Japanese Feudal Laws', *Transactions of the Asiatic Society of Japan*, 1st series, vol. xli.

Hanabusa Sakitarō (1942) *Kizokuin kaku kaiha no kenkyū*, Tokyo.

Hara Monjo Kenkyūkai (1984–9) *Hara Takashi kankei monjo*, 11 vols, Tokyo.

Hattori Shisō (1961) *Meiji no seijikatachi*, 2 vols, Tokyo.

Havens T. (1970) *Nishi Amane and Modern Japanese Thought*, Princeton University Press, Princeton.

Hayashi Shigeru (1951) 'Kizokuin no Soshiki to sono Seikaku', *Shakai Kagaku Kenkyū* vol. 3, no. 2.

Hayashida Kametarō (1927) *Nihon seitō shi*, 2 vols, Tokyo.

Hayward A. (trans.), F.K. von Savigny (1831) *Of the Vocation of our Age for Legislation and Jurisprudence*, Littlewood, London.

Hirao Michio (1935) *Shishaku Tani Kanjō den*, Tokyo.

Hisho Ruisan Kankōkai (ed.) (1935) *Hisho ruisan teikoku gikai shiryō*, 2 vols, Tokyo.

Hōrei Zensho (1885) *Naikaku Insatsu Kyoku*, Tokyo.

Hoshino Tōru (1943) *Meiji Mimpō hensanshi kenkyū*, Tokyo.

Hoshino Tōru (1944) *Mimpōten ronsōshi*, Tokyo.

Hoshino Tōru (1969) *Mimpōten ronsō shiryōshū*, Tokyo.

Iguro Yatarō (1968) *Enomoto Buyō den*, Sapporo.

Ike N. (1950) *The Beginnings of Political Democracy in Japan*, John Hopkins Press, Baltimore.

ILO (International Labour Organization) (1933) *Industrial Labour in Japan*, ILO Studies and Reports Series A (Industrial Relations) no. 37, Geneva.

Inoue Kiyoshi (1955) *Jōyaku kaisei*, Tokyo.

Ishii Ryōsuke (trans. W. Chambliss) (1958) *Japanese Legislation in the Meiji Era*, Pan-Pacific Press, Tokyo.

Itō H. (1906) *Commentaries on the Constitution of the Empire of Japan*, Tokyo.

Itō Hirobumi Kankei Monjo Kenkyūkai, (ed.) (1973–4) *Itō Hirobumi kankei monjo*, 9 vols, Tokyo.

Itō Sumiko (1976) 'Roesler shōhō sōan no rippōshiteki igi ni tsuite' in Shiga Shūzō (ed.), *Hōseishi Ronshū*, Tokyo.

Iwasaki U. (1921) *The Working Forces in Japanese Politics*, Columbia University Press, New York.

Jansen M. B. (1970) 'Mutsu Munemitsu' in Craig A. and Shively D. (ed.), *Personality In Japanese History*, University of California Press, Berkeley.

Jones F. C. (1970) *Extraterritoriality in Japan and the Diplomatic Relations Resulting in its Abolition*, New York.

Kanazawa Makoto (1968) *Kazoku Meiji hyakunen no sokumenshi*, Tokyo.
Kasumi Kaikan (1967) *Kazoku kaikan shi*, Tokyo.
Katō Fusazō (1927) *Hirata Tōsuke den*, Tokyo.
Kawai Yahachi (1954) *Ichiki sensei kaikoroku*, Tokyo.
Kenseishiryōshitsu, National Diet Library (Tokyo), Mss. as follows: *Kenseishi hensankai shūshū monjo mokuroku; Kondō Eimei monjo mokuroku; Kyūkizokuin hensan shūshū monjo; Nomura Yasushi monjo; Shingawa Yajirō kankei monjo; Toki Akira monjo mokuroku*.
Kobayashi Kazuyoshi (1987) 'Yamagata naikaku "Shūkyō Hōan" to kizokuin nai kaiha', *Nihon Rekishi* no. 473.
Kokuritsu kokkai toshokan: see Kenseishiryōshitsu.
Konoe Atsumaro Nikki Kankōkai (1968) *Konoe Atsumaro nikki*, 5 vols, Tokyo.
Konoe Kazankai (1924) *Konoe kazan kō*, Tokyo.
Kudō Takeshige (1901) *Teikoku gikai shi*, 3 vols, Tokyo.
Kumagai Kaisaku (1967) 'Shōhōten ronsōshi josetsu' in Matsuyama Shōka Daigaku Shōkei Kenkyūkai (eds), *Hōshigaku oyobi hōgaku no shomondai*, Tokyo.
Kuruma Yasushi (1931) *Nihon seitō antō shi*, Tokyo.
Lone S. (1989) *General Katsura Tarō and the Japanese Empire in East Asia, 1874–1913*, unpublished Ph.D. thesis, ANU, Canberra.
McClain J. (1976), 'Local Politics and National Integration: The Fukui Prefectural Assembly in the 1880s', *Monumenta Nipponica* vol. 31.
McLaren W. (1914) 'Japanese Government Documents', *Transactions of the Asiatic Society of Japan*, 1st Series vol. xlii.
Maeda Renzan (1971) *Seihen monogatari*, Tokyo.
Maejima Shōzō (1964) *Meiji chūmatsuki no kanryō seiji*, Kyoto.
Mason R. (1969), *Japan's First General Election, 1890*, Cambridge University Press, Cambridge.
Mason R. (1979) 'Suematsu Kenchō and Patterns of Japanese Cultural and Political Change in the 1880s', *Papers on Far Eastern History* no. 20.
Mason R. and Caiger J. (1972) *A History of Japan*, Cassell, Melbourne.
Masumi Junnosuke (1965–80) *Nihon seitō shiron*, 7 vols, Tokyo.
Matsumoto Shigetoshi (1926) *Tsuzuki Keiroku den*, Tokyo.
Mayo M. (1966) 'Rationality in the Meiji Restoration: The Iwakura Embassy' in Silberman B. and Harootunian H. (ed.), *Modern Japanese Leadership: Transition and Change*, University of Arizona Press, Tucson.
Meiji Hennenshi Hensankai (1934–6) *Shimbun shūsei Meiji hennenshi*, 15 vols, Tokyo.
Meiji Nyūsu Hensan Iinkai (1983–6) *Meiji nyūsu jiten*, 9 vols, Tokyo.
Meiji Taishō kokusei sōran (1929) Tōyō Keizai Shimpōsha, Tokyo.
Naikaku Insatsu Kyoku, see *Hōrei Zensho*.
Nakamura Kichisaburō (1962) *The Formation of Modern Japan As Viewed From Legal History*, Centre for East Asian Cultural Studies, Tokyo.
National Diet Library: see Kenseishiryōshitsu.
Newspapers: *Chōya shimbun; Kampō; Kokumin shimbun; Mainichi shimbun; Nippon; Tokushima nichi nichi shimbun; Tōkyō nichi nichi shimbun; Yūbin-Hōchi shimbun*; all available at Meiji Shimbun Zasshi Bunko, Tokyo University. Also *Japan Weekly Mail (JWM)*.
Nihon Kokusei Jiten Kankōkai (1953–8) *Nihon kokusei jiten*, 10 vols, Tokyo.
Nobukane Kazunosuke (1969) *Nihon kindaika to sozei*, Tokyo/Osaka.

Noma Gozō (1926–7) *Rippō ichigen ron*, 2 vols, Tokyo.
Oda Kichinojo (1929) *Kaga han nōseishi kō*, Tokyo.
Ogura Takekazu (1951) *Tochi rippō no shiteki kōsatsu*, Tokyo.
Oka Yoshitake (1958) *Yamagata Aritomo*, Tokyo.
Oka Yoshitake (trans. A. Fraser and P. Murray) (1986) *Five Political Leaders of Modern Japan*, University of Tokyo Press, Tokyo.
Ōmachi Keigetsu (1924) *Sugiura Jūgō Sensei*, Tokyo.
Ōsumi Kenichirō (1957) *Shōhō sōsoku*, Hōritsugaku Zenshū no. 27, Tokyo.
Ōtsu Junichirō (1927–8) *Dai nihon Kensei shi*, 10 vols, Tokyo.
Oyama Hironari (1956) 'Meiji zenki ni okeru chiso keigenron no hatten', *Shakai Kagaku Kenkyū* 7, no. 6.
Ōyama Ujirō (1934) *Matsuoka Kōki Sensei den*, Tokyo.
Robertson Scott J. W. (1922) *The Foundations of Japan*, John Murray, London.
Sakamoto Tatsunosuke (1930a) *Nihon teikoku seiji nempyō*, Tokyo.
Sakamoto Tatsunosuke (1930b) *Shishaku Mishima Yatarō den*, Tokyo.
Sakamoto Tatsunosuke (1940) *Shishaku Makino Tadaatsu den*, Tokyo.
Sakeda Masatoshi (1978) *Kindai Nihon ni okeru taigaikō undō no kenkyū*, Tokyo.
Sansom G. (1950) *The Western World and Japan*, Cresset Press, London.
Sansom G. (1958–64) *A History of Japan*, 3 vols, Cresset Press, London.
Satō Tatsuo (1943) *Kizokuin taiseibi no kenkyū*, Tokyo.
Sawada Minoru (1924) *Kizokuin kaikaku mondai to kizokuin seido no kenkyū*, Tokyo.
Senda Minoru (1986) 'Kazoku shihon no seiritsu tenkai: ippanteki kōsatsu', *Shakai Keizai Shigaku* 52, no. 1.
Shidō Motokazu (1954) 'Nihon ni okeru kinhonisei no kenkyū', *Keizai Ronsō* 73, no. 6.
Shinobu Seisaburō (1954) *Taishō seiji shi*, Tokyo.
Shinobu Seisaburō (1976–82) *Nihon seiji shi*, 4 vols, Tokyo.
Shively D. (1965) 'Nishimura Shigeki: A Confucian View of Modernization' in Jansen M. (ed.), *Changing Japanese Attitudes Toward Modernization*, Princeton University Press, Princeton.
Shōyū Kurabu (ed.) (1971) *Kizokuin no kaiha kenkyūkai shi*, Tokyo.
Shōyū Kurabu (1983) *Kizokuin seiji nempyō*, Tokyo.
Shumpo Kō Tsuishōkai (ed.) (1943) *Itō Hirobumi den*, 3 vols, Tokyo.
Small A. (1924) 'The Thibault–Savigny Controversy' in *Some Contributions to the History of Sociology*, Chicago.
Snellen J. (1934) 'Shoku Nihongi', *Transactions of the Asiatic Society of Japan*, 2nd Series vol. xi.
Strong K. (1977) *Ox Against the Storm: a Biography of Tanaka Shōzō, Japan's Conservationist Pioneer*, Paul Norbury, Tenterden.
Taguchi Sukekichi (1931) *Teikoku gikai no hanashi*, Tokyo.
Takahashi Hidenao (1985) 'Yamagata batsu kizokuin shihai no kōzō', *Shigaku Zasshi* 94, no. 2.
Takayanagi Kenzō (1963) 'A Century of Innovation: the Development of Japanese Law' in A. von Mehren (ed.), *Law in Japan: The Legal Order in a Changing Society*, Harvard University Press, Cambridge, Mass.
Takizawa Naoshichi (1968) *Kōhon Nihon kinyū shiron*, Tokyo.
Terabe Tetsuji (1953) *Ginkō hattatsushi*, Osaka.
Toby R. (1977) 'Reopening the question of *Sakoku*: Diplomacy in the

Legitimization of the Tokugawa Bakufu', *Journal of Japanese Studies* 3, no. 2.
Tokutomi Ichirō (1933) *Kōshaku Yamagata Aritomo den*, 3 vols, Tokyo.
Totman C. (1967) *Politics in the Tokugawa Bakufu*, Harvard University Press, Cambridge, Mass.
Uyehara G. E. (1972) *The Political Development of Japan*, Constable, London.
Uzaki Rojō (1915) *Batsujin to tōjin*, Tokyo.
Washio Yoshinao (1959) *Kojima Kazuo*, Tokyo.
Watanabe Ikujirō (1944) *Meiji shi kenkyū*, Tokyo.
Waters N. (1983) *Japan's Local Pragmatists: The Transition from Bakumatsu to Meiji in the Kawasaki Region*, Harvard University Press, Cambridge, Mass.
Wigmore J. (1891) 'Starting a Parliament in Japan', *Scribner's Magazine* 10.
Wigmore J. (1928) *A Panorama of the World's Legal Problems*, 3 vols, St Paul, Minnesota.
Wigmore J. (1969) *Law and Justice in Tokugawa Japan*, 10 vols, University of Tokyo Press, Tokyo.
Yamaguchi Aikawa (1932) *Yoko kara mita kazoku monogatari*, Tokyo.
Yasuda Hiroshi (1990) 'The Modern Emperor System', *Acta Asiatica* 59.

OTHER WORKS CONSULTED

Duus P. (1983) 'Imperialism and Domestic Politics in Later Meiji Japan', *Waseda Journal of Asian Studies* no. 5.
Inoue Kakugorō Kun Kōrō Hyōshōkai (1919) *Inoue Kakugorō kun ryaku den*, Tokyo.
Mason R. (1965) 'The Debate on Poor Relief in the First Meiji Diet', *Journal of the Oriental Society of Australia* vol. iii, no. 1.
Mason R. (1975/1976) 'Debates on Foreign Affairs in the First Meiji Diet', *Papers On Far Eastern History* nos. 12 and 13.
Mason R. (1985) 'The Peace Preservation Ordinance and the First Meiji Diet, 1890–1892', *Papers On Far Eastern History* no. 31.
Mitchell P. (1982) *The Japanese Commercial Code and its Fate in the First Two Sessions of the Imperial Diet*, unpublished Honours dissertation, ANU, Canberra.
Mitchell R. (1976) *Thought Control in Prewar Japan*, Cornell University Press, Ithaca.
Ramsdell D. (1992) *The Japanese Diet: Stability and Change in the House of Representatives, 1890–1990*, University Press of America, Lanham.
Shida Kōtarō (1933) *Nihon Shōhōten no hensan to sono kaisei*, Tokyo.
Siemes J. (1968) *Herman Roesler and the Making of the Meiji State*, Sophia University, Tokyo.
Steele M. (1984) 'Integration and Participation in Meiji Politics', *Asian Cultural Studies* no. 14, ICU, 1984.
Takayanagi Kenzō (1931) *A General Survey of the History of Japanese Commercial Law*, Tokyo.
von Mehren A. (ed.) (1963) *Law in Japan: the Legal Order in a Changing Society*, Harvard University Press, Cambridge, Mass.

Index

For Product Safety Concerns and Information please contact our EU
representative GPSR@taylorandfrancis.com
Taylor & Francis Verlag GmbH, Kaufingerstraße 24, 80331 München, Germany